D0758392

THE
SQUEAL
MAN

MARTIN FLUSSER

THE SQUEAL MAN

THE TRUE STORY OF MATT BONORA, SUBURBAN HOMICIDE DETECTIVE

WILLIAM MORROW AND COMPANY, INC.

NEW YORK   1977

Printed in the United States of America.

1 2 3 4 5 6 7 8 9 10

Library of Congress Cataloging in Publication Data

Flusser, Martin.
    The squeal man.
      1. Bonora, Matt. 2. Detectives–New York (State)–Nassau Co.–Biography. 3. Homicide investigation–New York (State)–Nassau Co.
    I. Title.
HV7911.B656F56   364.12'092'4   [B]   77-1768
ISBN 0-688-03193-5

BOOK DESIGN   CARL WEISS

To my parents

and

especially to Jane

AUTHOR TO READER

FOR YEARS Matt Bonora of the Nassau County Police Department maintained a reputation among newsmen as a good "source." Whenever a problem arose in Long Island police reporting–an unexplained change in the administration or a new departmental order or merely a criminal investigation wanting in color and background information–Bonora was the man reporters turned to. Occasionally fear of harming an investigation might silence him. More frequently, he was prepared to respond to pertinent inquiries. Accessible and knowledgeable, he was a strong proponent of the public's right to know. He further felt that the work of the police department would be more fully appreciated with a freer exchange of information and ideas, a point of view not necessarily coincident with departmental policy.

Throughout all his commentary Bonora was a modest but articulate spokesman. Though he might point to another detective's endeavors as exemplary, his own achievements were invariably presented in the first-person plural. Reporters, dissatisfied with the terse, back-patting statements emanating from the public relations offices of the Police Commissioner and the District Attorney, returned to him often. They enjoyed his refreshing candor and his sense of humor, the pithiness of his observations. Besides, he was not a man who spoke out of ignorance. A true student of police investigation, he had allowed few books on the subject to escape his scrutiny. He had even taught at the Police Academy. But his knowledge was more than theoretical. As a top investigator, later as Homicide commander, Bonora had participated in almost every major investigation on Long Island in the past decade. He loved his work. He was proud of the accomplishments of the Nassau County Police Department. He wanted others to feel the same way.

I first met Bonora as a reporter for Long Island's *Newsday*. For three years I had heard others in the newsroom speak highly of the detective, and from time to time my curiosity peaked, reading of his exploits in the paper and noting his uncommon outspokenness. Then in the spring of 1972 a former model living in New York City, a young woman from a monied and influential family, was found dead on Long Island. With rumors of her involvement in a nationwide drug ring the paper's managing editor, Don Forst, became interested. Specifically, he wanted to know how, from a background of finishing schools and debutante parties, her life had come to end in a deserted lot in Massapequa. I was given the assignment.

During the next two months as I searched for clues among the singles-bar set of the Upper East Side of Manhattan, traveling to Massachusetts and Washington, D.C., Bonora was also in pursuit. He was looking for Patsy Parks's murderer. In a sense we were chasing the same story though, I hasten to add, from decidedly different angles. (For reasons mostly involving health I have long refrained from enrolling in the Clark Kent-Jimmy Olsen school of crime-fighting journalism.) A number of Patsy's friends had already been interviewed by Bonora by the time I reached them. Questioned about this experience, they spoke of the detective's warmth and compassion, predicting I would be surprised by his unpolicemanlike demeanor. They urged me to make an effort to meet him. In subsequent interviews I learned a similar suggestion had been made to Bonora.

At one point a Homicide detective did telephone to suggest a "trade" in information. But fearing I might be forced to compromise my sources, I avoided setting up an appointment. Yet by the time the investigation ended (see Chapters 10-12), I had heard enough about Bonora to make me truly anxious to meet him. So early one morning in June, 1972, I telephoned the detective at home and invited him to lunch. He accepted with enthusiasm.

We met in the John Peel Room at the Island Inn on Long Island and drank and talked through most of the afternoon. There was almost a twenty-year disparity in our ages, to say nothing of the differences in upbringing, politics and social outlook. But the predictions of Patsy's friends proved accurate. We got on like old college roommates. Placing immediate trust in one another's discretion, we talked openly about our lives and ambitions. Bonora enthralled me with his "inside" view of the Parks investigation and with other anecdotes he recounted from his long career. I was particularly impressed by his memory for details—times, dates, names, sequences of events—an attribute that was largely responsible for his frequent employment as a prosecution witness. By meal's end I confessed I had contemplated writing a book about him. The project, as envisioned, would portray the major investigations of Bonora's career as well as provide a peek into the variegated world of the suburbs. While I would need the detective's assistance in researching the material, I advised him that I intended to treat the controversial aspects of his career as objectively as possible, gathering and presenting other points of view.

Bonora agreed to consider the proposal and discuss it with his wife that evening. The following day he offered his full cooperation.

The Squeal Man is the result of that informal agreement. The scenes of the book have been constructed from information gathered through close to one hundred interviews, from police documents and court papers, as well as from my own independent research. In many instances the direct quotations have been taken verbatim from trial testimony. In scenes where this was not possible I have based the conversation on the recollections of several witnesses. Parts of the book have been read to the individual participants and corrected for authenticity.

It is certainly easy to foresee objections to the type of methodology used in constructing the novel-like atmosphere of the book (Dwight Macdonald once called it parajournalism). Critics might justifiably complain there are sections impossible for the writer to have fully documented, and that therefore he is speculating on what actually happened rather than merely reporting. I would answer that objection by stating, first, that all reporting (and this from my own experience) involves some sort of speculation or conjecture. Moreover, nothing that was extrapolated in the book contradicts the truth of what happened. Where this extrapolation does occur (and it is rare) my belief is that the reader's overall comprehension of the scene has been aided by it. Not long ago a fundamentalist preacher stopped me on a street corner to offer his view of the Bible. "Not every single thing in there is true," he said, "but it's all the Truth." In a more modest way I would hope that description fits *The Squeal Man*.

My gratitude is extended first to Matt Bonora and his wife, Hazel, without whose complete cooperation this project would not have been possible. Invaluable assistance was rendered by the women of the Nassau County Courts record room and by Alan and Nancy Warshow, my cousins on Long Island, who furnished me with bed and board, and that most necessary accouterment of suburban life, a car. My thanks also to Julian Bach, my agent, who stuck with me through the long haul, and to my editor, Hillel Black.

THE
SQUEAL
MAN

CHAPTER

1

SHE HAD BEEN MURDERED as she slept.

Sgt. Matthew Bonora took one look through the gauze of semidarkness at the woman lying in her bed, at her broad, almond-shaped face that was caked in blood and at her thickly matted ebony hair; and he knew from sixteen years as a detective, from more than three thousand homicide investigations, that the woman lying there, twenty-nine-year-old Brenda Pobliner, had neither feared nor expected her execution, that she had neither screamed nor resisted, that she had died in the peacefulness of a dream.

She lay on her back, the blue blanket still covering her smooth, pale shoulders. Her head rested comfortably on its side on the top of her right arm; the eyes were closed. Bonora stared impassively at the lurid scene, at the blue pillow that had turned the color of burgundy. He wasn't shocked; his thoughts were moving forward. He bent down and through the gray sheath of early morning his eyes scanned the floor for a weapon. Finding none, he started toward the door, stopping before a walnut dresser whose high veneer reflected the light in the hall. It appeared to have been ransacked. The uppermost drawer stood halfway open, a strand of pearls hanging over its side like spittle from a baby's mouth. On top a leather pocketbook with a gold clasp sat open. Directly in front of the bureau on the floor lay two tiny jewelry boxes, their contents splayed out before them on the carpet. Bonora passed out of the room into the hallway and telephoned police headquarters.

"The works," he said, and gave the Long Island address of the Pobliner home. In the next half hour the laconic request would bring the Nassau County Homicide Squad, the Identification Bureau (I.D.), the Scientific Investigation Bureau (S.I.B.), the Medical Examiner (the M.E.) and the coroner's black van and stretcher (the wagon and basket).

Through the years Bonora had investigated countless deaths on the still-affluent North Shore of Long Island, that once-fabled "Gold Coast" where in the 1920's flourished the characters and four-hundred-acre estates of F. Scott Fitzgerald's romances. He had investigated in the poverty pockets of the county and in the black ghettos as well. But the preponderance of his work was directed, as it was this twenty-seventh day of December, 1968, to the great wash of the middle class. That sector of society whose tidal exodus from New York City had turned Nassau County (with 1,500,000 inhabitants) into the largest suburban governmental region in the nation, whose quarter- and half-acre developments have stamped her face irrevocably into the apotheosis of "suburban sprawl."

Waiting for his associates to arrive, he began to wander through the Pobliner home, a modest split-level possessing in outward appearance neither individuality nor great charm. His movements were cautious and deliberate like an archaeologist surveying a new excavation site, not certain what he might find but concerned lest he disturb it. Upstairs there were two other bedrooms besides the master. One was neat and apparently undisturbed. The other contained a small child sleeping soundly, with a partially filled milk bottle clasped between his hands. On the next level down were the kitchen, living room and dining room. From the dining room a canal was visible in the backyard, a significant asset certain to increase the value of homes in the area to upward of $60,000. The dining room and living room were both decorated with thick pile rugs and silk-covered furniture in an Oriental motif. Neither evidenced signs of disturbance.

As he moved into the kitchen the clutter of dirty dishes in the stainless steel sink momentarily whetted the sergeant's interest. So did an empty vodka bottle and two half-filled highball glasses he discovered in the finished basement, a large comfortable room with a mirrored and full-stocked bar. But on later consideration he concluded that neither the dirty dishes nor the alcohol was remarkable in a home of this sort—with its two-car garage, its boat, its fine furniture, its maid's room, the almost perfect reflection of a young, active, affluent suburban couple.

Presently inspecting the rear windows and doors of the house, Bonora was surprised to find a German shepherd pacing the fenced-in back yard, dogs normally serving as a deterrent to the most insistent burglar. He made a mental note to determine its whereabouts during the murder, then returned to the living room, where the uniformed patrolmen and the other detectives were gathered. One of the patrolmen pointed out the neighbor who had discovered the dead body, Mrs. Adele Pober. She was standing near the kitchen. Bonora directed a detective to interview her. He ordered a second detective to inspect the back yard and assigned a third to interview the neighbors. Watching the men jump to their appointed tasks and considering the prospect of a full-scale investigation, Bonora found himself growing excited. There were few things in life the forty-year-old sergeant enjoyed more than a challenging murder investigation.

Handsome in a very masculine way, dark with a high-sweeping forehead and prominent straight nose, Bonora had joined the police force as a hedge against the vacillations of the postwar economy. Yet after his first week as a rookie patrolman, when he single-handedly solved a murder case that had stumped the local detectives, he realized it was not security that would keep him a cop. Indeed, eighteen months later he turned down a $25,000-a-year offer from his former boss, a real estate developer who wanted him to become a broker in New York City. Promised a gold shield by the Police Commissioner, the twenty-two-year-old patrolman remained on the county payroll for another six months until his promotion was finally announced. In May, 1952, he became the youngest detective in the history of the department.

Since then Bonora had gained a reputation as the county's top investigator, an eminence firmly established during his seven-year tenure as a member of the Homicide Squad. But in September he had been transferred out of Homicide to become deputy commander of the Seventh Squad. The transfer was actually a promotion though Bonora was disgruntled nonetheless. Activity in the Seventh was mostly routine and he had felt his investigative abilities sorely neglected. He craved the challenge and involvement of a lengthy investigation, the mystery and excitement, the close camaraderie that inevitably develops among the men, the nurturing of contacts and leads. Administrative jobs were for other types of detectives.

At 9:30 A.M. the other investigators started to appear. Those who arrived now came alone and in groups, soon filling the living room and front yard with their dark suits and grim expressions. First to appear was Frank Godsman, commander of Bonora's Seventh Precinct Squad; then the Homicide Squad commander Daniel Guido and several of his detectives. Afterward the commander of the Scientific Investigation Bureau and his deputy, then the agents of Identification. Bonora remained in the living room observing with satisfaction as each investigator registered with the patrolman he had assigned to the front door immediately upon his arrival. Only a veteran homicide detective could appreciate the importance this timetable might hold in the event of a subsequent prosecution. So often a defense attorney tried to inject doubt into the incriminating testimony of a detective by confusing him with questions concerning the exact times of his arrival and departure. Or, to impeach the Medical Examiner's autopsy, the attorney might dispute the moment the corpse left the house. The "timetable," which recorded all movements in and out of the crime scene, provided an automatic safeguard against such tactics.

Bonora led Lieutenant Guido and several photographers from Identification into the master bedroom. As the cameras started to flash, a splattering of human matter became visible on the ceiling for the first time, a blood-red pancake six by three feet. Bonora's first reaction was characteristically professional: the thick splattering automatically ruled out bludgeoning as the cause of death. At once, before another thing was touched, the detectives called an S.I.B. ballistics specialist into the room to examine the blanket and carpet for gunpowder. By tracing the gunpowder that is known to fall in even, concentric rings from the point of shooting, the ballistics man would determine where the murderer had stood when he killed the victim.

The two detectives did not await the findings but returned to the living room and began to brief the other arriving investigators. Men were continuing to stream in from the Seventh Precinct Squad as well as the Homicide Squad; supervisors arrived from police headquarters. Bonora spoke to them for less than a minute before the front door burst open with a wood-splintering crack.

"What happened?" shouted a young man, leaping up the first few stairs to the living room and heading for the second set that ascended to the bedrooms. "What . . ."

Lieutenant Godsman, fearful that evidence might be destroyed, stepped into his path. For a moment the intruder tried to continue forward, pressing against the policeman in anger and confusion. Then his body sagged, and the tall, graying commander turned him around by the elbow, leading him to the love seat in front of the living room window.

"I've got some bad news for you," Lieutenant Godsman said gently, seating the young man, whom he recognized from a family photograph. "Your wife is dead."

An anguished look seized Jay Pobliner's face. His head sank between his hands. From across the room Bonora studied the reaction. (Emotion, like other kinds of evidence, was often not easy to evaluate.) A minute later he approached the husband who was still hunched over, soundless and unmoving. Pobliner looked up vaguely as the sergeant suggested they talk at the nearby Seventh Precinct stationhouse where the atmosphere was less emotional. With little urging he rose and accompanied Bonora and Det. Daniel Stark of Homicide to the awaiting squad car, climbing into the front seat between them.

As Stark pulled away from the curb Bonora took his "rights" card out of his wallet and began to read aloud from it. He advised the witness that he was not required to respond to their questions, that any answers he offered could be held against him, that he had the right to have an attorney present, and that if he couldn't afford a lawyer, one would be provided.

Pobliner's face blanched. He turned indignantly toward Bonora. "Are you accusing me?"

The sergeant assured him he was not. Advising an individual of his constitutional rights was standard police procedure, required by law. He added that the police had no assumptions as to his guilt. He was just being questioned for information about his wife and family.

The explanation was delivered promptly and without much reflection, a response given on numerous occasions. Yet no sooner had it been offered than Bonora felt perhaps he had spoken too quickly. Pobliner had turned away with a peculiar expression on his face. He sat gazing out at the horizon, his black, hooded eyes vacant as if his mind had settled in some strange, private world. What happened next Bonora could only attribute to the kind of instincts detectives develop through years of investigations. In truth, it was just a feeling that told him: "Pobliner didn't look right." Stark turned east on Merrick Road and suddenly Sergeant Bonora said in a low, firm voice, "Let me have the gun, Jay."

The demand brought silence to the car. Even the mewling of the engine and the hum of the wheels against the cement road seemed to fade in the face of the interior tension. Pobliner's right hand started to move. It left his lap, traveling deliberately up the outside of his overcoat, disappearing inside, groping, exiting with a double-barreled Derringer pistol. Bonora stiffened. As he moved slowly for the gun his own image flashed before him, bent over in the car with blood rushing from his chest. Then he felt the cold steel in his fingers and the vision disappeared, though only after fitting the weapon into the outside pocket of his tweed overcoat did his heart stop racing.

Not a word had been uttered during the exchange. In the silence that ensued Stark continued to drive as if nothing had happened, past four miles of gas stations, carpet stores and franchise restaurants on Merrick Road. When they reached Seventh Precinct headquarters, a former farmhouse that had been converted for police use, Bonora addressed the witness again.

Standing near Pobliner in the squadroom on the second floor, he demanded brusquely, "All right, Jay. What have you got to tell us?"

Pobliner looked quizzically at Bonora until the detective pulled the Derringer from his pocket.

"Oh that," he murmured. "I have a license." He offered the permit from his wallet for inspection.

Noting the Derringer's listing on the creased yellow sheet, the sergeant opened the gun and shook it empty of two copper-clad .22 caliber long cartridges. He held the gun to the light and peered through both barrels. The narrow steel tubes were lined with dust and lint—certain evidence the small, elegant pistol had not been fired in weeks.

Bonora spent six hours with Jay Pobliner that day, interviewing him and later supervising a series of tests to substantiate his statements. Bonora was a good interrogator—perhaps that was his strongest suit as a detective. He had a history of persuading the most hardened criminal to "go for it," that is, confess the crime, and of turning unfriendly accomplices into willing participants in the police investigation. But he also had the ability to draw witnesses out, getting them to recall what they might consider detail after boring detail, but which is often the key to a successful investigation. His muted brown eyes could easily feign empathy. His mouth too was deceptive. Set above a tilted, narrow chin with a small cleft, his thin lips shifted almost primly in conversation until things got tough. Then suddenly his chin would jut as his voice rose to stentorian tones.

Bonora used little theatrics in talking to Pobliner, employing an earnest expression and a soft, mellifluous voice that he hoped would relax him and elicit his full cooperation. Yet nothing he said or did seemed to set the young man at ease. Pobliner slumped in his chair and refused to face Bonora directly as they spoke. His voice was tense and uncertain. This diffidence finally did disappear, but it was not of the sergeant's making. In the middle of the interview Herman Pobliner, Jay's father, unexpectedly appeared in the squadroom. He was a tanned, handsomely attired gentleman whose features–the nearly identical broad but shapely nose and lips, wide-spaced hooded eyes–identified him to the detectives even before his introduction. Embraced by his father, Jay straightened up and his face brightened. As the interview continued, his eyes fastened confidently on his interrogator.

At twenty-eight, Jay Pobliner was already a wealthy young man. A graduate of New York University, he was the vice president of Rosalind Sportswear, a ladies' clothing manufacturer in New York City that was a family business. He also held a partnership in the Cloud Tours Travel Agency on Madison Avenue, which his father had purchased for him. He had traveled considerably and pursued a wide range of interests that challenged and tested him. He hunted and enjoyed target shooting, studied judo and magic, rode motorcycles and drove fast cars (a Ferrari until it was stolen a month before his wife's death).

In relating his previous night's activities, Jay told the detectives he had brought home a friend, an Estonian-born market analyst he had known since college. The friend, Illis Jurisson, had spent the night with Jay and returned with him the following morning to New York City. Before leaving the house Pobliner said he had kissed his wife, Brenda, good-bye–she was still sleeping–and turned off the burglar alarm in the bedroom. Then together with Illis he had walked his dog, returning to the house shortly thereafter and letting in the

German shepherd through the connecting door in the garage. When he reached his office at eight o'clock he phoned his wife at home, which was his normal routine. He received no answer. Fifteen minutes later he tried again. Still no answer. He called his mother. She had not heard from Brenda, and after several unsuccessful attempts of her own, urged Jay to phone a neighbor. Adele Pober lived only several houses away on Bay Drive. Pobliner reached her, and after he explained his concern she left to check the house. Moments later Donald Pober, her husband, returned Pobliner's call. He said that Brenda was bleeding but that she was alive and Adele had called an ambulance. Hanging up the phone, Pobliner had raced downstairs to the garage where his car was parked and hired one of the attendants to drive. He arrived at his home in the South Shore village of Merrick within the hour.

Finished with his account, Pobliner settled back into the chair. He glanced at his father, who nodded encouragingly.

"Did anyone have any motive, any reason to kill your wife?" Bonora inquired.

Pobliner replied that Brenda was without enemies, that people naturally liked her.

"How about prowlers? Have you had any experience with burglars or prowlers?"

"Actually about two weeks ago Brenda thought she saw someone in the backyard," Pobliner said. "We were sitting in the kitchen with some company at the time. I ran outside to check, but I didn't see anyone."

"What about you and Brenda? Were you having any problems?"

"No, not at all. We had a beautiful relationship. In fact we had plans to go away over New Year's to Asheville, North Carolina. A kind of second honeymoon."

After further questioning Bonora took Jay to police headquarters, where he agreed to undergo the standard examinations that corroborate witness testimony. He had his clothes inspected for blood and gunpowder as well as his body and hair, which was searched with a special, fine-toothed comb. His fingernails were scraped for pieces of foreign flesh, which often lodge there during a struggle. Later he was given a paraffin test to determine whether he had fired a gun. The results of all these exams were negative.

It was four o'clock before Bonora and Detective Stark returned with the two Pobliners to the house on Bay Drive. The temperature had been falling all day and now the skies were dark, lending credence to the predictions for snow. As the four men climbed out of the squad car several detectives, their overcoats buttoned tight, were searching the Pobliner front yard for footprints. Their work had to be completed before the snowfall. Others in neighboring yards and by the canal were hunting for the murder weapon with mine detectors attached to the ends of long wooden handles.

Pobliner, apprised that his mother was waiting, hastened up the front walk, oblivious to the activity around him. He unlocked the door and found her gazing down at him from the top of the first landing. She was an elegant, silver-haired woman, whose tremulous face was marked by two bright red eyes rimmed in black mascara. The two hugged one another emotionally. Mrs. Pobliner, sighing despairingly, whispered, "The bubble burst."

The remark intrigued the few detectives within earshot, including Bonora and Lieutenant Guido. They made no effort, however, to decipher its meaning. Instead the investigators began at once to inspect the house with Pobliner as guide, a room-by-room search for missing property they hoped might eventually lead to his wife's killer. Pobliner's actions during that half hour search struck the detectives as peculiar. Escorted from room to room, he refused to take more than a cursory glance inside before declaring in a low, distant voice, "Nothing is missing." Bonora and Guido explained that the Nassau County Police Property Recovery Bureau records and exchanges information with similar bureaus all over the country, that there was a strong chance of recovering anything stolen and that this could prove decisive in solving the murder. At their insistence Pobliner reentered several rooms, positioning himself in the center and taking a brief look about. But in each instance he repeated his earlier assertion and left abruptly.

Frustrated, Bonora walked out into the back yard, approaching the edge of the nearby canal. This was an attractive part of Long Island. The water in the canal was fresh and clear, the homes bordering it on each side substantial and well maintained. Yet the sergeant's thoughts were on murder that day, and when he looked at the man-made waterway he thought not of summer swimming and sailing but of the drowned children he had pulled from other canals along the island's South Shore. He peered over the edge and the blackness he discerned was as deep as the county morgue wagon. He was doubtful the police frogmen would find anything in tomorrow's search for the murder weapon.

Yet for a moment longer Bonora remained gazing into the darkness, unable to move. For seven years his work as a member of the Homicide Squad had orbited around the daily loss of life. He had learned to rationalize accidental death and suicide. Acceptance, cynicism toward man's baser instincts—these are an inevitable development in a detective's outlook, and Bonora had nurtured a hearty strain. But murder was different. More than just one man killing another, murder created a dangerous tear in the social fabric that demanded immediate repair. Such a vision, almost biblical in its moral overtones, rendered the sergeant incapable of conducting a homicide investigation with only the partial interest one often brings to a job after so many years. A murder turned him into Ahab chasing the white whale, a man whose attention and energies were obsessively consumed. This had been true from his very first investigation, when he had found a man with his head blown off by a shotgun. It was no different now as he contemplated the tragic death of Brenda Pobliner. Returning to the house that bitter cold December day, Bonora wanted more than anything else to be a part of the subsequent investigation.

Inside, detectives had moved a large trunk from the basement into the living room and were filling it with an assortment of household artifacts to bring to headquarters for further examination. Included in the collection were two of Pobliner's pistols stored in a small suitcase used by target shooters to transport their guns between ranges, and the bedroom draperies and bedcovers, which the S.I.B. agents had carefully folded between plastic sheets to preserve the bloodstains in their original state. Brenda Pobliner's address book had been impounded as well as Jay's checkbook, which would be used to compile a list of companies and individuals who served the Pobliner home. When the packaging was finished, Guido would give the contents a final inspection. Then the Homicide commander would formally relinquish the crime scene to its owner, a more than ceremonial gesture since future visits to the house would require the permission of either Pobliner or the court, dispositions that were unpredictable at best. As the men awaited this ultimate transaction Homicide Detective Henry Andreoli motioned Bonora aside and recommended with a wink that he examine the freezer in the basement. Bonora descended the first flight of stairs past the finished basement room into the storage area. He found a birthday cake inside the large white freezer in the rear. Its two-word inscription read: "Fuck You."

The Nassau County government complex is located in the approximate center of the county, on the border of the villages of Garden City and Mineola. Reflecting the region they represent, the buildings are a mixture of the new and the old—all interconnected by vast asphalt parking lots. In addition to the turn-of-the-century County Courthouse and scattered postwar office buildings such as those that house the District Court, the Planning Commission and the Sheriff's office, there is a brand-new marble State Supreme Courthouse, a ten-story Executive Office Building and a modern, all-white Social Services Building.

Several blocks away to the west is the headquarters of the 4,000-member Nassau County Police Department. Set back twenty yards from Franklin Avenue—a mildly busy four-lane road edged with trees as well as branches of some of New York City's most distinguished department stores (Saks Fifth Avenue, Lord and Taylor, Bloomingdale's)—the complex seems less like a government structure than perhaps a large mail-order house. It is a sprawling two-story tan brick building that over the years has grown into the shape of a squared six. In front there is a manicured lawn where bright tulips, geraniums and violets bloom in the spring. In the center of the main building one finds a grassy courtyard, in the rear several acres of parking lot presided over by a towering radio antenna. The Detective Division, of which the Homicide Squad forms a part, is housed on the second floor, along with the laboratory and the Commissioner's office.

The Homicide Squad occupies a suite of five offices. The commander and his deputy share the large room in the rear, which overlooks the interior courtyard, separated from the rest of the suite by a glass partition. Two desks placed head-to-head, two secretarial swivel-back chairs, a row of the omnipresent gray filing cabinets are the room's sole effects—a purposely spare decor that had been radically transformed by 11 P.M., the evening of the Pobliner murder. After four hours of discussion the room was cluttered with detectives, notebooks, paper coffee cups and a haze of blue cigarette smoke. In addition to the detectives there were agents from the lab and the Identification Bureau, and Jack Lewis, head of the District Attorney's Homicide Trial Bureau. Nassau County detectives are taught to work closely with the District Attorney's office from the start of a case since the legality of so much of their investigative work is later placed under careful scrutiny by the court. Lewis, a portly, forty-year-old lawyer, enjoyed the action and excitement of an investigation more than most of District Attorney William Cahn's staff. He had been in attendance at the Pobliner home throughout the day. Like the other investigators present he was now digesting the information that had been reported by all the detectives, throwing out hunches and theories on the scant evidence so far collected.

"You know that's strange that Pobliner said his wife was

bleeding," he mused out loud as another round of coffee was distributed. "Are you certain that's what Jay said, Mattie?"

"Of course I'm certain," Bonora answered. "We went over this several times. Danny has the notes."

Detective Stark nodded. "No doubt in my mind that's what he said."

"The statements of the garagemen back it up," volunteered James Short, a young detective from the Seventh Squad. "We spoke to two of them involved, this guy Masucci, who drove Jay out to Merrick, and the boss in New York, Larry Fleming. Both of them specifically recall him saying his wife was bleeding. That's why he said he was too nervous to drive and wanted someone to take him out."

Lewis was not the only one to have noticed the apparent discrepancy between the statements of Adele Pober and Jay Pobliner.

"Was Mrs. Pober positive she hadn't mentioned that Brenda was bleeding?" Guido asked, leaning anxiously across his desk toward Det. Louis Ryf.

Ryf nodded uncertainly, admitting his failure to press Mrs. Pober on the exact words used to deliver her message. "But I took the statement very carefully," he added defensively. "We went over it several times before she signed it."

"It is possible then that she was mistaken," Bonora suggested.

"You know, there was another strange thing about Pobliner's statement," Short said, interrupting. "It was so damned cold out this morning, why the hell did he take his dog for a walk? I found gobs of shit in the backyard, which means he had no compunctions about letting the dog go out there."

"Good hunting," one of the men quipped.

"No, that's an interesting point," Lewis acknowledged seriously when the laughter subsided. "How long did he say he was out walking the dog, Matt?"

"About ten minutes."

Guido said, "We checked the distance to the woods. It's one thousand thirty-three feet. Ten minutes is accurate if he walked the dog at all."

Lewis nodded reflectively, flattening the sides of his hair down with both hands, a gesture that gave renewed emphasis to his sharp features. "You know, if Jay is involved in this murder, that walk gives him the time for this alleged burglar to come in when the dog's not there and the burglar alarm is off. Did we get a time of death from the M.E.?"

"It'll be a few days before we hear anything," Guido said, turning then to Bonora. He suggested the sergeant and Detective Andreoli reinterview Mrs. Pober and her husband.

"Let's not forget about Illis Jurisson," Andreoli said, speaking of Pobliner's houseguest. "I've got a hunch Illis could be our man." Andreoli was the squeal man from Homicide, the detective who had answered the call ("the squeal") from Bay Drive when it came in that morning and would thereafter be responsible for the investigation. He had driven into New York City in the afternoon to speak with Pobliner's houseguest, but had found only his mother at home.

Bonora disagreed with Andreoli's suspicion. Picking up the stack of photographs on Guido's desk, he handed Andreoli several that Identification had taken of Brenda Pobliner's head.

"That's one hell of a grouping on her skull," he said. "And you heard what ballistics said. There weren't any powder burns on the skin, so the gun was fired at least a yard away. You need a shooter to do that. It's Jay with the credentials."

"What did Jay actually say about his shooting?" Lewis asked.

"He said he did quite a bit of hunting and that he was a target shooter and belonged to a gun club in Westchester. Stark took it all down. Tell them what guns he had, Danny."

Stark read from his notebook. "I own three pistols, four rifles and a shotgun. The Derringer, a three fifty-seven Magnum Colt Python and a Colt thirty-eight Special, snub-nose revolver are registered in New York City. I did have a twenty-two automatic down in North Carolina that I got from a good friend of mine, Lieutenant Welborn of the Asheville Police. But I gave it back to him. And my ex-father-in-law gave me an unregistered gun once but I turned this over to Mr. Waxmann in 1965. He's a Treasury agent I knew then when

I was working part time as an undercover agent for the FBI."

"I wonder if he really was an undercover agent," Short said.

Det. Gene Schoenberger, the squeal man from the Seventh Squad, remarked, "I've been wondering about that 'bubble burst' statement of Mrs. Pobliner's."

"Maybe she thought she knew what Jay had been up to," Stark suggested.

Bonora said, "I was standing right there at the time and that's what I assumed she meant. But now I'm not so sure. What do you make of it, Lieutenant?"

Guido shrugged.

"Who knows," Lewis said, "it could have been just an innocent statement of remorse on her part. You know, that they had had such a good relationship and now it had ended."

"I don't buy that at all . . ."

The meeting continued for another three hours and by the time Bonora reached home it was 2:30 A.M. He drove slowly into the driveway, parked the car in the garage and quietly pulled the metal door shut. Upstairs in the second-floor bedroom of the colonial-style ranch house, Hazel Bonora, his wife of nineteen years, was still awake, finishing a story in the *Reader's Digest*. She heard footsteps crunch across the gravel driveway. A moment later the back door to the house opened, and she smiled to herself as she recognized the sound of her husband climbing the bare wooden stairs, his steps quicker than normal. Earlier that evening she had been uncertain what to expect when Bonora phoned to say he would be home late, though the exhilaration in his voice had given her a premonition. In the months since September she had become deeply concerned as she watched her husband's growing listlessness, his habit of falling asleep in front of the television, his lethargy leaving bed in the morning. And though she was certain the new job at the Seventh Precinct was responsible, Bonora had assured her he enjoyed the lighter working schedule, the change in pace after the work in Homicide. It gave him an opportunity to spend more time with the kids, he said, and in the backyard greenhouse, where for the past few years he had raised begonias and geraniums. Yet from the moment Bonora entered the bedroom that night and kissed her cheek Hazel knew she had been right all along. When her husband wasn't investigating a homicide, when he came home every night at six o'clock finished with work he was feeling useless.

Bonora's present exuberance was the result of more than just the protracted day's investigation. Along with the two squeal men who would normally handle the investigation (one from the local precinct squad, Schoenberger; the other from Homicide, Andreoli) he had been assigned full time to the case as the supervisor. He spoke to his wife now about the day's work, laying out in vivid detail each aspect of the investigation. Hazel listened to his enthusiastic chatter for nearly twenty minutes before she could interject some of her own equally gratifying domestic news. The new medicine, she said, was working well for Betty, their eleven-year-old, who had been hospitalized twice in recent weeks for severe asthma attacks. And a letter had arrived that morning from their son, John, who was spending his high school senior year in Switzerland with Hazel's sister and brother-in-law, a Westinghouse corporate executive.

Unfortunately there was also a less cheerful development to consider. A month ago the Bonoras had been forced to sell their home when the construction of the new junior high school in town had driven up property taxes to over $1,800. The new owners were scheduled to take possession in ten days, and Hazel had so far been unable to locate a less expensive place for them to live. That afternoon she had visited three houses for sale but none had proven satisfactory. As she went on to recount the inadequacies of each home her tone grew more emotional.

Bonora offered a few encouraging remarks, but clearly his mind was elsewhere. Climbing into bed, he again launched into his account of the Pobliner case as if the problem of finding a new house were merely incidental. Hazel recognized the symptoms. Seeing the distant, eager expression in her husband's eyes, she knew she was losing him. Maybe for a week. Perhaps a month. She had been through it hundreds of times in the past, though that didn't make things any easier. She dreaded the long days and nights alone, the decisions and domestic traumas that became solely her own. (One time their daughter, Jeanne, had broken her leg and she was taken to the hospital, operated on, the leg put in a cast, and brought home before Bonora could even be contacted.)

Suddenly Hazel felt herself enveloped in self-pity, a feeling that embarrassed her with its selfishness. Yet like countless police wives before her she couldn't stop thinking how easy life would be should her husband become a businessman dealing with fine, educated people at regular hours. Or if he studied to become part of the higher paid police hierarchy that worked in headquarters in Mineola from nine to five. Of course, that had never been Matt's way. While most of his fellow classmates from the Police Academy had been struggling through the department's *Rules and Regulations* so they could earn their promotions, Bonora was studying criminal and investigative theory, social psychology, the psychopathic personality and reading books like *Practical Fingerprinting, The Informer in Law Enforcement* and Aubry and Caputo's *Criminal Interrogation.* These were subjects that would contribute little should he want to become a lieutenant or captain through the Civil Service examination. However, combined with his work experience, these studies would help build his reputation as the department's finest investigator.

That reputation infused Hazel Bonora with great pride, pride that had not been dimmed by the occasional loneliness and the financial struggles of the passing years. In truth it had been just as much her decision as Bonora's to forgo the real estate offer and the other lucrative job openings that tempted them both from time to time. She knew what police work meant to her husband. Now, however, the children had to be considered, especially with Betty so ill. (The Bonoras had two other daughters at home, Nancy, sixteen, Jeanne, thirteen.) With a major case like this one looming, Hazel knew the responsibility for locating a house and moving would ultimately rest on her shoulders. What if she couldn't deliver?

Bonora saw her troubled look, an expression he had no difficulty interpreting.

"Please don't worry," he said as he turned off the bedside lamp and put his arm around her. "We'll find a new home. It'll work out. I'll see to it. I promise."

CHAPTER

2

BRENDA POBLINER FEARED a man named "Joe" from Asheville, North Carolina. Detectives learned of this fear from her psychiatrist, but neither he nor Brenda's Long Island friends could identify "Joe" or explain why she might fear him. Bonora and Homicide Detective Andreoli were assigned to find out. Early Monday morning, January 6, they arrived in Asheville on a Piedmont Airlines flight, looking much like the businessmen aboard, though they carried pistols underneath their tan raincoats, gold badges in their wallets and Homicide files in their attaché cases.

A once-celebrated resort area of the Old South, Asheville rests on a rolling plateau elevated several thousand feet between the Great Smoky Mountains on the western Tennessee border and the Blue Ridge Mountains in the east. Descending the landing stairwell, Bonora could see the mountains in the distance, old rounded heaps, rimming the airport like the sides of a soup bowl, their frozen forests of pine and spruce a silver-gray beneath the sunlight. He was excited by the dramatic scenery, realizing he was away from Long Island on a special investigation. Yet he was exhausted from the rigors of the past four days. On Thursday, Hazel had located a renovated stone farmhouse with enough bedrooms for the four children and at a rental they could afford. The sergeant had not stopped moving since then, trying to stay abreast of the Pobliner investigation while keeping his promise not to abandon the family until they were resettled. In between interviewing witnesses he had transported the furniture by himself until finally Sunday afternoon he was able to enlist the aid of two moonlighting patrolmen who owned a furniture van. The last of the moving had been completed by 3 A.M.

Feeling the ache in his muscles now, Bonora crossed the runway with Andreoli by his side. Entering the low-slung terminal building, the detectives recognized no one. Nor, by design, was anyone there to meet them. Aware that Herman Pobliner owned a large manufacturing plant in town and that Jay was friendly with members of the local police department, Bonora and Andreoli had decided to use false names and addresses at the motels where they would stay. The proximity to New York City, whose police ranks have been rife with corruption, made them cautious when operating in the jurisdiction of other departments.

Bonora rented a sedan from Avis, and the detectives started immediately on the ten-mile trip into Asheville. Turning the radio to a local station, the two visitors began to chuckle over the Southern twang of the announcer. Then he introduced his first song. "I'm gonna didicate this nex numba to ma ole budda, Jay," he said, and the music began: "Ooh wah, ooh wah, ooh wah ditty, here come the boys from New York City . . ."

With the words *New York* Bonora stiffened. Could Jay Pobliner have that much power in this small town that he had already been apprised of their presence?

Andreoli, struck by a similar thought, brushed it aside with a wave of his hand. "It's just a coincidence, Matt," he said, then sensing Bonora's anxiety added confidently, "There's nothing to worry about."

Bonora glanced at his partner and the sight was enough to reassure him. For at six feet, 275 pounds Andreoli was nothing short of overwhelming in appearance, his feats of strength legendary in the department. Forty-seven and the father of seven, the outsized detective had once dispersed a group of labor demonstrators preparing to storm a factory just by picking the leader off the ground with one hand and warning the crowd he would be waiting for each of them at the gate. He sat now staring straight ahead, his powerful jaw crushing the chewing gum inside with a smooth, even motion. Bonora relaxed and settled back into his seat, turning his thoughts to the countryside as they curved gently past acres of deserted forests and streams and an occasional ramshackle farmhouse with windows patched by rags.

When they reached town the detectives were surprised to find none of the rambling retreats and hotels for which Asheville had long been famous. In their place were scores of new motels and franchise restaurants, servicing salesmen and executives on their visits to the manufacturing districts that have mushroomed in the city's outlying regions. Construction was in progress everywhere: modern, prefabricated glass and brick structures replacing old dilapidated dwellings, highway spurs soon to connect to major federal thruways.

The detectives checked into one of Asheville's two Holiday Inns, ate lunch, then drove to Black Mountain, where Brenda Pobliner had been raised and her parents, Al and Mabel Perkins, still resided. The tiny community was fifteen miles from Asheville, rural and impoverished. Dotting the surrounding landscape were numerous boxlike churches, each offering a variant of the evangelical religion espoused by the Reverend Billy Graham, who lived nearby.

Mr. Perkins, the owner of a wholesale florist shop, remembered Andreoli from a brief meeting at Herman Pobliner's apartment in New York City after his daughter's funeral. He welcomed both unexpected visitors into his tiny whitewashed ranch house. A kindly, taciturn man in his late sixties, Mr. Perkins was wearing a wrinkled brown wool suit and sported a Mason's tiepin that gave Bonora a convenient opening for conversation as the sergeant's uncle was a member of the same fraternal order.

"Wish I could spend more time there. Yessir, a real good organization," Mr. Perkins agreed as he ushered the two detectives into the humbly furnished living room and offered them seats on a stiff-backed couch.

"We dislike visiting people under circumstances such as these," Bonora said apologetically, directing his remarks to Mrs. Perkins, who sat in the corner of the room near the window knitting a shawl. She looked up from her handiwork with gray eyes that were pained and distant.

"There's no need fo' 'pologizin', Sergeant. We understand your business." Her almond-shaped face was sharper and smaller than her daughter's, the umber-colored skin drawn tight.

"No, I certainly don't know who would want to kill our poor Brenda," she declared in a twangy, clipped voice. "There wasn't nobody who didn't cater to her. Why she had a group of friends longer than a three-week grocery list. People liked her 'cause she was so good and simple. She was a hard-workin' gal too. Nothin' really ever came easy to her. We had to take her from college 'cause of nervousness. Worked herself near into a fit. Doctor said she'd go into a hospital if we left her there. Problem was grades came easy to the gal she roomed with. But Brenda, poor soul, she had to work for everthin' she git."

Mr. Perkins looked up from the floor smiling. "She made the Dean's List that second semester, didn't she, Mabel?"

Mrs. Perkins nodded. "Arthur persuaded her not to go back. She really wanted to return, but she always listened to Arthur. Why Arthur Clayton!" she exclaimed, seeing the perplexed look on the detectives' faces. "Arthur Clayton was Brenda's first husband."

A former marriage was a revelation to Bonora, and he pressed the Perkinses about Clayton, aware that nearly 85 percent of all murders stem from personal relationships. Mrs. Perkins discounted the possibility of revenge, insisting that the divorce had been amicable and that Clayton was happily remarried. Nevertheless, Bonora tactfully inquired into his present work and whereabouts. Then he asked about Brenda's former boyfriends

"Didn't really have none after Arthur Clayton," Mrs. Perkins said. "Not really."

"How about Joe Hall?" The detectives had found only one "Joe" from Asheville listed in Brenda's address book—Joe Lyle Hall. They thought he might be the man she feared.

Mrs. Perkins regarded Bonora curiously.

"Joe Hall?" she said. "Why Brenda never dated him. He already got hisself a wife and children."

"They were friends?"

"They jist worked together over at the television station. He's the one that introduced them two, Jay and Brenda."

"Oh, I see. Joe is a friend of Jay's," Bonora said.

"That's right."

"And they hung around together in Asheville?"

"Far's I know."

"Is there any reason Brenda might be afraid of him?"

"Who?"

"Joe Hall."

The elderly woman paused, glancing at her husband, whose eyes were riveted to the floor. Then she shook her head. "Not that I know. I don't think she even seen him in a year or two. He still lives here. He's a disc jockey on the radio."

Bonora turned the questioning to Jay Pobliner, and Mrs. Perkins's tone became suddenly cool. She and her husband had been slightly aloof all along—a reaction Bonora had not been unprepared for, having been warned of the native suspicion toward outsiders in this part of the South. Now, however, as the replies became more abrupt, Bonora grew concerned. Normally the family of a murder victim was eager for help, grateful for the detectives' interest. Instead the Perkinses were making him feel like an interloper, observing his every action with a wariness he suspected the Pobliners might have implanted. For the moment it was merely a hypothesis on the sergeant's part, but it did seem to be borne out shortly thereafter as he began inquiries into Brenda's relationship with Jay. No sooner had he raised the first question than Mrs. Perkins pounced on him, cross and reproving.

"Now Jay had nothing to do with that killing," she said, setting aside her knitting. "He's a fine boy and was a good husband to our Brenda. You couldn't want no better."

"We're not accusing Jay, Mrs. Perkins," Bonora protested. "We simply want to find out as much about your daughter as possible. We always try to get as much information as we can. Sometimes even the most inconsequential fact can lead you to the right suspect."

The elderly woman shook her head, measuring him harshly with her faded eyes. "They had a beautiful marriage, Jay and Brenda did. They loved each other." Suddenly her expression softened and her voice turned wistful.

"Oh, it was like a Cinderella story for her. When they first met, Jay used to fly Brenda up to New York on the weekends and they went everywhere together—all the best restaurants, the movie shows, museums. One day he showed up here carryin' a suede overcoat with a mink collar across his arm for her. They always had such fun together. And Brenda loved that chile mo' than anythin'. Why when it were sick she'd be up all the night. I never seen her so happy befo'."

Mr. Perkins supported his wife's assessment of their son-in-law.

"Jay is a good boy," he said, nodding his pink face soberly. "I s'pose y'all heard about the ten-thousand-dollar reward he's offered for the capture of Brenda's killer. Workin' himself real hard on this investigation, too. Wrote us only 'bout a week ago askin' for Brenda's letters. Says he was gettin' 'em fo' you folks.

"Sent 'em? Sure, we done just like he ask. Mabel sent 'em right up. Weren't nothin' much in 'em far as we could see. Jist 'bout what she did during the day and 'bout Neil and Jay a course. As you say, though, you never know where somethin' like that is liable to lead."

Bonora continued to forage through Brenda's background, including not only Jay in his inquiries but also her other acquaintances, intent on convincing the Perkinses that the Nassau County Police Department did not intend to shape the crime to fit one suspect. Eventually the broad scope and general nature of his questions did seem to ease their doubts. An hour later, sitting around the kitchen table sharing angel-food cake and coffee, the Perkinses began to divulge a few of those confidences normally reserved for only the closest of relatives and friends but which the homicide detective must eventually learn if he is to succeed.

"You know," Mrs. Perkins confessed with pride, "Brenda really was a Black Mountain girl. She converted to Judaism for Jay and his people and accepted all the ways of the New Yorkers, but she wrote me so many times she felt Black Mountain was her home. She hoped one day to persuade Jay to return here to raise Neil in these hills. You know, it's quiet here and peaceful like no place else on earth.

"Oh, the Pobliners was very generous to her," she continued, cutting the men another slice of cake. "You can't fault them none. They gave her all types of expensive clothes and jewelry. But she never did cotton to gaudy things. She wrote me she never wore them 'cept when her in-laws paid a call."

Afterward, as the detectives prepared to leave, there was unexpected warmth in the Perkinses' demeanor. Mr. Perkins personally helped both detectives on with their coats, and when they started for the door made certain to shake hands.

"Y'all come back now," he said.

Bonora promised to apprise them of new developments in the case. As he opened the door Mrs. Perkins looked him directly in the eye. She whispered, "Good luck and God bless you both."

Early the next morning the Nassau-county detectives drove to Greenville, South Carolina, a one-hundred-mile trip taken on the chance that Arthur Clayton might be involved in the murder of his former wife. He was not. An employee of the local Westinghouse plant, Clayton's alibi was corroborated through talks with his employer and several neighbors. Returning to Asheville the following day, the detectives interviewed a few of Brenda's close girlfriends, ostensibly to learn more about Brenda but actually seeking information on Joe Hall. They gained little. At that point Bonora made the decision to contact the Asheville police. He was still skeptical of their loyalties. His suspicions had actually been magnified since learning the Chief's name was also Joe Hall. But it appeared that on their own the detectives would not be able to unearth sufficient background information to properly interrogate Hall. Furthermore, Bonora feared that in a small, close-knit town like Asheville the police were bound to learn detectives *from up North* were about asking questions. The insult of failing to contact their local counterparts might foreclose future cooperation should it be needed.

The Asheville Police Department shares its headquarters with the city fire department. It is located in Pack Square, a dismal cement plaza downtown that is dominated by a seventy-five-foot granite obelisk erected by the United Daughters of the Confederacy to honor Zebulon B. Vance, a rebel Senator and twice Governor of the state. Late Thursday afternoon Bonora parked in front of the two-story gray stone building. The two detectives entered the waiting room, where patrolmen were turning out for the four o'clock shift. In serried ranks, they were undergoing a careful inspection, ramrod-stiff in their gray Confederate uniforms with the blue stripe down the leg, their heads shaven like soldiers in boot camp. The officer in charge was a squat, feisty lieutenant, who became solicitous when he heard the detectives' Italian names and learned they were New Yorkers. The lieutenant's own name was Pipitone and he had come from Brooklyn twenty years before. Now, however, he spoke with a distinct Southern drawl.

"Sure enough," he said, "the men always rib me 'bout being a Yank. But I tell 'em hell, they's only been bawn he-uh. I'm a Suthner by choice."

While they were talking, a nattily dressed man in his late twenties stepped from behind the front desk.

"Are you the two boys from New York?" he demanded in a gruff voice. He was wearing dark sunglasses and a slanting brown suede fedora that obscured his face and matched his double-breasted sport jacket.

Bonora, who thought him some sort of promoter, said, "That's right. We're detectives from Nassau County."

"I heah y'all been lookin' fo' me, askin' a lot a nosy questions. My name is Joe Hall."

Bonora tried to conceal his astonishment. "Well, as a matter of fact, Joe, we were looking to talk to you," he said slowly, trying to give himself time to think.

"Okay, do it now," Hall snapped. "Let's get this sheet over with 'cause I got nothin' to say to y'all anyhow."

Bonora appealed to the Asheville lieutenant and Pipitone led them into a room off the reception hall that resembled a closet. It was cramped and windowless, the walls painted a muddy brown. Light was supplied by a bare bulb hanging on a wire from the twenty-foot-high ceiling. Hall slouched confidently into a chair, gazing at the detectives with cold black eyes that signaled he was no neophyte in the world of police interrogations. When the questions began, he spoke in a voice that was both arrogant and cutting. He did admit introducing Pobliner to Brenda Perkins at the television station, but other than offering that information he was consistently unhelpful. As for the days surrounding Brenda's death, December 26 and 27, Hall claimed he had been on the air at WISE radio station from noon to 8 P.M., afterward going to the Some Place Else, the discotheque he owned.

"Do you know how to fly an airplane?" Bonora asked, thinking a private plane would have been the simplest means to travel to Long Island and back in the short amount of time between the two radio shows.

"No," Hall answered.

"You have any friends that do?"

Hall stretched out his legs along the floor and smirked. He was a sturdy, straw-haired young man, six feet two inches tall, with a thick nose and a hard mouth. He said, "Sergeant, I got friends in this heah town that can do anything."

"What about guns, Joe? You like to play with guns?" Bonora's tone had soured. He felt the witness toying with him.

"No, not at all. Why do you ask?"

Bonora pointed to Hall's jacket buttons which had been made from the brass ends of shotgun shells. "What's with those?"

Hall glanced down, then noticed Bonora's miniature shotgun shell tietack. The Winchester Firearms Company had awarded it to the sergeant for consecutively downing twenty-five clay pigeons at one of their trapshooting ranges.

"How about you, cop?" he said. "You like to play with guns. I see that shotgun shell on your tie."

Bonora exploded. "Let's cut the bullshit, Joe. We're not here to fuck around. If you want to play games, you better know the goddam rules. In New York State the law says we can lock your ass up if we find you have information about a murder and have been holding back on us."

"You guys don't scare me."

"We're not here to scare you. Actually we're here to help you. And to get your help. And we're going to do just that if we have to follow your ass all over this town or any other goddam town. Let's get that straight, Joe. Here and now."

"Well, don't you'all be comin' 'roun' my club," Hall warned. "That's private and I'll have y'all thrown out on yo' asses."

Bonora turned on him, his gaze steady. "Don't you worry," he said in a low, confident voice. "We'll be there. You're going to be seeing plenty of us."

Hall smiled thinly. But during the remaining five minutes his voice seemed to lose its edge. He even suggested a possible suspect in Brenda Pobliner's murder, an American Nazi party member named Frank Gaddis. According to Hall, Jay Pobliner had reported Gaddis to the FBI for allegedly threatening to assassinate President Lyndon Johnson. Gaddis despised Pobliner, he said, and would do anything to gain revenge. As the meeting broke up, Hall also seemed to reconsider his lack of hospitality to the Northern visitors. He offered to buy the detectives a beer if they stopped by his club that night, though with Bonora's courteous acceptance, this unexpected touch of magnanimity quickly evaporated. Hall's upper lip curled into a sneer and the swagger returned to his voice.

"Cops are the same all over. Always happy to snatch a free beer."

Bonora ignored the taunt, but he saw his partner bristle as Hall rose, adjusted his jacket and walked confidently out the door. "Why that lousy son of a bitch," Andreoli growled.

Chief Hall was waiting for the two investigators when their interrogation ended, as unrelated to Joe Lyle Hall in disposition, it turned out, as he was by blood. Dressed in a dark blue suit, he was a distinguished-looking man with fine, well-matched features and a shock of wavy gray hair. His manner was soft and gracious.

"Anythin' we can do fo' you men, why don't hesitate to call on me," he told his guests after they explained the purpose of their visit. Then he brought in his deputy in charge of day-to-day operations, Deputy Chief Gene Jarvis. Jarvis was considerably younger than his boss and more nearly resembled the kind of policeman the detectives expected to find in this Southern hill town. The deputy looked and acted like a retired marine drill instructor. He had a quarter-inch-high crew cut and wore his horn-rimmed glasses pushed up tight against his face. Though the highest educated officer in the department—he was a graduate of Springfield Teachers College in Massachusetts and numerous police seminars conducted across the country, including those at Yale and the University of Michigan—Jarvis seemed more interested in impressing the visitors with tales of his physical prowess. "No sir, I'm no man fo' sittin' behind a desk," he commented while leading them down a hall to his own office.

As they entered the drably furnished room Bonora's eyes bulged at the stacks of rifles and shotguns heaped on the floor, at the shelves above the desk coruscating with military helmets, the pea-shell-shaped American variety as well as the squared-off German and Prussian models with ornate spires.

"We been gettin' some riot gear together," Jarvis explained, picking up one of the rifles and cocking it with a brisk snap. "The federal government is sending us new equipment but in the meantime the boys brought in what they had from home."

"You expecting trouble?" Andreoli asked.

"Don't rightly know for sure. We got our share of Black Panthers though. You can bet on that."

Bonora mentioned his surprise at seeing a black patrolman in the four o'clock turnout.

"Oh, we're not all that backwards down heah, Sergeant," Jarvis said, smiling. "Despite what you read up in your New York papers."

"I meant he looked kinda short," Bonora added quickly, trying to cover his blunder.

"Well, let me tell y'all sumthin'," Jarvis said, leaning across the desk with an air of confidentiality. "That lil' ole boy turned out to be one helluva police officer. They don't mess around with him in this town.

"He patrols the colored section and when he first started he didn't waste no time showin' them who's the boss. His first night out he walked right into a bar where all the big bucks hang out. A couple of 'em shouted they was gonna take his gun away and shove it right up his ass. You see, he was the first colored officer we had. But our lil' ole friend he-uh, well he pulls out his pistol and picks the first three guys off the first three bar stools."

The deputy leaned back in his chair and winked. "We don't have no trouble down they-uh anymaw."

The two Nassau County detectives laughed uncomfortably and the conversation settled into the customary comparison of police departments and job conditions that is almost ritual when policemen from different locales get together. (With its nearly four thousand employees the Nassau County department is the largest suburban police force in the nation, the seventh largest overall. Starting salary was close to $10,000 in 1968. Today it is $12,500. A new recruit in the one-hundred-member Asheville Police Department receives only half that amount. Retirement benefits are also better on Long Island. It takes a Nassau County patrolman only twenty years' service to gain a lifetime pension of half-salary. An Asheville patrolman must work until he is sixty-five with no less than thirty years' service.)

Proper protocol observed, Bonora turned the conversation to the Pobliner investigation. Jarvis admitted knowing little about Jay

Pobliner other than that he had managed his father's manufacturing plant for several years in Asheville and maintained friendships with a number of men in the police department. He assumed the factory position must have been a sinecure, for young Jay seemed to spend most of his time riding about town in his Cadillac convertible, carousing with friends or picking up girls.

Joe Hall, on the other hand, was a subject in which the deputy was extremely well versed. Not only had Jarvis been personally responsible for his arrest on several occasions when he kited checks, but he lived on the same block as Hall. Agnes Hall, Joe's wife, visited Jarvis periodically to discuss problems with her husband, the most recent his abandonment of the family to live with Nancy Hensley, a twenty-two-year-old go-go dancer in his nightclub.

"You know, Agnes Hall is from a very fine Asheville family," Jarvis remarked. "But that Joe is a real character. He could sell snow to the Eskimos. Wouldn't surprise me 'tall if Joe killed that Pobliner gal, nor many of the people roun' heah either, I reckon. You see none of us is too happy with that club a his and those topless dancers."

"Topless dancers?" Andreoli exclaimed.

"Sure," said Jarvis, smiling mischievously, "though they don't start the evening out that way."

"What about that Gaddis fellow?" Bonora said. "Did Pobliner report him to the FBI?" Jarvis was uncertain, nor did Chief Hall, who soon joined the men in conversation, know.

"Well, was he a Nazi?" Bonora persisted.

"Oh yes," Chief Hall observed gravely. "But he hasn't been any trouble for at least a couple of years. The last time he was in town marchin' round heah with that swastiker I went out and spoke to him myself. I told him I had fought in Europe in World War II against that flag and I had seen a lot of my pals die on a cause of it. He wasn't gonna be carryin' it round in this heah city anymore. It was jest that simple."

Bonora indicated his interest in talking to Gaddis, and Hall promptly volunteered to find him. The Chief kept his word. By Saturday, Asheville detectives had located Gaddis forty-five miles outside the city in rural Yancey County. Bonora and Andreoli drove immediately to his cabin as Gaddis had no phone, and the three men spent six hours together. Pale-skinned and anemic-looking, with widespread, slow-blinking eyes, Gaddis seemed not at all vindictive toward Pobliner but rather much in awe—a circumstance that seemed to indicate Joe Hall had been purposely misleading. Calling Jay "jest a good ole boy," Gaddis said he admired Pobliner's proficiency in judo and his excellence as a marksman. The two had met at a local motorcycle shop and had biked together and occasionally hunted.

Gaddis informed the detectives that he had been working as a department store guard on the day of Brenda Pobliner's death. His attitude was open and cooperative. Though he offered little that was new to the detectives, he did mention in passing that Jay used to practice target shooting in his Asheville apartment, recalling that a number of the plastic bullets were embedded in the walls. At Bonora's insistence he later drove them to the hills outside of Asheville and pointed out Pobliner's former residence in a two-building housing complex.

The following day, Sunday, the detectives returned to the Asheville hills, accompanied by Sgt. Buster Ingle, an Asheville police detective, and knocked on the door of the designated apartment. Bonora reasoned that by finding the bullets he could corroborate Gaddis's story, thus tending to substantiate his innocence. But at the back of the sergeant's mind was another thought, indicative of his suspicions at the moment. If the bullets were .22 caliber, perhaps they could be matched to those that had killed Brenda Pobliner.

The present tenant of the apartment, Terry Cullen (not his real name), was another radio disc jockey. He kept the detectives waiting in the hallway almost ten minutes, explaining in a nervous, high-pitched voice that he was "cleaning up." When he finally opened the door Bonora stepped into the living room and glanced about in disbelief. Covering the floor and furniture were reels and reels of film, the strips of celluloid hanging from canisters ensnarled and entangled with one another like a den of snakes. Bonora held several strands of film up to the ceiling light, awed by the variety of sexual gymnastics depicted. Then he dropped them to look more closely at the room walls. They were papered in a collage of lewd photographs and magazine cutouts.

"Well, what can I do for you boys?" Cullen asked uneasily.

"We want to examine the walls," said Sergeant Ingle.

Cullen paled.

"We're looking for bullet holes," Bonora added hastily.

"Bullet holes?" said the disc jockey, exhaling with relief. "Sure, go ahead."

The detectives spread out through the apartment and began carefully to inspect the three rooms. They found a continuation of the mosaic of salacious photographs in the bedroom and kitchen, but there were no bullet holes in the entire apartment. In the living room, however, Bonora noticed an inflatable rubber mannequin that had been hidden behind a couch near the window. It was the perfect likeness of a naked woman complete with all sexual parts.

"What's with the rubber dummy, Terry?" he asked, as they were about to leave.

Cullen walked to the window and picked the mannequin off the floor. Standing, it was just about his size.

"Y'all ever heard the song 'Paper Doll'?"

Bonora nodded, smiling inwardly as he recalled the old tune that described a man who decided to purchase a paper doll to take the place of a real girlfriend.

"This heah's my paper doll," Cullen said. And seeing no adverse reaction from the detectives, he led them to the living room closet. "She looks great in anythin'," he declared, beaming. He opened the closet door to reveal an entire wardrobe of women's clothes.

"But what do you do with her?" Andreoli inquired innocently.

"Why she ken do anythin' any woman ken," Cullen replied. He pulled a plaid skirt from the closet and wrapped it around the naked model. "Anythin' I want. And I don't have to worry no maw that she won't be heah when I come home."

"Sure, that's right," Bonora agreed. "A gal like that's not about to run away on you. What do you do, Terry, blow her up each night?"

"Nah, you don't have to. Hell, she'll stay inflated forever if I want."

Andreoli said, "But do you actually, uh ... I mean do you—"

Before he could complete the question Bonora had wedged his arm under the hulking detective and turned him to the door.

"So long, Terry. Thanks for everything," he said. And the three detectives quickly left the apartment, marching down the hallway in an anxious silence that erupted into raucous, hysterical laughter when they reached the squad car, then moments later died as their disappointment struck home. The failure to find the slugs or even the bullet holes meant that Gaddis would now require further investigation.

Yet the detectives did not return immediately to Yancey County. Going over their notes that night they found an inconsistency that instead prompted them to appear early the next morning at the real estate office managing the apartment complex. A two-hour review of the rental records confirmed their suspicions: Gaddis had pointed out the wrong apartment! Jay Pobliner had actually occupied the same corner apartment as Cullen but in the adjoining building.

Ordered to return to Long Island that afternoon, the detectives rushed back to the complex and located the superintendent, who obligingly opened Pobliner's now vacant apartment. The bullet holes were visible from the doorway—precisely in the spot Gaddis had described. With the superintendent's help the wood paneling was quickly removed. Then Bonora used his pocketknife to scrape out the plastic bullets buried deep within the fiberboard wall. As each bullet dropped onto the floor the detectives examined it with intense anticipation. There were twelve in all. Not a .22 caliber slug in the lot.

CHAPTER

3

Two WEEKS after their return to Nassau County, Andreoli learned through a telephone conversation with Mr. Perkins that his son-in-law was planning a visit. As the investigation had not progressed significantly on Long Island, it was decided the detectives would return to Asheville. Jay Pobliner was still under suspicion for the murder of his wife. Moreover, Joe Hall's alibi had not yet been fully corroborated.

On the scheduled day of Pobliner's arrival Bonora and Andreoli were positioned inside the conning tower of the Asheville Municipal Airport, their eyes gazing intently down on the runway from behind the green windows. Interested in whom Pobliner might contact in North Carolina, they were utterly astonished by what subsequently occurred. As the 2 P.M. Piedmont flight from Newark, New Jersey, landed, Lt. Clarence Welborn of the Asheville Police Department pulled onto the runway with the emergency light of his patrol car flashing. A moment later Pobliner, followed by a black maid cradling his young son, walked off the plane carrying two full-sized suitcases. He handed the suitcases to the Asheville lieutenant, who locked them into his trunk. Then the two men exchanged a few words, shook hands and parted: Pobliner and the maid entering the terminal to rent a car, Welborn leaving the airport with the suitcases.

From the viewpoint of the two Nassau County detectives the transfer of suitcases constituted retribution to the Southern lieutenant for some past personal service. But during the next few days as they surreptitiously followed Pobliner about town Bonora's inbred cynicism gained the upper hand. The curious transaction assumed increasing degrees of criminality: from smuggling cigarettes and alcohol to procuring girls to transporting stolen jewelry until finally, the distribution of hard drugs became the most reasonable explanation.

Yet none of these theories concerning Welborn's involvement proved accurate. When the Nassau County detectives questioned him about his activities he made no attempt to dissemble in describing the airport trip. A slow-talking man in his late forties with an appearance and manner suggesting some kind of bumbling though well-meaning Andy Devine character, Welborn explained that Pobliner had asked to be picked up ("Jay, he loves to ride in the po-lice car") then apparently changed his mind. He decided to rent his own car at the airport, the lieutenant said, and asked him to deliver his suitcases to the home of a friend where he would be staying while in North Carolina.

"As I told yuh, Sarge, he always been a good boy 'round heah. Course he do spend money like the devil," Welborn observed, his horsey mouth spreading into a smile that exposed his missing back teeth. "Used to come in, you know, and take the whole squad out to dinnah."

Bonora spent the next half hour trying to shake Welborn out of his naiveté. He planted the thought that the suitcases could very easily have been transporting drugs and that if federal agents were following Pobliner the lieutenant would be arrested for complicity. When

Welborn countered by declaring, "Jay, he told me you guys are after him," Bonora calmly denied the charge but added candidly, "He is certainly under suspicion." Then drawing upon all his dramatic skills, the sergeant ominously admonished Welborn against further involvement with Pobliner, suggesting he think about his wife and children first. "You could end up in real trouble," he warned, and with a menacing look exited from the lieutenant's office.

The histrionics took an immediate effect. Five days later, February 3, Bonora received a call to the office of Chief Hall. When he arrived he found Lieutenant Welborn staring mutely at the floor, his lips trembling. Beside him was an Asheville patrolman, who for good reason was as anxious as his superior. It seems that following his discussion with Bonora, Lieutenant Welborn had "chatted" with Patrolman Walt Masters and the two policemen had then visited Chief Hall. Masters confessed to purchasing a .22 caliber pistol for Jay Pobliner in the early fall, a weapon Pobliner had conspicuously neglected to mention to the Nassau County detectives.

"It wasn't 'til last weekend that I recollected," Patrolman Masters apologized, but Bonora waved off the explanation, insisting that his present cooperation was the important thing.

Masters's distress was obvious. He massaged his jaw vigorously and his wide, soulful eyes twitched as he recounted the purchase of the single-action revolver, a cheap German import called an R and W that Pobliner wanted "jest for target practice." Then with quick, nervous steps he began to pace the office as Bonora placed a telephone call to the Nassau County Scientific Investigation Bureau. The ballistics specialist, Inspector Glen Carpenter, had already concluded the murder weapon to be a Colt Frontiersman, but a second check of his records now made him reassess his opinion. Yes, the R and W might very well fit the necessary specifications, he said.

Masters seemed taken aback by the news. He wanted desperately to rid himself of any taint of wrongdoing, so Bonora gave him the opportunity.

Apprised of the need to retrieve the weapon, Masters telephoned

Pobliner who had returned to New York. Reaching him at his father's apartment on Central Park West in Manhattan, he explained in a worried voice that the Nassau County detectives were in Asheville and would soon be questioning him. Under no circumstances did he want to become involved in the murder of Jay's wife. Bonora, listening on another extension, heard Pobliner assure Masters that the gun he had purchased was not responsible for Brenda's death, that he had given the pistol to a friend in October and that it was still in his friend's possession. His voice was nonchalant but firm in its refusal to return the gun, until Masters threatened to reveal its existence to the Nassau County detectives. Then Pobliner grew palpably concerned and under continuing pressure from the patrolman finally agreed to contact his friend and call Masters at the end of the week to make arrangements for the pistol's return.

Bonora was jubilant. Pobliner's agreement meant that the gun had been neither destroyed nor lost. It was the break he had hoped for.

February 6 was bitter and wet on Long Island. At nine o'clock that morning Hazel Bonora stood in her winter coat glancing about the kitchen, satisfied by what she observed. The breakfast dishes had been cleared from the table and placed in the dishwasher, the sink left spotless, *The New York Times* added to the growing stack awaiting her husband's return. An hour before, the children had departed for school. Her final inspection completed now, she carefully locked the kitchen door and walked through the rain to the garage where the Ford station wagon was parked, determined to make this day seem like any other.

She pulled out of the driveway and turned south toward the Harold Johnson Real Estate Agency, proceeding slowly along the village of Wantagh's quiet morning streets, the curbs still bordered by patches of snow. The darkness of the day and the rain required her full concentration while driving. But it was difficult to focus her attention so completely, difficult to close her mind to the fact that this was her twentieth wedding anniversary and her husband was still six hundred miles away.

She arrived before 9:30 A.M. at the small red-brick house that served as the real estate office. Finding herself alone, she prepared a cup of instant coffee and began at once to busy herself, checking the classified advertising to record the new properties on the market, reviewing her own files and preparing lists of potential houses for the day's expected customers. For six months she had worked as a real estate saleswoman and it was a period in her life that made her feel content and proud. She appreciated the independence the work allowed, the opportunity to meet new people and the money she earned ($3,500 so far) that enabled her to afford new clothing and larger allowances for the children as well as certain luxuries the family couldn't otherwise have enjoyed. (They had recently visited Bonora's parents, who had retired to Arizona.) She was pleased Matt had insisted she accept the job offer their neighbor, Harold Johnson, had made.

This morning, however, the challenge of matching customers' expressed desires to houses that never quite fit failed to divert her. She stared out the window feeling a touch of melancholy as the rain struck the black macadam of the road, turning the curbside snow into muddy pools of water. We *should* be together today, she thought, then quickly chastised herself. But the longing didn't stop.

She had known her husband almost thirty years, since their childhood days in Hempstead, Long Island, where both their parents had moved from Brooklyn. Bonora's father was a printer, her father a construction foreman. They had begun to date in high school when Matt was a skinny teen-ager with a mischievous streak that kept him out of school more often than in. She had been a cheerleader who everyone predicted would become a famous model or movie actress because of her delicate features and slender figure. But Hazel Johnsen had not gone to Hollywood or New York when graduation ended (nor did she regret the decision). With Matt's promise to return after a tour of duty in the marines, she found a job in the Arnold Constable department store in Hempstead working the teletype machine. And when he finally did return three years later they were married as planned in the Trinity Lutheran Church in West Hempstead, the reception following in the American Legion Hall.

During the twenty years they had spent together the Bonoras' relationship developed into a strong and protective bond. Hazel felt no qualms about her role as wife and mother and continued to impress Bonora with her ability to handle the children, to cook and clean, to manage the finances and to stay young and attractive. Rarely did they disagree over items of major importance such as how the children should be raised. Both upheld the orthodox moral code of their parents and made demands on their children that might be considered excessive in light of today's liberalized conventions. Yet they prided themselves in being decidedly more lenient than either of their own parents had been. For instance, when Nancy attended the junior prom she would not have to be home at midnight as Hazel's Norwegian immigrant parents had required of her. But Hazel did want to know where Nancy was going afterward, with whom, and at what time she would return. John was allowed to wear his hair modishly long though not unkempt. The girls wore washed-out jeans and t-shirts if they were freshly cleaned and neat. All four were properly respectful of their elders, intensely loyal to one another— "good kids" in the most traditional sense of that term. When instructed to do something by either parent, they did it without quibbling.

During most of the years of their marriage Bonora had sheltered Hazel from his police work—at least from the gruesome part. (A born raconteur, he couldn't resist those curious incidents that begged recounting, especially if amusing dialects were called for in the telling.) She was grateful for this preclusion initially though after the transfer to Homicide she began to dread the interminable days that passed without an indication of the dangers her husband faced. Though the thought of Matt being shot rarely troubled her—this was the suburbs after all—she did worry about him in other ways. Assigned to a murder case, he was like a dog with a bone, refusing to let go, working ninety to one hundred hours a week with never a moment's rest. Hazel had a recurring nocturnal fantasy that Matt had fallen asleep at the wheel driving home late from an interrogation and had been killed in a highway crash. This nightmare would awaken her and the anguish of not knowing where he was or what he was doing would intensify. Her fears for her husband had finally given her an ulcer.

Fortunately, since the beginning of the Pobliner investigation, Bonora had kept Hazel informed of the case's daily progress. He felt guilty about his prolonged absences from home and hoped the knowledge would ease her concern as well as convince her of the importance of his presence in Asheville. Pleased at first, Hazel wondered now whether it wasn't better to remain ignorant. Aware of the investigation's present state, she could no longer delude herself into thinking it would soon end. It would be weeks until their normal routine could resume.

The thought of this dismal prospect distressed her and for a moment longer her eyes lingered wistfully on the rain-splattered window. Then she turned back to her desk and continued her research in an even more concentrated effort, working diligently through the next half hour until the front door opened. Looking up and seeing the blue uniform of a Nassau County patrolman, she felt her heart start to run, assuming he had come about her husband. The patrolman proceeded to explain his presence, but Hazel sat there shaking her head as if disputing his words until finally she realized he wasn't talking about Matt at all. He was merely inquiring about a nearby robbery that had occurred some hours before.

The patrolman's departure was followed soon afterward by the arrival of Harold Johnson, her boss, and several of the other saleswomen. The disquieting silence was replaced by the normal hum of activity, and Hazel returned to her work, making several appointments for the afternoon, then selecting suitable houses to show the customers. The next thing that happened was a memorable event in her life. She recalled it this way:

"It was almost noontime and I was on the telephone trying to fix an appointment with a landlord. All of a sudden one of the gals in the office started shouting and pointing toward the window as if she had gone mad. I looked outside, and coming up the front walk was Matt. It was still raining out, really pouring. And he was soaked to the skin. He saw me through the window and he started to smile. It was as if the sun had begun to shine. He was carrying his suitcase in one hand and a dozen long-stemmed roses in the other. He had just flown in from Asheville. I ran to the door and we hugged and kissed in the doorway just like school kids. Then I brought him into the office and everybody joked about how forlorn I'd been without him. He smiled and looked exhausted. His face was drawn and there were dark rings under his eyes. I think he must have lost fifteen pounds since the investigation began.

"He told me he had to return to Asheville in the morning for some phone call and suggested we go have lunch together. He was trying his best to be romantic, but he was falling asleep on his feet so I sent him home for a nap. I had appointments for the afternoon anyway. Frankly I was a little worried about him. He was almost forty then, but you know Matt. He didn't let age interfere with anything he ever did. He was probably driving himself just like a rookie down in Asheville."

Bonora didn't need much coaxing to "nap." He returned home, and not until ten hours later did he awake. He jumped out of bed and immediately began to upbraid Hazel for allowing him to sleep so long. He hadn't flown all the way home from Asheville just to rest, he complained good-naturedly. Over her protests he dressed for the evening, putting on his dark blue suit, the one he had bought the year before for the Detective Association dinner, and a new Countess Mara silk tie that had been a Christmas present from the children. A few minutes later Hazel joined him downstairs, secretly glad he had resisted her arguments about the lateness of the hour. Her blond hair was wrapped high around her head and sprayed in place. Her shapely but now plumpish figure was adorned by a gray wool gabardine outfit with a mink collar and cuffs that she had bought on sale two months before and kept in hiding.

Bonora was delighted by the surprise. He opened a split of

domestic champagne, which they drank in the living room over an exchange of "ancient memories." Then the detective drove his wife to the San Su San, a nightclub not far from police headquarters in Mineola that had been a favorite in the early years of their marriage. In those days it boasted an orchestra, a brightly lit dance floor and round tables covered in thick white linen. But "those days" were gone. The place now bearing the San Su San name turned out to be nothing more than a local gin mill, dark with jukebox music, the customers in their Banlon shirts and sweaters looking as if they had just come from the nearby bowling alley. Determined to celebrate their past, the Bonoras stayed for one quick drink, though Hazel felt much too overdressed and out of place to enjoy even that. Afterward they decided to try the Banjo Inn, a nearby nightclub that seemed the only alternative other than driving into New York City, which Hazel ruled out since Matt was leaving early in the morning. The Inn's atmosphere was an improvement—the main room was more festive-looking and there was live music—but the youthful ambience seemed much more appropriate to a high school graduation party than a twentieth-anniversary celebration. The patrons were predominantly teen-agers in jeans and sweaters who could very well have been the Bonoras' own children or their friends'. Still, the evening was not one they would soon forget. Matt and Hazel each had a few Scotches and spent a couple of hours singing along with the banjo music, enjoying each other with a poignant awareness that they were lucky to be together that night.

The strobe light flashed, reflecting vividly off the towering granite walls of the Asheville Post Office. "Okay," Bonora instructed, "open it slowly so the photographer can shoot each step."

Patrolman Masters nodded and began to untie the string holding the cardboard shoe box that Jay had finally mailed to him after numerous conversations and arrangements. When the knot was undone, he stepped aside to give the photographer room, and the camera flashed again. Then Masters removed the box from the outside wrapping paper. Flash! The inside of the box was lined with brown paper. Flash! Wrapped in the paper were several dress shirts and two ties. Flash! Concealed between the shirts and ties was a nickel-plated .22 caliber revolver. Flash! There it was. Jay Pobliner's gun at last!

Bonora scooped up the entire package, grabbed the film from the photographer and left immediately for the airport with Andreoli. En route the two detectives stopped at Finkelstein's Gunshop in Pack Square and by comparing the registration numbers verified that the pistol Pobliner had mailed was the one Masters had originally purchased. Then they were on the plane to New York, then in Mineola waiting outside the ballistics laboratory in the Scientific Investigation Bureau. Three hours later at ten o'clock Inspector Carpenter called them into his office. He had test-fired the gun several times, comparing its slugs with those that had killed Brenda Pobliner. The test slugs were grooved six times with a right twist, the murder slugs six times to the left. Pobliner's R and W was not the murder weapon.

Bonora's astonishment was complete. For a moment, unable to speak, he stood there gazing at the inspector. In the excitement and expectation of the past few days he had stopped considering the possibility that Pobliner's gun was not the murder weapon. It made such sense in his mind. It explained his reluctance to return the pistol. It explained his mysterious behavior at the house the day of the murder. It explained . . .

Bonora thanked Carpenter for his assistance and left, returning slowly through the second-floor corridor to the Homicide Squad. When he arrived he found the detectives sitting around the reception desk drinking coffee, their somber expressions indicating the news had already reached them. "C'mon," Bonora said, "let's get some dinner."

The men piled into two squad cars and drove to Lorenzo's in nearby Hempstead. The restaurant-bar was a detective hangout, a long pine-paneled room dimly illuminated by strings of Christmas lights and featuring cop talk and Italian specialties made with a thick Neapolitan sauce. It was a place to relax and unwind, to rethink and consider new alternatives. The detectives were given a large table in the rear and Bonora ordered a double Scotch. He was badly disappointed by what had just occurred and not a little disillusioned. The case was close to two months old and detectives had still not recovered the murder weapon nor did they even have a motive for the crime. He felt as if they were starting almost from the beginning again, a thought that discouraged him, though he had no intention of giving up the pursuit. A murder had been committed and the killer would have to be found. That was the challenge of his profession.

Andreoli suggested they press Illis Jurisson harder. Several of the other detectives wanted to reinterview Jay Pobliner, believing he knew more than he had so far revealed. Bonora was of the opinion Joe Hall was the key. He had a background of criminal activity, and no doubt possessed the proper connections to manage such a skillfully executed crime. Over heaping plates of spaghetti in red clam sauce the detectives appraised the case further, discussing their personal theories and reviewing possible avenues of approach. As the evening wore on, it was decided that Andreoli would pursue the investigation of Illis Jurisson. Pobliner would not be reinterviewed, but his neighbors and acquaintances would be. Bonora and Seventh Squad squeal man Gene Schoenberger were to return to Asheville. They would concentrate on Joe Hall.

By the middle of February, when Bonora and Schoenberger arrived in Asheville, Joe Hall's life had become a shambles. He was still estranged from his wife and children but increasingly uneasy about the situation. He had no money and the Some Place Else, the club he had dreamed would make him both wealthy and content, was about to fold for his inability to pay the back taxes. Neither of these conditions, in Hall's own words, however, were worth a "bucket a piss" compared to his concern over the murder of Brenda Pobliner.

Unaware of this "concern," the Nassau County detectives elected not to reinterview Hall because of their previous poor reception. Instead they decided to pressure him indirectly. They did this first by having stories published in the two local newspapers, the Asheville *Times* and the Asheville *Citizen,* that described their continuing interest in the case. Next they began interviewing more of Hall's companions and his fellow employees at the radio station. Finally, one evening a week later, an Asheville detective was sent into the Some Place Else to tell Hall the Pobliner investigation was "all sewn up." He indicated that the Nassau County detectives were preparing to make arrests and that Hall had "better come clean."

Neither this ruse nor the detectives' other activity forced Hall to break his silence. Yet when Bonora and Schoenberger returned to Mineola at the end of February they carried within their briefcases information that would send the investigation a giant step forward. During the week of their stay Asheville detectives had managed to locate the Pobliner maid, who had fled to North Carolina a week before the murder. Her interview presented them with the first hint of a possible motive.

Dark and rawboned, with two small children and an estranged husband, Effie Mae Rosiere punctured the illusion of an idyllic marriage that both Jay Pobliner and Brenda's parents had so enthusiastically painted. She described a household filled with unhappiness and wracked by quarrels.

"Mr. Pobliner hisself out two or three nights a week," she said, "comin' home two in the mornin'. He used to say he was goin' shootin' wid hiz gun, but y'all knows what kinda shootin' he be doin'. He'd go up to dat gas station wid dat friend a his Butch and dat other fella wid the red hair and no legs. Dat's right. Red hair and no legs. Miz Pobliner didn't like it none. She oways beggin' him to stay home, but Mr. Pobliner, he never listen to her much. He pretty strong-headed.

"Fightin'? Yes, dey fightin' all de times. One time, oh dere was a big fuss. The phone rang and Miz Pobliner picked it up but dere wasn't no answer. She come to de dinnah table screamin', 'Dat was your girlfriend callin'.'

"Sure he had a girlfriend. Lily, her name was Lily. I took a message from her one time, I remember . . ."

Effie Mae Rosiere's statement sent detectives scurrying through Merrick, checking the local gas stations for a red-haired, legless man who they hoped would lead them to Pobliner's mistress. As easy as this might appear, it became a prodigious task, for Merrick, like the rest of the South Shore of Nassau County, is the epitome of automobile-dominated suburbia. Merrick Road alone boasts ninety-four service stations, more per mile than any road in the state. And if the density of gas stations were not enough to burden their search, the detectives were, in addition, proscribed from questioning the attendants for fear of alerting the elusive witness. They could only observe.

For almost two weeks detectives from Homicide and the Seventh Squad scoured the tiny village with no success. Then it was decided that the legless man's description would be given to the county patrolmen–information that had been withheld as a precaution against leaks. Finally, a week later, a highway patrolman spotted the red-headed amputee in Stan's Automotive Center, a yellow-tiled Sinclair gas station on Merrick Road less than a mile from the Pobliner home. When Bonora and Andreoli arrived there they found Butch Pezold working in the garage, the "Butch" mentioned both by Effie Mae Rosiere and Mrs. Perkins, who had met him in November when he accompanied Jay on a hunting trip. It was Butch, under threat of arrest for withholding homicide information, who eventually brought the detectives to the home of Jay Pobliner's girlfriend. Two days later, on March 13, Liliane Scudder gave her statement.

"She was easy," Detective Schoenberger recalled. "We just walked into the house and told her we knew the whole story of her relationship with Jay. It was a bluff, but she bought it. She was worried about her husband. He was a big guy and she said he used to beat her. We promised to keep him out of this and she agreed to cooperate."

Seeing Liliane that first time when she answered the door in a partially opened bathrobe, Bonora readily understood Pobliner's attraction. While Brenda's nature had been demure, even genteel, Liliane Scudder radiated a kind of shadowy animalism. The daughter of a French farmer, she was slender and small-breasted with a smooth, firm, adolescent quality to her legs and hips. Her eyes were bright and liquid; her fine, flesh-toned lips moved sensuously over the words of her heavily accented English.

The statement she gave the detectives encompassed twenty typewritten pages and described in detail her entire two-month affair with Jay Pobliner from the initial meeting at Stan's Automotive Center, where her car was serviced, to the day of Brenda's death, when she claimed they stopped seeing one another. During that period they met several times a week, but always on Thursday nights when Liliane told her husband she was attending a PTA meeting and Jay told Brenda he was going to the Westchester gun club. Often they double-dated with her best friend Kathy Schuster and Jay's good friend, Eddie Gaines. The evenings were spent at the Outrigger Motel in Freeport.

Liliane denied knowing anything about Brenda's murder and staunchly proclaimed Jay's innocence. She conceded that on numerous occasions he had complained that his wife was "cold," but after the murder he was "very upset." She had spoken to him twice that December day. Jay had called her in the morning from his office to say he was driving back to Merrick because his wife was bleeding and being taken to a hospital. Later that evening he called from his father's home and told her Brenda was dead.

Liliane refused to characterize their relationship as anything more than a casual affair. Yet despite Liliane's own attitude, Bonora was convinced the relationship was something very special to Jay Pobliner. From Liliane he learned that Pobliner had introduced her to his son by a former marriage, as well as to his partner in Cloud Tours, not something a married man ordinarily does with a mistress. He had given her two substantial presents, a ring for her birthday and a jeweled bracelet for Christmas. And on the day of his wife's death he did have time to phone Liliane though he had stated to detectives he couldn't wait for his father to accompany him back to the Merrick house.

If indeed this was the motive for the murder of Brenda Pobliner, it would have to be corroborated. The detectives moved quickly to do so in the next few days, taking a statement from Kathy Schuster that confirmed the liaison and from the night manager of the Outrigger Motel who recognized Pobliner from his photograph as a "Mr. Rogers." Mr. Rogers had given the manager the two biggest tips in his career, ten dollars the first time, five dollars as a Christmas bonus. Andreoli and Bonora spent two days sorting through the registration cards of the motel—amazed and amused by the frequency with which the name of a certain, much disliked Inspector in the Nassau County Police Department appeared—and they were able to place Pobliner there on eleven different nights. These cards were then brought back to the Identification office, and the handwriting matched to other samples Pobliner had unwittingly given the police.

This work completed, Bonora, Andreoli and Schoenberger climbed into a squad car and drove to a modest, split-level home on Frankel Boulevard in Merrick. Schoenberger rang the bell and a young woman with a timorous smile answered the door. Perhaps if she had sensed the ominous purpose of their visit, could have foreseen the dilemma that would ultimately confront her husband, the young woman might have acted differently. But suspecting nothing, Mrs. Edward Gaines welcomed the detectives into her home, calling for her husband, who she said was upstairs taking a shower. Without awaiting a reply, Bonora and Andreoli brushed past her and started up the stairs. Gaines met them coming out of the bathroom, a twenty-five-year-old man with the face of a boy, still slightly pudgy with baby fat. He was dressed in a terrycloth robe, his wiry brown hair dripping, his bright eyes wide open. He demanded to know who his visitors were and what they wanted.

Bonora introduced himself and the others, and Gaines flushed, even before the sergeant could explain the purpose of their visit. He quickly agreed to talk with the detectives but insisted they wait in the den while he dressed. Bonora did not like the arrangement, unhappy about the time Gaines would have to collect himself. Still, rather than argue, he returned downstairs, deeming it more important not to alienate a potentially helpful witness.

Mrs. Gaines led the detectives into the back den, a large orange-carpeted room with a walnut bar and a picture window overlooking a canal similar to the one behind the Pobliner home. For a while she sat uneasily among her strange guests, fidgeting in the growing silence. Then she thought to offer coffee or liquor. The offers were politely refused.

"Say, what's going on anyway?" she asked.

Bonora put her off. "It's just some private matter we want to discuss with your husband."

"Can't you tell me about it?"

Bonora shook his head. A moment later he glanced at his watch: ten minutes had elapsed. He stood up impatiently and strode to the foot of the stairs.

"Eddie, we're waiting for you," he shouted.

"I don't want to talk to anyone," Gaines yelled back.

"You're going to talk to us whether you like it or not, you hear?" Bonora said, his harsh rejoinder bringing the other two detectives to his side.

After a long moment Gaines responded in a husky voice. "All right. I'll speak to the Jewish guy."

The three detectives turned to each other with quizzical expressions. Then Schoenberger, a man of German extraction with small, uneven features and pebble-grained skin, shrugged his shoulders, grinned and started up the stairs. He found Gaines trembling violently in the master bedroom and began at once to console him. He explained that he was not in trouble, that the detectives were only interested in Pobliner. But the witness's distress was profound. Through twenty minutes of placating and coaxing, he cried before being persuaded from the room, and downstairs he refused to go to the Seventh Precinct stationhouse. Eventually, though, he did agree to accompany the detectives to the squad car after Bonora subtly reminded him the alternative might be discussing the situation in front of his wife.

Seated in the back seat with Schoenberger, Gaines looked apprehensively at the detectives positioned around him. Bonora observed him silently and without apparent emotion. Then he said softly, "Eddie, we're going to give you the opportunity to tell the truth. If you want to tell us the truth, we're going to work with you, we're going to help you, we're going to protect you. You're making a decision that will affect not only you but your kids, your wife and your parents. And you have to make it all by yourself."

The sergeant continued, his voice still gentle, friendly. "You're in way over your head, Eddie. Don't forget, when that money starts working, it's going to be working for one person, and it ain't lil' old Eddie Gaines. The Pobliners are getting ready to feed you to the wolves." Bonora grinned. "Of course the wolves are not all that bad. You need a friend right now. Desperately. And you've got three of the best you'll ever have sitting here with you."

He paused, looking deeply into Gaines's attentive eyes.

"You've got to make a decision, Eddie. Do you want us as your friends or not? Bear in mind, we know the whole story from beginning to end."

Gaines said, "I don't know what the hell you're talking about."

Bonora's jaw suddenly tightened. "You're a fucking liar," he shouted. "Don't give us any bullshit because we know your whole involvement. And if that's the attitude you're gonna take, your ass is going to go up for murder."

Schoenberger said calmly, "Give him a chance, Matt. He's not a real criminal. He just needs some time." The ploy had started, the standard "good guy, bad guy" routine. Bonora was playing the heavy, the "bad guy," so as to control the situation. Andreoli had been set to play Gaines's "friend" but the witness had unexpectedly chosen Schoenberger.

"You know Jay Pobliner?" Bonora demanded.

"Yeah, I know him."

"How long have you known him, Eddie? Now before you say anything let me caution you that we know the answers to nine out of ten of these questions. We just want to see whether you're capable of telling the truth and are willing to cooperate."

"I grew up with him," Gaines said promptly.

Bonora nodded encouragingly. "Eddie, if you don't think we're here to help you, why do you suppose we're sitting out here in this car?"

Gaines shrugged.

"C'mon, Eddie," Bonora said with forced weariness. "You know damn well we could just as easily have talked in front of your wife. But I didn't think she wanted to know about Liliane and Kathy Schuster and some of the particular sexual positions you seem to relish."

Gaines squirmed restlessly and Schoenberger interceded on his behalf. "Let him collect his thoughts. I know he's going to work with us. He just got caught up in this thing, didn't you, Eddie?"

Gaines smiled gratefully at the detective. "I wa-want to cooperate with you guys, but I need my lawyer."

"See, I told you, Matt," Schoenberger exclaimed. "He wants to help us. Who's your lawyer, Eddie?"

"Herbert Handman," Gaines replied, naming the attorney who represented the Pobliners.

Bonora laughed. "Herbie Handman, huh? Herbie Handman's your lawyer?"

"Yeah."

"What did I just get through telling you."

"What do you mean?" Gaines said.

"Herbie Handman's not your lawyer."

"Don't tell me," Gaines said defensively. "He's my lawyer."

"Herbie Handman is not *your* lawyer. He's Jay Pobliner's lawyer," Bonora said.

Gaines looked helplessly at Schoenberger.

"You've known Jay all your life. Did you ever see him swing for anything?" Bonora continued.

"No," the witness responded faintly.

"Well, you think things have changed?"

"I told you. I'm willing to talk to you, but I need my lawyer."

"Fine," Bonora said. "You get your own lawyer who's going to have the interests of Eddie Gaines at heart."

Schoenberger cut in. "Matt, I think he understands now we're here to help him. Don't you, Eddie?"

Gaines's eyes flickered fearfully at the detectives seated about him, a vein pulsing thickly on the side of his forehead. Then he nodded and left the car in a state of terrified confusion.

CHAPTER

THE DISCOVERY and interrogation of Jay Pobliner's mistress had a ripple effect on the investigation, reaching all the way to Asheville. By the third week in March, Joe Hall could no longer stand the pressure. "If you threw a firecracker in front of Joe's house, the boy would probably never come out again," one acquaintance recalled. On the one hand, the twenty-eight-year-old disc jockey believed that the police were coming momentarily to arrest him. On the other, he had convinced himself Jay Pobliner had ordered his execution.

"I feel like an orange being squeezed from both sides," he complained desperately to Nancy Hensley, his go-go dancer friend. And telling her the intimate details of Brenda Pobliner's murder, he explained why he had to leave town.

But Hall never had the chance to flee. The following morning Nancy Hensley went secretly to Deputy Chief Jarvis and told him all she knew. Jarvis called Hall into police headquarters.

"He told me he knowed everythin' there was to know about the murder," Hall related afterward, "and either I was gonna come clean or it were gonna be my ass fo' Brenda's murder. He said if I talked I wouldn't get hurt. I guess I didn't have no choice. I weren't gonna take no one else's ration a shit."

Deputy Chief Jarvis telephoned Bonora in Mineola.

Joe Hall's association with the murder of Brenda Pobliner had begun in November, 1968, when Jay and Butch Pezold arrived in Asheville on a purported hunting trip. Instead of hunting, Pobliner had divided his time between the Some Place Else and a motel room he shared with Evelyn Rice, a bar waitress he had picked up the first night in town. He had left Brenda and their young son, Neil, in Black Mountain.

On Sunday, November 17, Pobliner had approached his old friend, Joe Hall, with an urgent request. A buddy in New York, he said, needed an unregistered gun to kill someone. He handed Hall fifty dollars, which the disc jockey readily accepted, assuming the matter was part of a charade. But during the next few days Pobliner continued to badger him about the gun. Convinced that Jay was serious, Hall contacted another disc jockey at WISE named Glen Bell. He made arrangements to purchase a Colt Frontiersman, a .22 caliber single-action revolver, black with a white-pearl handle. The gun was registered, but Hall, determined to rid himself of the obligation, decided it wouldn't make any difference. He paid Bell eighty dollars.

Jay came for the gun that night at the Some Place Else, accompanied by Evelyn Rice. Hall took him behind the pantry and after receiving an additional thirty dollars handed Pobliner the weapon and a yellow box of fifty copper-clad .22 caliber long cartridges. Evelyn Rice and Norma Sue Freeman, the club barmaid, watched Jay heft the gun in his hand, dry-fire it several times, then stick it under his coat. Later that same evening Pobliner asked Hall for one more favor. He said that he and his friend Eddie had decided to murder their wives in Asheville over the New Year's holiday. They planned to drive the women into the hills outside of Asheville with the idea of taking in a nighttime view of the city. They would shoot them there, leaving their bodies in the car with their pocketbooks gone as if they had been robbed. Pobliner wanted Hall to obtain a stolen car that the two men could use for their return trip to town. He insisted that Hall owed him this "favor," since it was Hall who had introduced him to Brenda.

"What do you want to kill Brenda for?" Hall had inquired.

"She's just not the same girl we used to know," Jay said. "She doesn't like to go out and have a good time. All she likes to do is just sit around the house and bitch and gripe all the time."

"Can't y'all di-vorce?"

"No," Jay said. "It just wouldn't work. My father wouldn't buy it. This is the only way."

Hall had no further contact with Pobliner regarding the Asheville murder plan, though a month later reading the newspaper accounts of Brenda's death he deduced some modifications had been made. That deduction was subsequently confirmed at the end of January when Jay paid him a visit at the Memorial Mission Hospital, where he was confined for phlebitis. Alone in the hospital room, Pobliner recounted how he had shot his wife with the Asheville pistol before going to work, dumping the murder weapon into the East River as he crossed the Queensboro Bridge into Manhattan. He assured Hall that Brenda had been asleep and "did not feel a thing."

What happened to his friend Eddie and the Asheville plan, Hall wanted to know. Jay remarked that his friend had "gone chickenshit," so he had brought in another friend as an alibi, Illis Jurisson, who was standing right alongside him when he did the shooting.

How then had he managed to pass the paraffin test?

Smiling, Pobliner slipped his coat sleeve down over his hand so that nothing was exposed. Pointing his forefinger like a pistol he clicked his tongue three times.

On the morning of March 26, 1969, the Nassau County Grand Jury met to indict Jay Pobliner for the murder of his wife. While the fifteen-member panel considered the evidence, Bonora and five other detectives were gathered in a coffee shop on Madison Avenue in New

York awaiting the call from the District Attorney. The detectives planned to arrest Pobliner as soon as the indictment came down, fearful that once apprised of the formal accusation he might try to flee the country. Certainly as a travel agent and the son of a millionaire Pobliner possessed both the knowledge and means to plot an escape. Nor did he seem to have compunctions about leaving his own country. Several weeks before, he had confided to Joe Hall his plans to emigrate to Israel. His father, Pobliner said, was making a sizable contribution to the Israeli government so that he could become a general in the army. He offered Hall the position of his aide-de-camp.

At 10:30 A.M. the indictment was handed down. Moments later the detectives entered the Cloud Tours Travel Agency with guns drawn. They wanted to give Pobliner no opportunity to demonstrate his proficiency as a marksman or his ability as a judo expert. They found him standing by a window in his shirtsleeves, with no gun visible on his person.

"You're under arrest, Jay," Bonora said, his gun pointed at the suspect.

Pobliner peered out the window at the sidewalk fourteen floors below. When he turned back to the detectives the color had drained from his face, his lips were pressed tightly together. Andreoli approached him quickly. He was frisked, handcuffed and brought to Mineola for booking.

But the investigation did not stop there. In suburban, middle-class murders it is rare that a defendant agrees to plead guilty since with a good attorney and ample funds for a legal defense, there is a strong possibility he can win his freedom in court. Once Pobliner was settled into the Nassau County Jail to await a bail hearing, Bonora returned to Manhattan to arrest Illis Jurisson as a material witness. The detectives were concerned that he too might try to leave the country.

Jurisson had been interrogated on several occasions without much success, but it was hoped that given immunity he might be persuaded to testify against Pobliner. He had suffered a nervous breakdown in January, and in Bonora's mind that tended to corroborate Joe Hall's story. For just prior to his two-month hospitalization he had begged and pleaded with the librarian at his company's headquarters to secure a copy for him of a movie called *The Girl on the Red Velvet Swing*. Bonora and Andreoli had obtained the film in New York and viewed it one Friday evening at home with their wives. They were intrigued by one scene in particular. A camera moves in slowly on a dead woman. She is lying sleeplike in her bed, the blankets pulled up to her shoulders, her jet black hair matted with blood and lying halo-like about her almond-shaped face. She is the mirror image of Brenda Pobliner as the detectives had found her—as Jay Pobliner had left her!

Jurisson was living with his mother once again in a five-story limestone building on West Sixty-fourth Street. Bonora sent homicide Det. Matthew Brennan to guard the rear of the building while he and Det. Ralph Betz from Burglary proceeded up the stairway to the third-floor apartment. The detectives rang the doorbell several times but there was no response. Opening his wallet and assuring himself he had not forgotten the search warrant, Bonora instructed Betz to get ready to pick the lock. Then he left to notify Brennan of the decision.

Once outside, however, the sergeant's attention was diverted by the sight of the unmarked Nassau County squad car being slowly maneuvered from its parking spot on the hook of a New York City police tow truck.

"Hey, what the hell are you doing?" Bonora yelled, running toward his car. "That's a police vehicle."

The driver looked skeptically at Bonora, who was wearing a glen plaid, double-breasted, six-button suit. He said, "Listen, buddy. You're in a no-parking zone. That means no cars are allowed to park here."

"That's not a goddam car. It's a police vehicle. We're locking a guy up here," Bonora insisted, pulling out his detective shield.

The driver looked at the gold medallion in its black-leather case then handed it to his partner. The partner returned the shield, unimpressed. "We see identification like that all day long. You can buy it all over the city."

"For Christ's sake," Bonora protested. "This is ridiculous."

The driver shrugged indifferently, but at Bonora's suggestion agreed to call the Nassau Communications Center on the car radio. A few minutes later he was out of the truck unhooking the sedan, apologizing and chuckling at his mistake.

Bonora was not at all amused, but by the time the tow truck had pulled away, his interest had moved elsewhere—to a nearby vacant telephone booth. With the same kind of intuition that had led him to ask Pobliner for the gun the morning of Brenda's death, he now deposited a dime in the coin box and telephoned the Jurisson apartment. After three rings Illis picked up the receiver.

"Jesus, Illis, will you open the goddam door?" Bonora said.

"Who is this?" Jurisson inquired suspiciously.

"You know very well who this is. It's Sergeant Bonora. Now either you open that door or we'll slam it down with sledgehammers."

There was silence on the other end. Then a resigned voice. "All right. All right."

The following day Eddie Gaines appeared before the Nassau County Grand Jury. He denied the testimony of Joe Hall, that he and Jay Pobliner had together conceived a "plan" to murder their wives. But Bonora continued to see and speak with him over the next few weeks, stopping at his house or calling on the phone in a concentrated effort to convince him of his sincerity, to prove to Gaines he did not intend to punish him if only the truth would come out.

Recalling those efforts much later, Gaines said: "The funny thing was that this big tough guy, Bonora, the man who scared me half to death that first night—well, he turned out to be the sweetest guy of the lot. You see, I knew I was going to have to tell them about Jay's idea, but I was worried about its effect on my wife and my marriage. I had broken down one day in the Homicide office—I was crying like a baby—and Matt offered to speak to my wife. He said he wanted to try to straighten everything out for me. That was it. I was sure then everything was going to be okay."

The "plan," it turned out, was much as Joe Hall had remembered—a sightseeing trip of Asheville ending with a murder in the hills that would look like robbery. Gaines insisted, however, that he had never taken Pobliner seriously. The plan was merely a "joke" between them, a husband's wild fantasy. They kidded each other about the plan, he said, until after a while he began to question its humor. Finally on the Monday before Brenda's death he instructed Pobliner never to repeat the "joke" again. He had decided it was no longer funny.

On March 29 Bonora returned to Asheville for his sixth and final time. He found the sun shining brightly and the landscape metamorphosed from the bleak days of December. It was a splendid time to be there. The hills, now a deep blue-green, were stippled with bright patches of flowering white dogwood. Even the gray, weather-beaten farmhouses appeared rejuvenated, their gardens aflame with yellow jonquils and azalea. Thinking of the freshly manicured golf courses and the ice-cold mountain lakes, Bonora and the three investigators accompanying him vowed to return to Asheville someday for a vacation. As for now, they were much too busy to take more than wistful glances at the lush countryside.

The four investigators were gathering corroborative evidence to support the lengthy statement of Joe Hall. Pobliner had refused to plead guilty, instead hiring Maurice Edelbaum, a New York criminal attorney with a national reputation as a trial lawyer, to defend him. This decision meant a protracted court fight, a fight that would be won or lost, the detectives believed, on their ability to convince a jury of the truth of Joe Hall's testimony. And they would have to do so without producing the murder weapon. Boats from the Marine Division of the Nassau police had unsuccessfully dragged the East River underneath the Queensboro Bridge for two days. They had managed to salvage seventeen revolvers but not a Colt Frontiersman.

The five days Bonora spent in Asheville during this trip were tense and exhausting. Concerned that Pobliner might reach a witness before them and buy a change in testimony, the four investigators raced back and forth through the hills of the town. The three detectives took detailed statements from the witnesses and gathered supportive documents; Jack Lewis, the Assistant District Attorney, questioned the witnesses under oath in the presence of a court stenographer.

Running like men being chased, they worked early in the morning and late at night—whenever witnesses were located and ready to talk. And slowly they began to close their case. Statements and sworn testimony were taken from Glen Bell, who sold Hall the pistol; from Norma Sue Freeman, the barmaid, who saw Hall give Jay the gun and was able to describe the distinctive look of the Colt Frontiersman; and from Evelyn Rice, Pobliner's local girlfriend, who had observed the pistol transaction in the bar and whom Jay later told about the Asheville murder plan. Al Huntzinger, Hall's bartender, also gave written testimony. He had banked a $1,500 "loan" that Jay had sent Hall and for which no repayment was expected—"hush money," as Joe characterized it. Huntzinger's bankbook supported Hall's testimony that the payments had been made in three weekly installments of $500 each. A certified copy was made of it.

On Thursday, April 3, Bonora turned his efforts to the confession of Jay Pobliner. That the confession had been given to a bedridden witness was of distinct advantage to the prosecution's case, for no one could contend physical or psychological pressure had been used to induce it. And Pobliner's presence in the hospital on January 28 had already been confirmed through the statement of Agnes Hall, Joe Hall's wife. She also was able to attest that Pobliner had spoken to her husband alone.

But there remained the very crucial question whether Hall was in sound enough mental condition at the time of the confession for his testimony to stand up in court. It was this question Bonora was still in the process of resolving as he entered the office of Joe Hall's personal physician, Dr. Robert Moffitt. With Bonora was Detective Andreoli and Joe Hall who, apparently seeing the error of his ways, had become a committed ally of the detectives', guiding them about town and helping to round up the witnesses needed to support his account.

All three men had been working since early that morning. Informed that the doctor was with a patient, they slumped into the vinyl-upholstered chairs of the waiting room. Hall sat next to Andreoli on the couch, his sprawling legs outdistancing the detective's, his sturdy six-foot-two-inch frame looking puny in comparison. Bonora sat opposite them in a single chair pressed against a wall decorated with medical certificates and plaques. He was tired and for a moment his eyes closed. He began at once to think about Pobliner, wondering how Jay had so completely deceived his parents-in-law, who up until the arrest continued to speak of his unassuming, decent nature, his modesty, thoughtfulness and generosity. The characterization was so antithetical to what the detectives had witnessed—to the picture Pobliner's first wife had drawn. Harriet Pobliner had grown up with Jay in Riverdale, a haven for successful businessmen and foreign diplomats just north of Manhattan. She depicted her former husband as a young man intimately aware of his wealth and social position. She recalled that Pobliner carried a gun under the front seat of his car and waved it threateningly at drivers who cut him off. Once, she said, he had even punched a subway rider in the nose for staring at her, doing the same thing a week later to the beautician who had cut her hair too short. . . .

Bonora opened his eyes and found Joe Hall staring at him, a peculiar expression on his face.

"Something wrong, Joe?" he asked.

Hall's eyes glimmered. "Remember that night I tol' y'all to stop by fo' a beer at the club?"

Bonora leaned forward. "Sure, you asked us at the police station that first day we met you." How could the sergeant forget? The invitation had precipitated a bitter argument with Andreoli in which he had finally been forced to pull rank on his old friend. Andreoli, still fuming at Hall's contemptuous attitude, had insisted upon going to the club. Bonora had forbidden it, sensing some risk, a possible setup.

Hall lowered his face, trying to hide a breaking grin.

"I had a pal a mine waitin' on yuh by the name a Haystacks Calhoun. He's a professional wrestler—goes about six hundred pounds. I told him that a couple a tough guys from New York are comin' in to bust up my place and I gave him a hundred bucks to handle you two. He was there till near two in the morning. But y'all never showed."

Bonora arched his eyebrows at Andreoli. "Yeah, we were pretty tired that night, weren't we, Andy?"

Andreoli set down the magazine he had been reading and replied frostily, "I still think we should have gone for that beer." Bonora laughed loudly and when Andreoli began to smile, Hall joined in.

Dr. Moffitt entered the room, looking to Bonora like a James Stewart model of a country practitioner. He was tall and slim with thick gray hair and a gentle Southern drawl. Informed of the detectives' needs, he checked his records and confirmed Hall's assertion that he had not been given sedatives or drugs that might cause hallucinations during his confinement. Then at Bonora's behest he accompanied the three men to the Mission Memorial Hospital and inspected their records. They too indicated that no drugs had been dispensed to Hall that might have impaired his mental health.

Moffitt willingly signed a statement to that effect and the hospital made a certified copy of the medical record for the detectives to take with them to Long Island. Still Bonora was not completely satisfied. What if the Pobliners came to Asheville and in their desperation managed to falsify the original records or even steal them? It was a bizarre possibility, almost inconceivable, and for a moment Bonora wondered about the depths of his own paranoia. Reflecting further, however, he decided he had no such neurosis. He had given more than three months of his life to this investigation and there was simply no reason to take chances. This crime was not some traffic violation. This was murder.

He persuaded the hospital officials to turn their original records over to Dr. Moffitt, who was also the Buncombe County coroner. Then he drove to a bank, rented a safe-deposit box, deposited the original records in the drawer and delivered the key to the doctor. He was certain now that the records would be safe until the trial.

It was almost six o'clock by the time the two detectives returned to the Holiday Inn, and they found Schoenberger and Lewis sprawled across the beds looking exhausted. A half-empty bottle of Dewar's Scotch was sitting between them and there were sandwich wrappers scattered on the floor.

"I hope you two have been taking it easy," Bonora said as he entered the room.

Schoenberger laughed and went to the bathroom for two more glasses.

"You all wrapped up?" Lewis asked.

"I think so," Bonora said.

"Good. You and Henry can put in for the ten-thousand-dollar reward Jay offered."

"I'm calling my attorney in the morning," Bonora joked.

"Say, what's the law on that anyway?" Andreoli asked seriously, taking a sip of the Scotch.

"Policemen can't accept rewards," Lewis answered. "You can be sure Jay wouldn't give it to you two anyhow. He might give you a birthday cake like he gave Brenda, though."

"Yeah, fuck you too," said Andreoli, grinning.

Bonora picked up the telephone and called Guido in Long Island.

"We've been working like crazy down here," he told his boss. Then, beginning with the statement taken from Glen Bell, he related all the work the men had accomplished during the past five days, ending his account with the storage of Joe Hall's medical records in the bank vault. When he was through, there was a long pause at the other end of the phone.

Guido said thoughtfully, "I guess you better come home, Matt. I can't think of anything else to do."

Nothing else was needed. On October 23, 1970, Jay Thomas Pobliner was found guilty of fatally shooting his wife by a jury sitting in Nassau County before Judge Paul Kelly. The decision was subsequently upheld by the Appellate Division and by New York State's highest tribunal, the Court of Appeals. Pobliner is currently serving a twenty-five-year-to-life sentence in the New York State Correctional Institution at Green Haven.

CHAPTER

_____

5

ON A CLEAR MORNING in early June, two months after the Pobliner investigation had ended, Bonora sat in the reception area of the Seventh Precinct squadroom sipping a cup of hot tea and watching with interest as a young detective posted the new squad statistics on the blackboard. The sun had suffused the room with a warm yellow glow and the sergeant was enjoying the quiet that filled the minutes before nine o'clock—the hour when the telephones were apt to start ringing. Across the top of the blackboard written in heavy block letters were column headings:

FELONIES	MISDEMEANORS	ARREST TOTALS	PROPERTY RECOVERED

Printed down its left side in the same yellow chalk were the names of the squad's twenty-five detectives. The numbers underneath the column headings were being erased by the detective-accountant and replaced with a current record of each detective's work.

This blackboard chart was Bonora's innovation. When he first became deputy commander in September, 1968, the Seventh Squad was in a dismal slump, the Police Commissioner threatening full-scale transfers. Arrests had fallen off significantly, property loss recovery was at a minimum and community leaders were incensed by the squad's recent failure to arrest even one of the young blacks who had driven over from the village of Freeport to Merrick High School and senselessly attacked and beaten twenty-three students.

Seeking to understand the malaise, Bonora had begun to review the case files. Much to his surprise, he discovered that the veteran detectives, those with experience and developed investigatory skills, seemed to be coasting. Conversely, some of the younger men, in particular Tommy Gulla, who Bonora had been informed was not a "team player," were driving themselves to their apparent limits but receiving little or no recognition. The statistics he compiled readily confirmed this: the younger men were making all the arrests. So one day the new deputy commander posted the statistics on the blackboard and directed that from then on they be updated week to week.

Naturally the chart provoked considerable controversy, especially among the older detectives. These men, angered that their work would be judged solely by the number of "collars" (arrests) and the amount of stolen property they managed to recover, warned that such comparisons would create a competitive divisiveness within the squad. The argument was not one Bonora could dismiss out of hand, though it did not dissuade him from his experiment. Shaking up the squad *was* precisely what he wanted to do.

Now, six months later, as the young detective stepped away from his work at the blackboard, the sergeant smiled to himself at the new order of the squad. Golder, Gulla, Ryf, Schoenberger, Sheehan, Glicka ... it began on this sixth day of June. Artie Golder had been his severest critic, no doubt because the veteran detective—recognized as the squad's most resourceful investigator—had found himself at the bottom of the comparative ladder the first day of the chart's posting.

His return to a position of rightful primacy was one more proof to Bonora of his success in changing the squad's attitude. In the last several months the arrest record as well as the property-recovery rate had increased 30 percent and squad morale was at a peak. The detectives were appearing in the office before their scheduled tours of duty and working overtime at their own insistence, cutting back or totally abandoning their moonlighting jobs. And just last month the arrest of three teen-agers who had set fire to the Massapequa High School and the conviction of two men who desecrated the Grace Episcopal Church, a nineteenth-century landmark in Massapequa, had brought about the first public praise in a year. Bonora felt pleased today not just because he knew the squad was more effective; rather because he felt he had given his men a sense of pride in what they were doing.

Still reflecting on that achievement a moment later when the first telephone rang, he answered in an unusually buoyant voice.

"Congratulations," replied the caller. It was Deputy Police Commissioner James Ketcham, a close personal friend.

"Hell, Jimmy, you know the squad has been working like we've got a torch burning our seat," Bonora said.

Ketcham chuckled. "I'm not talking about that, Mattie. Christ, I know you've been doing a good job down there. I called about McKie. You made state law. We just got the decision down from Albany."

Bonora fell silent. In the excitement of the Pobliner investigation and his own increasing involvement as deputy squad commander, he had almost forgotten about George McKie, a convicted murderer whose case had been pending in the Court of Appeals since February. McKie was not just another faceless statistic in Bonora's twenty-year record of arrests. He had tracked him some fourteen months. And though the prime suspect in a homicide investigation is always an object of intense scrutiny, fourteen months of eating, sleeping and working one suspect is like joining another man's family. One begins to understand his depths and subtler emotions, even read his psyche.

Bonora expressed it more simply: "I knew when George would spit."

Deputy Commissioner Ketcham explained that the high court had established a new precedent with its decision in the case, thus creating law for the state of New York. He congratulated the sergeant again and the two men rejoiced over "the victory" the court's decision had finally given them. But as soon as Bonora hung up the phone, a wisp of melancholy brushed against him and he realized his sentiments toward George McKie had never been so simple as to evoke a single emotional response. True, at times McKie did assume the role of his most hated enemy. Yet at other moments he appeared as just another hapless victim, an unfortunate product of destitute circumstances. Still, whatever his changing relationship with Bonora, McKie's demands upon the sergeant had been relentless.

A black former Golden Gloves boxing champion with a reported I.Q. of 163, George McKie was an inveterate nightwalker and a voracious reader. His basement brimmed with paperback mysteries and crime stories that were the staples of his reading and from which he seemed to gain many of his ideas. Bonora could envision him now, standing in front of 42 Wanser Avenue the moment he had placed him under arrest. He was forty-three years old then and nearly penniless. Yet there was no reproach in the intense black eyes. Nor shame either. His lips, thick and feminine in shape, held a faint smile as if he were proud to have fought off the police for as long as he had, had gone the full fifteen rounds. Later he even congratulated the detectives.

Ironically, Bonora had paid McKie little attention at their first introduction in March, 1965, on the porch of a home in the black ghetto of Inwood. Just having arrived on the scene, he was more interested in viewing the body of Mrs. Manella Morris, a fifty-three-year-old domestic. Mrs. Morris lay upstairs shrouded in a maroon blanket that was bound about her with three pieces of clothesline. One strand of the rope had been wrapped so tightly about the neck, Bonora just naturally assumed she had been strangled to death until McKie suggested something different, a suggestion that would focus the detectives' attention on him for the next fourteen months. It came about this way:

Bonora, returning to the squad car from viewing the deceased, read over McKie's statement, for it was the unemployed handyman who had discovered his upstairs neighbor's body. Bonora then asked one of those broad, open-ended questions experienced investigators use to keep a witness talking with the hope of extracting some previously unmentioned detail.

He said, "George, what are we going to do about all this?"

McKie shook his plum-shaped head tragically. "It's a shame po' woman got hit on the head like she were. We're gonna have to stop whoever's going 'round hittin' people on the head."

Bonora had cut short the interview, using the arrival of the Medical Examiner as an excuse. Now he returned to the house and raced up the inside stairs to Mrs. Morris's apartment, reaching the corpse before it could be disturbed. He studied the blanketed victim again, this time searching for outward signs of bludgeoning. He saw nothing. Informing the Homicide commander of McKie's curious remark, he received permission to cut the cord binding Mrs. Morris's neck. He did so, making certain to preserve the knot, which was an unusual variety. Then Dr. Leslie Lukash, the Medical Examiner, stepped forward and, pulling back the blanket, made instant sense of McKie's counsel. The left side of the victim's forehead was bloodied and crushed inward like a dented beer can.

Bonora returned downstairs and found McKie with Fourth Squad squeal man Santa Oliva and Detective Stark from Homicide. The three men were conversing casually on the front porch, which overlooked a neighborhood whose only sign of brightness that day was the harsh glare from the blue and orange paint of the Nassau County police prowl cars. As Bonora joined them he saw a mongrel dog feeding off scraps from an overturned garbage can. Nearby several black men, red-eyed and barely standing, were drinking from open bottles of wine. For a moment the detective forgot he was in Nassau County, forgot that less than a half mile away were the affluent villages of Lawrence, Cedarhurst, Woodmere and Hewlett, for whom black Inwood residents provided a convenient source of domestic labor. He felt suddenly as if he had stumbled into something unreal and odious, a kind of close, murky swamp. He turned quickly away and put his thoughts to the murder.

"Now let me get this straight, George. You found Mrs. Morris's body when you went to use her john, right?"

"Yessir, my toilet's broken. C'mon, I'll show you," McKie said, motioning the detectives toward his first-floor apartment. Bonora and Stark followed him through an empty living room and a bedroom bare except for a filthy mattress on the floor. The apartment was as cold and raw as the outside air. At the rear was the bathroom, its water frozen and the toilet bowl cracked as the witness had described. McKie explained that the landlord, who had officially evicted him several days before, had turned off the heat.

Satisfied that the bathroom was unusable, the detectives turned around and were starting out through the apartment when a quick, instinctual glance inside an open closet door made Bonora halt.

"What's that?" he inquired, pointing to the back of the closet.

McKie looked inside. "It's a hatchet."

"Is it yours?"

The witness shrugged. "Never did see it before."

Bonora lifted the tool from the closet, using his handkerchief to preserve any fingerprints, and tagged it for evidence. Within a few days the lab would determine it the murder weapon.

The detectives arrested George McKie later that day, convinced of his guilt and worried that he might murder again. They charged him with conducting unauthorized gambling in his apartment and illegally selling liquor to the participants, offenses that he himself had admitted to during his interrogation at the Fourth Precinct squadroom and which were further corroborated by his girlfriend, Annie Lou Turner. The detectives figured that while McKie was incarcerated, they would be able to gather sufficient evidence to indict him for murder. Yet the investigation proved far more difficult than expected.

Most of McKie's acquaintances, it turned out, distrusted the white detectives. Those who didn't spent the greater portion of their waking moments inebriated. To surmount these barriers Bonora had enlisted the help of Robert Monroe, a black patrolman he had worked with as a rookie. Monroe had patrolled Inwood for ten years and was something of a landmark in the community. He was six feet tall and 280 pounds with a face the size of a basketball and a chest and belly that resembled a tackling dummy. If all the local residents didn't know him by name, they certainly did by sight. And he in turn knew his constituents—their hangouts, habits and acquaintances.

Using both Monroe's knowledge of the community and his entrée, the detectives traced McKie's movements on the days surrounding Manella Morris's death. They learned that though the morning before Manella's murder the suspect had asked to borrow fifty cents from a neighbor, the following day he was spending money, said one acquaintance, "like that boy jest tapped the numbers." That day, according to the detectives' calculations, McKie spent twenty-three dollars, buying several pints of wine for his friends, buying drinks at a bar for another friend and his girl, repaying a long-time debt of one dollar and giving Annie Lou Turner, his girlfriend, five dollars. He also visited his widowed mother, who had been much comfort to him in the years following his return from the army in February, 1949, when he first learned his wife had deserted him for another man. He presented her with a ten-dollar bill.

What was the source of McKie's newfound wealth? The detectives believed they learned the answer when Peter Morris, Manella's common-law husband, returned home from the Cape Verde Islands, where he had taken his ailing brother to die. Morris informed the detectives that he had given his wife $400 before departing and that $275 was missing from the apartment.

The identification of the three knots that had bound the victim's body drew the net even closer about McKie as the murderer of Manella Morris. A knot specialist from the U.S. Merchant Marine Academy in Kings Point, Long Island, recognized them as an obscure variety originating in India that were used exclusively by the military for shipping cargo. That information fit neatly into McKie's background of service in a port battalion in the Mediterranean as well as with a report that he had taught knot tying during the early part of his seven-year army career.

As significant as these pieces of evidence appeared, they were not sufficient to convict a man of murder. So the detectives continued the investigation, delving deeper into the background of their suspect and the community in which he lived. By the middle of June, three months after Manella Morris's death, they had uncovered a series of crimes that they believed could be associated with George McKie in one way or another. Two of these incidents—a fire in an empty lot on the corner of Mott and Henry streets and an automobile fire on Kelly Place—had only the most tenuous of connections. Both had been declared arson with no known suspect. Nevertheless, the detectives knew from their research that McKie was living within a block of each fire at the time of its occurrence. Furthermore, each of the fires had started in the early morning hours before dawn when McKie was likely to be out on one of his nightly jaunts. His connection with a garage fire on Walter Avenue was less speculative. Monroe had personally witnessed McKie leaving the blaze and upon stopping him for questioning, smelled kerosene on his clothes. The patrolman's perception took on fuller meaning the following morning when the Fire Marshal's office discovered an empty kerosene can in the charred wreckage.

The crimes most closely connected to McKie were two incidents of assault and one attempted assault. In each case the suspect had a direct relationship with the victim. Juanita King, the young wife of a close friend, S. J. King, had been knocked to the floor by an intruder in her apartment. When she looked up she found a black man standing over her, dressed in a tan raincoat, his face partially obscured by what appeared to be a child's sweater. Flexing a hank of rope between his two hands, the intruder threatened to kill her in an affected Spanish accent. As he started to peel off his leather gloves Juanita jumped up and ran outside through the kitchen door. Using a neighbor's phone, she called the police, who appeared five minutes later with George McKie in their custody. McKie had been found a half block away. He was not wearing a raincoat then and Juanita was afraid to accuse him. But in recounting the incident for the Homicide investigators a year later, she expressed the firm conviction that McKie was her assailant, though she could conceive of no reason why he might want to kill her.

John King, or "Callahan," as he was known in the community (to differentiate him from S.J.), was perhaps McKie's best friend. In fact, the evening he was assaulted he had been drinking with McKie at the Twin Diner along with King's common-law wife, Maggie Kennedy, and Annie Lou Turner, McKie's girlfriend. That evening Maggie and Callahan had had another of their tempestuous altercations and Maggie left the bar in a huff, soon followed by McKie. Callahan took a taxi home and found his apartment door wide open. Whiskey-bold, he strode into the apartment and was reaching for the light when someone clubbed him unconscious. He was certain Maggie Kennedy was responsible. Yet when he finally awoke and checked the bedroom, she was fast asleep. He left the apartment immediately in search of the attacker, and who should he stumble into first but—George McKie. McKie readily joined his friend's search and within five minutes had discovered something shiny in the gutter. It was Callahan's missing key ring, from which the house key was conspicuously absent. The key ring, Callahan recalled, had "disappeared" several days before from the bar of the Sunshine Lounge where he had put it while drinking with two other friends and George McKie.

Christine Brown like Juanita King was alone in her apartment the night a stranger entered. Thinking the intruder was her husband, whom she had just fought with at the Sunshine Lounge, Christine began to scold him for his infidelity. As he approached her bed she warned him she was brandishing an ice pick and was prepared to "stick it in your motherfucking heart" (a threat she ultimately fulfilled two years later and for which she was sent to prison). The intruder sat silently by for twenty minutes accepting a hail of epithets.

Then he left. When her husband returned some time later she learned he had been at the Sunshine Lounge the entire evening.

Once again as in the Callahan incident there was no damage to the locks to indicate forced entry nor did the victim want to speculate as to the identity of the masked man. But Christine did remember that George McKie had done some handiwork for them just a month before the incident. He had installed their new locks. . . .

As each of these crimes came to light and was connected with McKie, Bonora began to look for a relationship between them—an intellectual expedition he had taken on countless occasions. A series of unlawful incidents occurring in one community was the usual cause for such mental exercise, turning detectives into scientists in their desire to synthesize, to build a modus operandi that would tie the crimes to a particular person and forecast his next actions. In the case of McKie detectives were hoping for a better understanding of his motives.

During his years as a detective Bonora had encountered a curious collection of M.O.'s, from the obvious to the obscure; from the house burglar who defecated in the middle of each living room to the rapist who repeatedly tied his victims' hands together with their brassieres and climaxed three and four times before intercourse, to the arsonist whose penchant for old abandoned buildings occurred only at four o'clock on Wednesday mornings. Yet through the end of June the sergeant was unable to discern any pattern among McKie's crimes aside from the recurrence of their February dates. Then one afternoon Detective Oliva prepared a written list of the incidents and the three investigators sat down around a table in the Fourth Precinct squadroom to study it.

February 23, 1962	*fire on Mott and Henry streets*
February 8, 1964	*assault on Juanita King at 11 Maiden Lane*
First week of February, 1965	*assault on Callahan at 62 Walter Avenue*
Second week of February, 1965	*thwarted assault of Christine Brown on Church Street*

February 22, 1965   automobile fire on Kelly Place
February 23, 1965   garage fire on Walter Avenue
March 15, 1965   murder of Manella Morris

It was the fires that had always intrigued Bonora and once again he began mentally toying with them.

"Do we know who owned the automobile that was torched?" he asked Oliva.

The detective shook his head. "It was abandoned. Probably stolen too."

"Bob, how about that garage. Any insurance on it?"

"No," Monroe said. "It was just about standing up."

Bonora returned his eyes to the list. He had started thinking about that fourteen-year-old boy he had arrested years before for setting fire to a vacant lot in West Hempstead. A rookie patrolman then, he had found the youngster watching the leaping flames as if mesmerized, a half-used book of matches clasped in his fist, an empty gasoline can lying at his feet. Bringing him into the bright lights of the stationhouse, Bonora was startled by what he saw: a dark stain on the boy's pants near the crotch, about the size of a maple leaf. The detectives later confirmed this was semen. The boy had ejaculated in his excitement over the fire!

With a sudden hunch Bonora reached into his briefcase and pulled out a notebook. He began thumbing the wirebound pages in earnest, looking for the interview with George McKie's mother. Something she had said was on the edge of his mind. He remembered her sitting in a sway-backed couch with a floral chintz cover, her face warm and hopeful, her moist yellow eyes patient with the detectives' troubling inquiries.

He found the interview in the middle of the notebook. Reaching it, a date flashed at him. February, 1949. Then he heard Mrs. McKie's voice, a soft and injured lament that had brought a pathetic look to her face.

"George," she said, "he just couldn't believe it when they placed the handcuffs on him. I'll never forget it. Him standing there in the middle of the room looking at me with tears in his eyes. And repeating over and over, 'She's having *me* arrested. *Me!*' "

Bonora quickly scribbled in February, 1949, at the bottom of the crime list and the eyes of the two detectives brightened with recognition. That was the date of McKie's return from the army when he learned his wife, Thomasina, was living with another man. The shock, Mrs. McKie had told the detectives, devastated her son. On two occasions he had taken Thomasina into the vacant lot behind the Number Four School in Inwood and beaten her mercilessly about the head. It was after the second beating that she filed a complaint and the police arrested McKie.

"Sex was the common denominator," Bonora announced excitedly. "It applies to the fires. And remember Manella's nightgown? It was pushed up to her waist as if George wanted to take a good look.

"So Maggie Kennedy was obviously the object of McKie's attack, not Callahan," he went on. "Callahan must have walked in on George unexpectedly that night. You recall he told us he had taken a cab home from the diner instead of walking as he usually did."

"But why those four women in particular?" Oliva asked.

Bonora explained that both Maggie Kennedy and Christine Brown were having trouble with their husbands just like George and Thomasina. Then he stopped, puzzling, and Monroe filled in the gaps.

"Those other two women were also having trouble," the patrolman said, much to the surprise of the two detectives. "Peter Morris never really planned to return home from the Cape Verde Islands, at least according to the talk about town. That was the reason he was supposed to have left most of his cash with Manella. And Juanita, she's been having real problems with her husband, S. J. You know, S. J. has got a dong about as long as a horse. And the way he drinks it apparently takes him hours to get off. Anyway he already put Juanita into the hospital once and for the last couple of years she's been scared for him to come near her. It's a standing joke down at the Sunshine Lounge, only S. J. has never found it too funny."

The puzzle solved, Bonora could finally envision the sequence of events that had taken place that Sunday in March. It had begun early in the evening according to a neighbor who had been watching Mrs. Morris prepare for bed that night. ("I seen her playin' wid herself and I remember I says to myself—ole Nellie, she ain't got no man now and she scratchin' her pussy.") McKie had observed Manella too. The neighbor saw him studying the window, then watched as he walked to the corner of the block, returned, looked up at the bedroom window again and entered the house.

What McKie did in his downstairs apartment during the next several hours remains uncertain, but clearly his anger was rising. For sometime after midnight he decided that Manella Morris was not going to play her husband for a fool as Thomasina had once done to him. He marched upstairs and, opening the door on the sleeping woman, pulled the blanket off the bed and quickly enshrouded her. With three pieces of clothesline he bound the blanket tightly and carried his victim into the kitchen. Peter Morris's ax rested conveniently nearby. Picking up the tool, McKie began to beat Manella in the same place he had beaten Thomasina—about the left side of her forehead. He smashed her two, three, four times until Mrs. Morris's muffled screams had ebbed. Afterward he wandered the apartment until he found the bankroll Morris had left his wife. Then before departing he ripped up Manella's nightgown to her waist and took a satisfied look. She would never use that again to cuckold her husband.

The day the Court of Appeals handed down its ruling in the McKie case Bonora received a profusion of congratulatory telephone calls as news of the decision spread through the Detective Division. A precedent-setting case was rare. Nor was it so frequent anymore that the investigative work of the department passed muster with three different courts. In recent years rulings by the U. S. Supreme Court had given defense attorneys such a myriad of openings for overthrowing a conviction that many detectives had begun to picture their task as hopeless. They were pleased when one of their own succeeded.

Bonora heard from Detective Oliva in the early afternoon and the two men reminisced about the fourteen months they had spent together attempting to arrest McKie for murder. Oliva's fondest memory involved a discovery he and Monroe had made on their own several days after McKie's modus operandi was uncovered. On a pure hunch the two investigators had searched the vacant lot behind Inwood School Number Four, where McKie had taken his wife both times to beat her. There in the underbrush they had found a tan raincoat that matched Juanita's description. A hank of clothesline and a pair of leather gloves were cached in one pocket.

"I don't think I ever would have thought to check that lot," Bonora commented admiringly. "That's what I call real good detective work."

Oliva responded self-consciously, quickly pointing to the sergeant's own successes. But Bonora's thoughts were already directed to the general reaction the entire investigation had produced in the Inwood ghetto, perhaps the most profound reward he had taken with him when the Morris case was ultimately resolved. Now that the black communities in Nassau County, like their counterparts across the nation, had assumed a hostile and uncooperative posture toward the police, he was often nostalgic for that period in Inwood.

The black residents in Inwood, at first suspicious, ended up believing in and trusting the detectives, though this conversion had not come easy. Starting the day of the body's discovery, the three investigators had put in over four months investigating the murder, withdrawing only under bureaucratic pressure. In the early part of 1966 they served two more full-time stints. Still, they were not through. The District Attorney concluded that a judge would not permit the list of connected crimes to be used in McKie's murder trial. And the other evidence alone was, he felt, simply insufficient to guarantee conviction.

So the detectives continued to investigate, anxious to complete their case and to get George McKie off the streets. Even during the

months they were officially unassigned, the pursuit went on. Because
Inwood was Monroe's regular patrol, he took it upon himself to keep
track of McKie. Several times a week he would phone Bonora and
apprise him of their suspect's recent movements. At least once a week
during the fall and winter months of the investigatory hiatus Bonora
would drive to Inwood. After picking up either Monroe or Oliva, he
would pay a call on one of the witnesses previously interviewed.

The detectives spoke with Juanita King so often during those
months that she actually refused to see them at one point, turning
livid at the mere mention of George McKie's name. And Maggie
Kennedy, who had dubbed Bonora with the nickname JoJo—for
reasons no one could fathom—would complain when he dropped by:
"JoJo, you're driving me to drink with this McKie business."
Disturbed and uncomfortable in the detectives' presence, the community was nevertheless beginning to realize that the senseless murder of
Manella Morris was not about to be abandoned as just one more
"nigger killing."

This persistence had a decided effect on the Inwood ghetto. In the
spring of 1966 when the detectives rode through town the residents
milling about on the street corners would shout out their approval.
Often one of them would approach the squad car with news of
McKie's present whereabouts ("Up on Church Street, I seen him") or
with fresh rumors about the Morris murder ("A woman down at the
bus stop says you fellas gonna be real surprised when you find out
who kilt Nellie").

Remarkably, it was a product of this newly acquired trust that after
a month's absence finally brought the detectives back to the case on
that eventful day in May, 1966. Eva Mae Harper, a large, bottle-shaped
woman with a matronly demeanor, had replaced Annie Lou Turner as
McKie's girlfriend. Older than McKie and supporting him financially
through her work as a domestic, she was more resistant to the
detectives' inquiries than Annie Lou had been. Yet on Saturday, May
14, it was she who unexpectedly appeared in the Fourth Precinct
stationhouse seeking the detectives' help, distraught and terrified by

her last encounter with McKie. He had threatened her for talking with the detectives. "He told me he should have had me murdered long ago," she wrote in a five-page statement. "He told me he should cut my goddam, motherfucking head off.... He said I better get out of town and offered me fifty dollars to go home to North Carolina."

Four days later Bonora was on his way to Inwood, traveling south from Mineola along a route that in the past fourteen months had become as familiar as his nightly trip home. On the basis of Eva Mae's statement he had managed to wangle one more day from the Homicide commander Charles Spahr, and the deep-felt disappointment that had weighed on him for weeks had quickly evaporated. If McKie wanted Eva Mae out of the state, she obviously possessed crucial information.

He stopped first at the Fourth Precinct stationhouse to pick up Oliva, and the two men continued into Inwood where they located Monroe on his beat. Bonora negotiated the patrolman's release with his supervisor, relinquishing the driving wheel afterward to Oliva and moving into the back seat so that the prodigiously built Monroe could sit comfortably in the front. Then the three investigators drove to Eva Mae Harper's residence, a two-family house with a crumbling front porch and gray asphalt shingles that were peeling and blistered. When they learned she was not at home Bonora suggested they try to locate McKie.

Oliva began to drive slowly along Lawrence Avenue, the main thoroughfare through the Inwood ghetto. Bonora and Monroe searched both sides of the street, examining the fronts of the gray, decrepit houses and the narrow dirt alleys running between them. At the corner of Bayview Avenue, an open, plazalike area where many of the local residents gathered, Oliva turned right and headed into the parking lot behind John's Liquor Store. Six of McKie's friends were standing there drinking from a bottle of Thunderbird wine, neither their position nor occupation changed in the year since the investigation began. Oliva drew the car alongside and the men informed the detectives that McKie had not appeared all day. As the detectives remained a few minutes conversing, Bonora noticed that Franklin Bing was being purposely excluded from the wine-passing ritual.

"How come poor Franklin is missing out?" he asked with amused sympathy.

Clyde Roseman, slight-shouldered and withered, winked a sly red eye. "He hollers in the canyon."

The remark provoked a trumpet of laughter from the group and Bonora smiled questioningly at Monroe.

"It means he goes down on women," Monroe said, chuckling as the car pulled out of the lot.

The detectives continued their search through Inwood for the next half hour until Monroe spotted McKie near the Lawrence railroad station located just over the Inwood village line. He was talking to a young Negro woman in front of an abandoned house. A month before, the detectives had secretly trailed McKie for an entire week after women had been assaulted at home two nights in a row within a block of his residence. That secret surveillance had produced nothing, so this time Bonora directed Oliva to park the car in the railroad station where it could be easily observed. Perhaps psychological pressure would elicit better results.

A few minutes later McKie terminated his conversation and, noticing the investigators, began to walk away from them along the railroad tracks. One hundred yards down the line he veered sharply, disappearing into a vacant lot behind a series of wooden sheds.

Bonora cursed loudly with his disappearance, bemoaning the hopelessness of their present task. Fifteen minutes passed and when McKie did not reappear, Oliva started the car.

"Which way, coach?" he asked.

Bonora deliberated a moment then said brightly, "Hey, why not try McKie's lot? Maybe there's some other stuff up there you guys overlooked."

The forced optimism was transparent to his partners, but neither uttered a word and Oliva drove to the lot behind School Number

Four. For the next twenty minutes they kicked their way through the dense underbrush, picking up rusted beer cans and empty wine bottles—anything that looked unnatural. They found nothing.

Only once before had Bonora felt so frustrated, certain of a man's guilt yet unable to find the evidence necessary to arrest him. He had been much younger then, a detective only a few years, when a teenage girl had come to him with a frantic plea for help. Her father, a merchant seaman, had been forcing the child and her two younger sisters to have sexual relations when he returned home on his shore leaves. He both raped and sodomized them. Her mother would do nothing, she said, and her father had threatened to kill them if the subject were ever broached outside the family.

Speaking to the two younger sisters and receiving supportive stories, Bonora had brought the sailor into the squadroom. When he denied the accusations Bonora had begun to interrogate him, certain from the exacting congruity of the three sisters' stories that the father was lying, but knowing that only an admission of his transgressions would be sufficient to hold him. The interrogation continued for hours and Bonora, sensing the futility, became fearful for the young girls' lives. He considered what might happen should he release the seaman. Then he thought of his own small children at home and grew terrified transposing them into a similar predicament. The tension mounted. His head began to spin and he felt overwhelmed. The next thing he knew he had grabbed the sailor about the neck and was choking him with all his might while the other detectives tried to pull him off. When he finally did let go and was dragged from the room the sailor panicked and confessed. And his admission, detailed in a ten-page statement, corresponded perfectly to those given by his children.

Recollection of the incident always pained Bonora. He was ashamed of his loss of control even though his violent behavior probably kept the three girls alive. It was not the way a professional acted. Still the recollection came to him now that he felt the same keen frustration, knowing there was nothing more he could legally do. He bent down and picked up an empty beer can lying at his feet. Crushing it with one hand, he pitched it savagely against a nearby tree.

"Shit," he muttered and returned to the squad car feeling impotent and angry. He motioned to Oliva and they began once again to move through the ghetto, cruising slowly past the houses and small brick tenements and the vacant, trash-strewn lots that had once been wooded fields. For more than an hour they circled the small community until just before two o'clock Monroe sighted McKie walking near the railroad station. Oliva began to trail him in the car at a half block's distance, following him north along Lawrence Avenue past the parking lot filled with the shiny new cars of commuters from the surrounding villages. At the Bayview Avenue corner, where a number of his friends were gathered, McKie nodded hurriedly and continued along onto Wanser Avenue. He walked briskly forward for another half block, then stopped. With a darting look over his shoulder he turned into a yard and entered a tiny shed at the rear where one of his friends lived. Oliva parked adjacent to the yard in front of 42 Wanser Avenue, a faded, three-story red-brick building where another nocturnal assault on a woman had reportedly occurred. Monroe left to interview the victim while Bonora and Oliva waited. Soon afterward McKie pulled back the shed's flap door and gazed out at the two attendant detectives. He promptly withdrew when Bonora's eye met his.

A moment later the door swung open again. This time McKie came striding out at full force, his powerful legs churning the grass beneath him, his arms still pumping furiously as he stuck his head through the open passenger window.

"I've had it with you guys," he shouted. "You're bugging me. Now I've had it."

"George, what are you getting so upset about?" Bonora asked innocently.

"It won't work, Matt."

"What won't work?"

"Every time I turn around I see you. You're bugging me. Now when are you gonna leave me alone?"

Just then Monroe opened the apartment house door and approached McKie, unaware of the ongoing argument.

"Howdy, George," he said in an amiable tone.

McKie glared at him. "Monroe, I don't even want to talk to you."

"Well, I don't want to talk to you either," the patrolman shot back defensively, his broad smile disappearing. "I got nothing to say to people like you."

"What do you means, you black motherfucker— You're a goddam traitor to yo' race!"

"George," Monroe repeated calmly, "I told you I got nothing to say to you."

McKie moved toward him menacingly. "You know you can be killed too," he shouted violently, bearing his fist in the air.

Bonora motioned to Oliva and the two detectives slipped out of the car as Monroe was answering the suspect's challenge. He said, "Listen, I'm not some little old lady that can't defend herself. I'd take you on with one hand."

"I licked Callahan and I can lick you," McKie boasted, referring to a fight that had taken place outside the Sunshine Lounge two months before.

"George, you'd be no problem for me," Monroe replied.

Bonora moved in between the two men, picking up Monroe's rhetoric. "You know what he says is true. You're not talking to a little old defenseless lady lying down somewhere."

McKie glowered defiantly at the detective for a long moment. Then tight-lipped he answered, "Sure I did it. I did it but you guys can't prove it."

"Huh? What was that?" Bonora said, caught off his guard.

"You heard me. I said I did it and you guys will never prove it."

Bonora froze, gazing dumbly at McKie as if his actions and emotions had been caught in the stop-action lens of a television camera. Then he glanced at his watch to check the time of the confession, simultaneously realizing the absurdity of his gesture, as if a mechanical instrument could put the enormity of the last moment's words into perspective, could understand *really* what that admission meant. It had taken so long that for months now Manella Morris's murder had struck him as something unreal. George McKie had not been a man but an idea, an inexplicable force that had drawn him along like an echo chasing its author. Bonora thought of the fourteen months, the anxiety and pressure, the frustration, the distraction from his family. He knew it was all ending now, and when he peered up at McKie a broad smile had crossed his face.

"George," he said calmly, "you better get into the car. We're going back to the stationhouse."

The arrest of George McKie just about concluded the investigation into the murder of Manella Morris. But not quite. The following day during the afternoon session of the Grand Jury one final wrinkle was added. Callahan motioned Patrolman Monroe aside and informed him that McKie had been discussing the Morris murder at a party at Juanita King's house earlier in the week. Immediately the order of witnesses was halted and the guests at Juanita's party called to the stand. In the next three hours the twenty-one members of the Nassau County Grand Jury heard that McKie had forecast his disclosure only two days before—erasing those doubts that had naturally enough arisen over the improbable confession. According to the testimony that day, McKie had told his friends that he was too tired to run any longer, that he felt as though the police were surrounding him. "What do you do when you can't run anymore?" he asked plaintively. "I feel like tellin' 'em I did it." Two days later he did.

The Grand Jury hearing was the first of countless legal proceedings that would take two and one-half years to conclude as the McKie case wound its inexorable way through the state court system. In March, 1967, George McKie was convicted of second-degree murder and sentenced by Nassau County Court Judge Albert A. Oppido to serve a twenty-year-to-life prison term. Then his case went to the Appellate

Division and finally to the Court of Appeals in February, 1969. Now five months later on this warm June afternoon Bonora's thoughts turned charitably toward McKie's defense attorney, Lawrence McKeown, whose belief in his client's innocence had been as tenacious as was Bonora's certainty of his guilt. An old-fashioned firebrand attorney, a striking white-haired Irishman rarely without a legal lesson for the prosecution, he had carried McKie's cause through the three courts for only the small financial compensation the state would pay. All along he had argued that his client's confession to the three policemen was obtained in violation of the U. S. Supreme Court's Escobedo ruling, which stated he had a constitutional right to counsel.

Court of Appeals Justice John F. Scileppi wrote the final decision for the three-member tribunal, in which he opined that the "right to counsel" dictum was applicable only to an arrested defendant or a suspect in a custodial interrogation. He noted in the precedent-setting ruling that had the confession been made in the patrol car, such premises—like a squadroom office—would have been considered custodial. But George McKie was on the street, not under arrest, free to come and go as he pleased when he blurted out his admission of guilt.

Before leaving for home that afternoon Bonora heard from Monroe, who was now a detective. He told Bonora that he had learned McKie was bearing up well in prison, serving his time without causing problems, having secured himself an easy job where he could feed his enormous appetite for reading. Bonora felt a touch of compassion hearing of his prison life, aware of McKie's intelligence and his propensity to wander, thinking how difficult the constraints must be for him. Yet he felt no remorse for incarcerating him and would have been bitter had McKie submitted and the court accepted a plea of insanity. For time after time criminals immured in state mental institutions, for the "indeterminate" sentence murderers receive, were released in less than a few years. And Bonora knew McKie well enough to realize his mental wounds might take decades to heal.

Not that he had much faith in the prison system. Indeed, it occurred to him that its rigid control might well cause the tensions swirling within George McKie to boil still more furiously. Yet at present there seemed no other alternative. And given the choice, he wanted McKie away for as long as possible so he could do no more harm.

CHAPTER

6

"My bedroom has been ransacked. I just woke up from a dead sleep, found a piece of tape on my mouth. My wife also has tape on her mouth. I woke up my oldest son and together we tried to revive her but she doesn't seem to respond.

"Could you send an officer down? Eight seventy-three Fulton Street, Valley Stream. I have a couple younger children, could you tell the officer not to use his siren? I don't want my children to wake up."

BONORA RUMINATED on the message as he proceeded along the Northern State Parkway toward work. It had been received the previous day, August 27, 1970, in the Fifth Precinct stationhouse. The patrolman dispatched had found the woman dead and had called the Homicide Squad. A murder investigation was begun.

The message stimulated Bonora's curiosity. Experience had taught him that even in the worst crises people tend to react with an extraordinary degree of composure and order. They maintain their proper priorities. With a house on fire the woman grabs her child, not the fur coat. Yet this man, a husband aware that his wife is unconscious, telephones the police and describes to them first—the condition of the bedroom! The remarks about the children also gave the sergeant pause. Had the man checked their room before telephoning the police, certainly the natural reaction of any concerned father? He must have, otherwise how would he have known they were sleeping? Yet the message makes no mention of a visit to the children's rooms.

It was now specifically Bonora's job to raise such questions. Three months before, after twenty years' service in the department, he had been appointed commander of the Nassau County Homicide Squad. The promotion was the fulfillment of his earliest aspirations. The Homicide Squad was the jewel of the police department. Its investigations set the standard for all others; its members were hand-picked veterans, each with a proven knowledge of investigation and the law. Behind this preeminence was a well-considered rationale. A murder in suburban Nassau County, an uncommon and unexpected phenomenon, can terrify an entire village. As such, it attracts a profusion of publicity and local interest. The subsequent investigation, if completed expeditiously, greatly increases the department's reputation for crime solving—a far more effective deterrent to crime than severe jail sentences, studies have shown. A low incidence of crime in turn buoys the public confidence in the police. And that confidence spurs the morale of the entire department, increasing the effectiveness of the uniformed patrol and the Detective Division alike, or so it is theorized.

The man responsible for initiating and perpetuating this so-called cycle of effectiveness is the Homicide chief. Bonora's promotion to that post surprised many in the department for since World War II no Homicide commander carried a rank lower than lieutenant; many had been captains. Yet tradition aside, it was an understandable promotion. Over the years Bonora had demonstrated both resourcefulness and ingenuity as an investigator as well as a dedication to police work that was outstanding in a department known for the conscientiousness of its members. If he wasn't investigating ninety hours a week, then he was home perfecting some part of the craft on his own. One result of this extravocational activity was the invention of a revolutionary process for detecting fingerprints that brought him nationwide publicity, including an article in the *New Yorker*. (The traditional method for detecting fingerprints involves brushing powder across a latent fingerprint, a tedious and lengthy process if, for example, an entire home has to be dusted, and one that always threatened to damage the print itself when the powder was applied. The Bonora Method, as it was patented, uses a chemical mixture sprayed from an aerosol can for the "dusting" of the latent print.) Bonora was also the police department's top marksman, a member of its elite antisniper squad.

Yet beyond his abilities and his dedication to police work Bonora had shown a capacity for leadership, a willingness to defend his principles, that on countless occasions had gained him the respect of his fellow officers. When in 1955 the department refused to cover his hospital expenses for a back injury incurred while officially off duty, he fought the decision, believing it unfair. The injury was the result of his efforts to aid a stranded woman motorist. The woman's car had broken down on the edge of ice-coated Wantagh Parkway with three children in the back seat—an emergency situation that Bonora argued demanded the immediate response of any police officer. His position eventually received the support of the local newspapers and the Nassau County Executive. His victory meant the subsequent protection for all off-duty policemen operating on behalf of the public. More recently as Seventh Squad supervisor, Bonora gained the loyalty of his men by making certain their jobs were not sacrificed in his efforts to change the listless character of the investigations. He was equally protective of the men in the First Squad six months later, his tenure as Squad commander just as successful.

From the pragmatic point of view of Police Commissioner Francis Looney, Bonora was a natural choice. An ambitious and energetic

Commissioner, open to innovation and change, Looney moved commanding officers around like chess pieces to improve the working of the police force. When one of these men began to perform effectively, as Bonora had, he saw no reason not to reward him.

The Homicide chief, like those special battle commands in the armed forces that consistently produce generals, was the acid test of leadership in the Nassau Detective Division. Former Homicide commanders filled much of the upper echelon of its bureaucracy. The one notable exception, Chief of Detectives Edward Curran, received the appointment for his own decisive role in solving the Weinberger investigation, Long Island's most notorious kidnapping-murder.

Bonora had no such far-ranging designs, his ambitions tempered by a realistic awareness of where success in the department might lead him. If he studied the rules and regulations with sufficient diligence to pass his lieutenant's and captain's exam, he could begin the climb through the upper levels of the administration—to Deputy Inspector, Inspector, Deputy Chief Inspector, Deputy Chief. And what would all these promotions ultimately achieve? Only one thing, from Bonora's perspective: removal from the action.

Not that he possessed any illusions about his new post. He was well aware that much of the Homicide commander's job was routine. Of the 2,500 cases handled by the squad each year only some forty would require lengthy, full-scale investigations. The rest of the work would involve examining automobile accidents, suicides or drownings—in short, any unnatural death where a doctor had not been in attendance for the past twenty-four hours or refused to sign a death certificate attesting to the cause. For the Homicide commander there were reports to file, meetings to attend, requisitions to fill out for personnel and equipment, all interspersed by his required testimony in the County and Supreme Courts, the Grand Jury rooms and to the Medical Examiner—countless demands that would prove repetitive and tedious. Yet there was the certain knowledge that every so often a full-scale Homicide investigation *would* be launched into a real murder mystery. And that in Bonora's mind was worth all the rest.

The first of these full-scale investigations under Bonora's command had only just begun. On the evening of August 27, 1970, the home of Mr. and Mrs. Howard Holder had been entered and apparently burglarized. While asleep, the couple were drugged with chloroform, their mouths taped shut to prevent screaming. Mrs. Joan Holder had never recovered from the anesthesia.

When the detectives arrived to investigate, they found the master bedroom where the Holders slept in a state of disarray. Drawers had been pulled out and ransacked. Mrs. Holder's jewelry box was missing, containing about two thousand dollars' worth of jewelry, including her engagement and wedding rings. Mr. Holder's wallet was found on the floor, its contents—mostly credit cards—strewn about.

The crime had attracted immediate and widespread publicity throughout the metropolitan area for the Holders had made their mark on Long Island in the fifteen years since their emigration from Brooklyn. Mr. Holder, an elementary school principal in New York, had served for the past ten years as president of the Valley Stream School Board. In recent months there had been speculation he planned to run for higher office, perhaps countywide. Mrs. Holder had chaired numerous civic committees and fund drives, in addition to presiding over the local Parent-Teachers Association.

Aware that thousands of interested observers were scrutinizing his every move, Bonora wanted to be certain he overlooked nothing in his first major investigation as commander. That was why, on the morning of August 28, he was so intently reflecting on Mr. Holder's call to the Fifth Precinct stationhouse; so intently, in fact, that he failed to notice the strange silence in the Homicide squadroom when he entered. Only after he reached his own inner office did he stop to consider this irregularity, did it occur to him that it was already past nine o'clock and the men were not gathered there. Indeed, looking about him for the first time, the commander realized the entire squadroom was empty!

Ruth Fuller, the receptionist, answered Bonora's question with a cryptic shrug, motioning him across the hallway. The sergeant left with his sport jacket still hanging in his hand, halting abruptly at the entry to the supervisors' office. Seated inside around the perimeter of the austere sun-filled room were approximately twenty-five detectives, members of the Homicide Squad and the Fifth Squad from Valley Stream. In the corner of the room behind a sturdy mahogany desk sat Capt. George Archer, talking volubly about the murder, waving his hands like a maestro as he paired the detectives into teams and handed out assignments. Archer had been Bonora's predecessor as Homicide commander. He was an aloof man, always busy studying and working to get ahead, rarely present at squad functions and parties. After a year's service in the Homicide Squad he had passed his captain's examination and was promoted in May to supervisor of two of the county's eight precinct squads.

Bonora remained in the doorway, momentarily stunned; the direction of a murder investigation had always been the exclusive province of the Homicide commander. Then suddenly, with a comprehension that shook his confidence, he recalled Archer's remarks three months before at the party celebrating Archer's promotion to captain. Throughout that evening's festivities, which included skits and prankish toasts, the detective master of ceremonies had mimicked Archer continually by placing his hand on the new captain's shoulder and repeating in a mincing falsetto, "I wanna be a captain, I wanna be a captain, I wanna be a captain"—a sardonic allusion to Archer's reputation in the department as a man who would do anything for a promotion. When Bonora had sought him out, hoping for some insights into his new job, Archer had greeted him coolly, his conversation hiding none of the resentment he felt toward this sergeant who had been selected to replace him. He pointedly suggested that it was a mistake on the Commissioner's part to have picked such a low-ranking member of the department to fill his position. The Homicide commander was constantly dealing with men of higher rank and there would be contention when questions arose concerning jurisdiction over the investigations.

Bonora's confusion turned to anger as he recalled those remarks, yet he made no immediate attempt to interrupt Archer's control of the meeting. He did refuse, however, to disguise his aggravation.

When Archer tried to include him in the decision-making in an overly solicitous manner he remained purposely distant and laconic. He took no issue with Archer's approach to the investigation but, recalling his previous warning, he wanted to be certain the captain understood no amount of diplomacy would win him the right to interfere. He was thinking too of the ominous experience of Lt. Henry Koehl, his first Homicide commander, a tough, dedicated cop of the old school and somewhat of a legend in the department. For seventeen years Koehl had led the county Homicide investigations with a high degree of professionalism and commitment until a murder investigation was conducted in the village of Hicksville toward the end of his career. During that investigation a newly appointed Inspector, John Lada, interposed himself in so forceful a manner as to take over the entire case. He gave out all the assignments and handled the interrogation of witnesses. Koehl backed off from the investigation, turning his attention to the squad's other chores. The case was bungled.

During the next twenty minutes as the detectives received their assignments and filed out of the room Bonora remained in the doorway, controlling his rage. Finally alone with the captain, he demanded an explanation in words veiling none of his displeasure.

For a moment Archer said nothing, characteristically rubbing the underside of his nose with a horizontal movement of his forefinger. He was an aristocratic-looking man, tall and trimly built. Leaning back in his chair, he began to explain his actions in a conciliatory tone. He had arrived at work early and concluded it expedient to begin the men's assignments right away. There was so much ground to be covered in the investigation and since the supervisors' office was much larger than the Homicide commander's and since there were so many men . . .

Bonora cut him off. "Goddamit, George. You know damn well I should have been consulted first. I'm the Homicide commander. You were promoted, remember? You know these investigations have always been run from the squadroom by the Homicide C.O.!"

Archer conceded that what Bonora said had been true in the past. But as the present supervisor of the Fifth Squad he had no intention of "sitting on my hands."

"Well, I'm going to be running this investigation," Bonora said firmly. "And you just better understand that."

Archer's face reddened. And Bonora, deciding further conversation would only intensify their impasse, strode out of the office looking for his own supervisor. Failing to find him, he proceeded immediately to the office of John Cummings, the acting Chief of Detectives. He described the encounter with Archer, concluding with the warning: "There's going to be a lot of trouble if Archer persists. You remember what happened to Henry Koehl."

Cummings, Koehl's assistant during the Lada incident, needed no further persuasion. He agreed to supervise the investigation closely so as to constrain Archer—a promise the Homicide commander was confident he would keep. The two men had been partners in the old Seventh Squad during the early 1950's and Bonora knew Cummings to be a man of his word. When he left his office that morning he was greatly relieved, unaware that this encounter with George Archer was just the first of many that some two years hence would culminate in the destruction of Bonora's career.

Assistant District Attorney Jack Lewis was awaiting Bonora when he returned to the Homicide squadroom, seated at the commander's desk preparing a wiretap application. An anonymous caller had telephoned the Holder residence to claim responsibility for the murder, and the attorney needed Bonora's sworn affidavit. The two men spent the remainder of the morning drawing up a request for a thirty-day monitoring period of the Holder phone. After lunch they appeared before State Supreme Court Justice Harold Spitzer, who with few questions approved their application. But then, apparently conscious of the increasingly hostile posture the higher courts have assumed toward electronic surveillance, the judge restricted the wiretap to twenty days.

Returning to the squadroom, Bonora found the detectives beginning to report back from the day's assignments. First to appear were several members of the Fifth Squad who had been canvassing the drugstores in Valley Stream and its environs for sales of chloroform and two-inch-wide Parke-Davis adhesive tape, the kind used to seal the Holders' mouths. Their efforts had been unavailing. Chloroform, it turned out, was not a stock item in any of the drugstores. And the brand of adhesive tape carried locally was Johnson and Johnson.

The Homicide detectives who arrived afterward brought more encouraging news. Interviewing residents in the Holder neighborhood in Valley Stream, they had found several who reported hearing the sound of screeching tires in the early morning hours of August 27, information that would tend to corroborate the theory that a burglar had accidentally asphyxiated Mrs. Holder and left the scene in a frenzy. Those who had seen the car described it as a 1962 or 1963 Chevrolet sedan, dull black in color as if it had been finished with primer paint. Bonora commended the detectives and instructed them to continue the neighborhood canvass in the hope of learning the car's license plate number.

The squeal team came next, Frank Cardone from Homicide and Robert Madonia from the Fifth Squad. Cardone, thirty-six years old and in physical appearance the image of Pierre Salinger, President Kennedy's former press secretary, detailed the detectives' return visit to the Holder household. They had gone there to question Mr. Holder more fully about the property that had been stolen and the events that had led up to his wife's death. During the account Bonora received a telephone call from Homicide Detective Charles Karazia, who had been sent to the Brooklyn school district where Holder was employed, to speak with his boss. As far as the district supervisor was concerned, Karazia said, Holder's work as an administrator had been above criticism. The supervisor knew of no one who might want to do him harm.

"Do you want me to stick around and speak with some of the other administrators?" Karazia asked.

Bonora answered no, suggesting the detective try to obtain a school roster so that other teachers and administrators could be contacted in the future. When he hung up, Bonora turned back to Cardone. "What did you find out about Holder's son, Thomas?"

"Apparently, he's just like he come on to us," Cardone responded, flipping through several pages of his pocket-sized notebook. The detective spoke out of the side of his mouth with the voice of a Hollywood tough, his language spiced by a dry sense of humor. "He's supposed to be quiet, not too rambunctious a kid. The several teachers we spoke to had pretty decent things to say. All the regular garbage: friendly, kind, doesn't get into fights, keeps his desk neat, brings an apple on Wednesdays. The track coach said something strange, though."

"That's right," Madonia cut in. "When I told him about the murder he said something like, 'You know, it's been one hell of a rough summer for the Holders, what with Joan being hit on the head and now this.' "

"What the hell was he talking about?" Bonora inquired, his forehead furrowing in consternation.

"The coach was pretty vague. Apparently Joan showed up a few weeks ago at a Little League game with her head bandaged. He heard about it from his wife. His wife heard about it from a friend, who said Joan had been smacked on the head during the middle of the night."

"And that's all he knew?"

Madonia nodded. He was seven years younger than Cardone and dressed in bell-bottom trousers and bright, waisted sport jackets. "That's what he claimed."

"Did you speak to his wife?" Bonora inquired.

"She didn't know much more. She had heard the story from a woman named Jane Flood. We called her, but she won't be home until seven or eight o'clock."

"Well, I want that story nailed down tonight," Bonora said.

"I kind of figured that," Cardone said. "I've brought my sleeping bag, so if you don't mind me using your office . . ."

Bonora didn't mind.

Three days later, Monday, August 31, Bonora paid his second visit to the Holder household. It was not unusual that he should return, for further questioning often produces additional, previously unrecollected information. Yet his objective on this particular day was more specific than just a deeper understanding of the family background. Cardone and Madonia had managed to "nail down" the story of Joan Holder's head injury, and it suggested some highly peculiar activity in the Holder house. According to Vivian Grosso, the Holders' next-door neighbor and the original disseminator of the story, Joan Holder had been awakened early Saturday morning, July 25, by a blow on the crown of her head. Her husband had inspected the house and found no signs of forced entry. Yet Joan Holder was positive she had been clubbed, vehemently discounting Mrs. Grosso's suggestion that she might have injured herself on the bed's headboard. The laceration had required a visit to the doctor, she said, and there simply were no sharp edges to cause such a wound.

In all his conversations with the detectives Holder had not once mentioned this incident—a strange oversight, it seemed, for someone anxious to solve his wife's murder. The wiretap on the Holder phone had also stimulated the detectives' curiosity. On Saturday, Holder had received a phone call from a "Melvin" who informed him he would be going into the "building" Tuesday to pick up the "items" wanted. The use of such ambiguous terms seemed an obvious effort to conceal, and the detectives had been only partially successful in their attempts to decode the message. Believing that "building" referred to Holder's school, they had searched the faculty roster and found a "Melvin" listed, a teaching supervisor named Melvin Feil living in nearby Long Beach. On the afternoon of Bonora's return visit to the Holder home other detectives were examining Feil's neighborhood, mapping out plans to tail him the following day.

The Holder neighborhood was part of a modern development, one of hundreds built on Long Island during the postwar construction boom. It consisted of inexpensive boxlike houses sited on regular sixty-by-hundred-foot lots, selling originally for $20,000, now worth close to $50,000. The land was meticulously sodded and maintained; the merion bluegrass brushlike in front, the evergreen shrubbery and frail elm trees trimmed as if part of a formal garden. The residents were predominantly middle class: teachers, company salesmen, small shop-owners—family men who worked hard, often at two jobs, to meet their mortgage payments and escalating taxes.

It was a quiet, durable neighborhood, and on the Monday afternoon that Bonora and the two squeal men returned, there was nothing to indicate that much had changed in the past five days, that a violent death had ended the life of one of its most admired residents. Fulton Street was empty of police cars and the hundreds of friends who had trooped to the Holder residence to pay their respects, many of whom knew the family only from working together on village committees.

The Holders lived in a one-story, white-shingled ranch house with gray shutters. Mrs. Muriel Holder met the detectives at the front door. Calling for her son, she showed the visitors into the curtained living room, seating them on a long couch and illuminating one of the nearby glass and gold-painted lamps. Howard Holder appeared a moment later. Wearing a double-breasted sport jacket and a pleased look on his face, he greeted his guests warmly, almost as if they were old friends come to pay a condolence call. He seated himself with a weighty sigh that acknowledged how hectic and exhausting the past five days had been.

Bonora offered a general observation on the difficulties all homicides present. Then, not wanting to seem insensitive by pushing too quickly into the matter at hand, he mentioned the fine impression Holder's wife had left on the community. He cited the praises his detectives had been offered whenever Joan Holder's name was raised in the township. He commented admiringly on the size of her funeral, which had been widely reported in the newspapers, and on the eulogy of the rabbi, who had intoned, "Her life was taken not only from her family, but from the many who came to depend upon her for the help she gave in her work."

For his part Holder recounted how "touched" he had been by the overflow of visitors, "by the people you didn't expect" and by all who had come to visit him during *shiva*, the Jewish mourning period. And in his deep-pitched voice that moved in the easy, articulate manner of those who have spoken often in public he went on to express his qualms about the well-being of his three young children, wondering aloud how they would get along without their mother.

Listening to him talk, Bonora thought how in other circumstances Holder would have easily drawn his admiration. He was forty-three, tall and slender. His studious, hollow-cheeked face was dominated by a high forehead, large horn-rimmed glasses and a thickly boned nose that seemed pasted on rather than a natural extension. Yet his entire appearance exuded a strength of character that had apparently served him well over the years: from his promotion to vice principal of a Manhattan public school only four years out of college to his prestigious appointment as district supervisor of the summer Head Start program, and to his successive victories as president in the rancorous and highly emotional school board elections. He evidenced few personal doubts, seeming to know implicitly where he was headed, though at the same time he made his listeners feel their support would be instrumental in his continuing success. In light of the investigation's recent developments, however, Holder's ready affability made the commander slightly uneasy. His composure seemed perhaps too complete in the face of such a major tragedy.

Informed there was still some confusion over Wednesday night's events that would necessitate another review, Holder waved his hand nonchalantly. Standing up, he said, "Why don't we all go into the bedroom and I can show you exactly how everything took place."

The detectives rose and followed him into the sleeping quarters. Once again as they entered the narrow carpeted hallway Bonora noticed the floor squeaked noisily. Such noise was not an unusual phenomenon in the cheaply built homes of the postwar boom when contractors tried to save time and money by nailing only some of the floorboards. But Bonora wondered whether a burglar, startled by the sound, would have continued any farther, for one had to pass the three children's bedrooms to reach the master bedroom at the end of the L-shaped hallway.

The bedroom shared by Howard and Joan Holder faced the tiny backyard. A large, somber room, it contained a king-sized bed replete with built-in bookcases, end tables and lamps. Along one wall was a man's armoire; along another, a high walnut dresser with a double set of drawers. Facing the bed was a low vanity table and mirror that supported a portable television set. It crossed Bonora's mind that a normal burglar might have stolen the TV, but the sergeant's primary concern was the bed where Joan Holder's alleged clubbing had occurred. As Holder seated himself at its foot Bonora circumspectly studied the headboard, concluding at least the possibility, however slight, that Joan might have accidentally inflicted her own wound.

Holder's story of Wednesday night's events did not deviate appreciably this afternoon from his other previous accounts. Retiring with his wife at midnight, he recalled opening his eyes soon afterward and finding a man placing tape over his mouth. He had tried to struggle but was too drugged by the chloroform. The next thing he remembered was awakening with his mouth sealed; Joan was alongside him, unconscious, her mouth taped. He ripped away the tape and tried in vain to make his wife respond. Then he went to get his fifteen-year-old son, Thomas, and the two tried once more to revive her. Finally he called the police.

Thinking now of the phone call to the Fifth Precinct stationhouse, Bonora asked, "When did you check the two girls' rooms?"

"What do you mean?" Holder said.

Bonora clarified the question and Holder shrugged.

"I imagine right after I went to Tommy's room."

"But you're not sure."

"I really don't recall."

"No?" Bonora said. "Do you remember telling the desk sergeant on the telephone not to have the police use their sirens because you had two children sleeping?"

"Did I say that?"

"Yes, you did."

Holder shook his head. "Well then I must have looked in their rooms prior to calling."

"But you don't remember?"

"I was groggy, Sergeant. I was drugged."

"All right," Bonora said. "Now is there anyone you can think of who might want to kill you or Joan?"

"No one."

"No problems out here with neighbors or parents angry at the school board?"

"Not really."

"How about in Brooklyn?"

"The only problem I ever had in Brooklyn I've already told you about, Sergeant. When those troublemakers from the PTA brought charges against me for being seen too much with one of our teachers, Lynnor Gershenson. It was absurd, really. Joan and I had a good laugh over it."

Bonora nodded sympathetically. The district supervisor had told Karazia that the charges were brought before a board of supervisors and parents and dismissed as untrue.

"Let's get back to Thomas," the commander said. "You say you sent him to check the doors and he found the lock open on the kitchen door?"

"That's right."

"Who has the keys to that door?"

"Just Joan and myself."

"Was it normal for it to be left open?" Madonia asked.

"No, it wasn't. But I can't say that we didn't leave it that way at times. This isn't the city, you know." Holder chuckled faintly, and dimples like sword slashes creased his high-boned cheeks.

"Weren't you at all concerned about a burglary?" Madonia continued.

"It wasn't really something I gave much thought to."

"Certainly there have been burglaries in the neighborhood," the young detective stated with assurance.

Holder shook his head doubtfully.

"There haven't been?" the detective said.

"There might have been," Holder replied. "I just haven't heard of any."

"How about assaults?" Bonora asked. "Or any kind of suspicious incidents for that matter?"

Holder was sitting on the edge of the bed and he leaned forward, his chin sinking introspectively into the V of his right hand.

"No, I can't think of any."

"You know we're talking about anything out of the ordinary," Cardone explained. "Sometimes there's a pattern that develops."

"No, nothing has ever happened here," Holder reiterated. "This has always been a peaceful neighborhood ... until Thursday morning." He gazed absently at the floor for a long moment, then suddenly stood up. "Now is there anything else, Sergeant?" he said, his voice for the first time betraying a sign of impatience. "With the funeral over there is so much to be done."

"I'm sure there is quite a lot," Bonora said considerately, "but there is still one other aspect of the evening that I'm puzzled about. You see, your daughter Ellen told the other detectives that she bumped into you as she came out of the hall bathroom at about one o'clock. Now you've told us once again you went to bed at midnight and didn't leave the room again until three. These discrepancies are difficult to deal with, as I'm sure you can very well appreciate."

Holder smiled thinly. "She's a young child, Sergeant. She must have been confused." He suggested that perhaps it had been Thomas his daughter met in the hallway.

"Yes, it was Tommy," ten-year-old Ellen agreed a while later when the detectives had brought her alone into the bedroom. On Thursday morning, still unaware of her mother's death, the young witness had readily recalled the meeting with Holder for the detectives. She said her father had taken her by the hand and led her back to bed. She remembered him commenting on the coolness of the room as he bent over to kiss her goodnight and felt the air conditioner on the back of his neck. And she recounted how he had walked over to the window unit to redirect the flow of air away from the bed.

"Tommy?" Madonia said now with surprise. "That's not what you told me before."

"I know that," Ellen responded, her bright, long-lashed eyes averted to the floor. "They keep telling me it was my brother."

"Who keeps telling you?"

"Daddy and Tommy. After I talked to you we had a family meeting. Daddy asked me what I said to you and when I told him, he said I was wrong. He said it must have been Tommy who took me from the bathroom."

"But you recalled it was your father the other day," Madonia reminded the child.

"I know. I think it was my Daddy, but I'm confused."

Bonora said, "Sweetie, what makes you think it was Daddy?"

Ellen had been standing stiffly by the bed, arms at her side, her black curly hair still covering nearly all of her downward-turned face. With the question she looked up at the commander, her white, delicate features knotted in confusion. She said, "I saw Daddy's hair blowing with the air conditioner when he kissed me goodnight."

"Anything else, dear?"

"Tommy never kisses me."

"Never?" Bonora questioned gently.

The young girl reflected, biting her lower lip. "He kissed me only twice in my whole life. Once on his bar mitzvah and last year when he came back from Puerto Rico."

CHAPTER

7

EARLY TUESDAY MORNING Det. Robert Oehl was stationed near the home of Melvin Feil on the island of Long Beach. A member of the Nassau County Burglary Squad for almost ten years, he had been assigned to the investigation as soon as there was a report of missing property. It was Oehl who had examined the Holder house for signs of forced entry, who had removed and disassembled the kitchen-door lock, determining that it had not been jimmied open. And it was Oehl that Bonora had charged with the surveillance of Melvin Feil's car.

A quiet, serious-minded detective in his late forties, Oehl was reputed to know every important burglar in the county. Chasing this kind of criminal for a decade, he had become something of an authority in automobile surveillance, an exercise demanding no small degree of mastery. "Tailing," as it is commonly termed by the police, does not at all resemble the prosaic assignment portrayed on television, two men in one car merely following those in another. It is a highly coordinated effort among a series of detectives using a selected group of inconspicuous cars, an especially challenging task if the subject in question is suspicious, as he is likely to be if he is breaking the law.

On this morning Oehl had arranged to have with him three cars (on other occasions he had used as many as five or six), each different in style and color, each equipped with a three-way radio so that six detectives could communicate with one another as well as with headquarters. To avoid detection he had positioned them far apart in the tiny neighborhood—a development of split-level homes built side by side, each no larger than a beach bungalow. Slumped back into the worn seats, tentatively reading their newspapers, the men waited impatiently to begin. Four hours later at 10 A.M., Melvin Feil appeared at his front door. He was a diminutive man with a large, youthful face. Making several birdlike checks of the neighborhood, he crossed the street and started his car. Oehl observed his actions from down the block, following close behind as he sped west toward New York City.

Feil reached Long Beach Boulevard with the Burglary detective in his wake. Then as he turned north to cross the channel onto the mainland Oehl dropped back and the detectives in the second car took over the tail. They followed Feil for another mile, then they too dropped back, allowing the third car to pick up the surveillance. In the meantime Oehl had reached a parallel road and unknown to Feil was racing side by side with Feil's car, prepared at any moment to take over the surveillance. Before Oehl did resume his tail, however, Feil made an unexpected stop. Instead of turning west on Sunrise Highway, which led to Brooklyn, he continued north into South Hempstead and picked up a passenger. The third-car detectives radioed into headquarters the address and license plate number of the car parked in the driveway. A few minutes later the passenger had been identified as John Arato, the school custodian.

Oehl picked up the tail as they returned to the highway. Now, though, he was wearing a fedora and his partner had ducked below window level so that it appeared he was driving alone. For several miles he followed Feil in this guise until, concerned about his possible detection, he directed the second car of detectives to take over. They too had changed their appearance, switching drivers so that the first "wheelman" was now sitting in the back seat reading a newspaper. Then it was the third car's turn. Then Oehl again. Each time an attempt was made to change the appearance of the men in the car. They would don fake moustaches, beards, even women's clothing and wigs—anything to disguise themselves. And all the while those in sight of Feil detailed a running description of his movements over the radio so that each car would be instantly aware of any unusual developments.

In this manner they tailed Feil into Brooklyn, then into the Williamsburg section near the industrial quarter, where Holder's school, P. S. 157, was located. The neighborhood was similar to those from which so many suburbanites had fled, humbled by poverty and neglect. The school, a gloomy five-story brick building, had been defaced by graffiti. The bricks on its two majestic turrets were black, the windows dark under prisonlike iron mesh.

Feil parked on Kent Avenue, and the custodian, John Arato, let him into the school. The detectives stationed their cars within view of both the school's battered front door and Feil's new automobile, appalled by what they saw around them. Children played on the broken, oil-stained streets, and the detectives realized that families still lived here, that life went on however desperately among the crumbling warehouses and the specters of apartment buildings long ago abandoned by their landlords.

When Feil reappeared at the front door he was alone. Taking another quick survey of his surroundings, the teacher walked briskly to his car, climbed in, locked the doors, then headed east, in the direction from which he had come. Two police cars followed while the third waited for Arato. Oehl supervised the surveillance of the teacher's return home so he was in a convenient position to observe Feil's actions when he reached Long Beach. Feil parked across the street from his house and left the car carrying a handful of papers. As he crossed the street he tore the top sheet into pieces, depositing it in the plastic garbage can in front of his house. Then he went inside. A moment later Oehl cautiously approached the garbage can. Certain he was not being observed, he fished out the pieces and fitted them together. Printed in ink on the small sheet of notepaper were the words "I love you."

Eight hours later a second group of detectives entered Brooklyn, Bonora among them. They drove to the predominantly Jewish section of Borough Park and stopped before a row of two-story red-brick apartment houses with white cement stoops. It was a warm summer evening and several elderly women were sitting outside in loose housecoats. They watched the detectives' arrival with heightened interest, commenting among themselves in muted Yiddish as the three unfamiliar men in their dark sport jackets and ties entered the building owned by Murray and Betty Rosenblatt, the parents of Lynnor Gershenson. After repeated attempts to reach her, the young teacher at P. S. 157 had finally called the Homicide Squad that evening during the interrogation of John Arato. Bonora, Cardone and Karazia had departed immediately, leaving Madonia behind to finish the custodian's statement.

Mrs. Rosenblatt, wearing a pants suit, her short gray hair brushed up like a boy's, was waiting with her apartment door open. She greeted the detectives with a rigid smile, sucking nervously on her yellowed teeth as she showed the visitors into the living room, which was dark and sparsely furnished. Two small chintz couches were positioned at one end of the room; two Chippendale-style chairs protected by clear vinyl at the other. In the center along the near wall was a wooden table holding several graduation and wedding photographs and a gold and blue menorah.

Mrs. Rosenblatt called for her daughter. Her youngest son, a college student, entered from the bedroom and introduced himself. A moment later Lynnor appeared from the same room and approached the detectives with the casual, jaunty walk of a woman aware of her appeal. She was smiling broadly, confidently. Studying her entry, Bonora immediately understood why rumors of secret liaisons might circulate about her, justly or not. At age twenty-six she possessed the sexual presence of a much older and far more experienced woman, a provocative quality that radiated from her soft brown eyes and full mouth. She was no classic beauty—her nose was too long and gently curved, her forehead too high—but her slightly buxom figure was earthy and sensuous, her plump cheeks milk-white against the lavish dark swirl of her hair.

Lynnor spoke to the detectives in a gay, whispery voice, chatting easily about her summer vacation and the hot weather as she led them into the dining room, where they could talk in private. Bonora stayed behind in order to telephone headquarters. Cummings and Archer took the call together on two different extensions.

"Did she go for it yet?" Cummings asked playfully. Archer laughed heartily.

From his position in the kitchen Bonora glanced into the living room. Failing to see Lynnor's brother, he ignored the remark, responding with forced casualness. "Just thought you might want to know where we are. If you need us, here's the number."

Cummings understood at once. "Fine," he said. "We'll be here waiting for you."

The supervisors in Mineola hung up their phones but Bonora did nothing. Then he heard the slow, unmistakable click of another telephone extension in the apartment. He shook his head ruefully as he joined the others in the back room, wondering just how much the boy had understood.

The commander found the two detectives sitting at one end of a long, Formica-topped table, Lynnor at the other. He settled himself next to the witness, who was leaning back in her chair with her legs crossed, smoking a 100's-sized cigarette and sipping from a glass of ginger ale. Cardone had already begun the interview and Bonora asked to be briefed. He learned that Lynnor had joined P. S. 157 in

September, 1969, as part of a special program at Long Island University that allowed her to teach while completing her degree. She had been married five years to Ira Gershenson, another teacher, and had just divorced him in July during a trip to Juarez, Mexico. She was presently living alone with her four-year-old daughter, Debby, in a nearby apartment.

Bonora motioned to Cardone to continue his questioning. In the next half hour the detective elicited the witness's activities during the days surrounding Joan Holder's murder as well as details concerning her relationship with Howard Holder. On the night of Mrs. Holder's death Lynnor recalled that she had been at home watching television with her daughter. The following morning she and Connie Abbate, a teacher at P. S. 157, had taken their daughters to the zoo. In the afternoon she had gone shopping. Learning of the murder that evening on the six o'clock news, she had immediately telephoned Melvin Feil, Mr. Holder's best friend. He told her that Joan Holder had been killed by an intruder and that the house had been robbed. On Sunday she attended Mrs. Holder's funeral and the following week she drove out to the house in Valley Stream with several other teachers from the school to pay a condolence call.

Lynnor's first meeting with Holder had come about during the summer of 1969, when she came to tour the elementary school where she would be teaching in the fall. Since then he had been "extremely helpful," acquainting her with the school's procedures and helping her with teaching techniques. The principal's office was always open to the new teachers, and she had availed herself of the opportunity frequently because Mr. Holder was both "a knowledgeable educator and a very understanding man."

Lynnor faced each question directly, answering in a hushed, slightly throaty voice that grew warmer and more fluid as the interview proceeded. She added extra facts and bits of information that were often irrelevant to the question but that demonstrated a willingness to be helpful. She sipped demurely from her ginger ale and smoked, and from time to time found reason to grin and chuckle with the detectives. She laughed deprecatingly when Cardone raised the issue of the PTA accusations.

"That was the silliest thing," she said, shifting in her chair and waving her cigarette. "This woman who made the charges, she's a real troublemaker. You know the type. The head of the PTA. Of course it was ridiculous. The whole scene was actually a joke among the faculty members."

"Why did the accusations come up in the first place?" Bonora asked. "What was her reasoning?"

Lynnor took a long drag on her cigarette and shook her head.

"She must have had some reason," he said.

"I guess a woman like that has nothing else to do in that neighborhood but make trouble," Lynnor said bitterly. "Because there was nothing going on, believe me!"

"Well there must have been *something* if the board finally saw fit to discuss it in a closed meeting."

"Sure," Lynnor said. "We all ate lunch together, a bunch of the teachers. There's an Italian restaurant called Anselmo's a couple of blocks from the school. Actually it's the only decent place in the area."

"That was it?"

"I guess so," Lynnor sighed.

Bonora asked the names of the luncheon members and Lynnor listed in addition to herself and Holder, Connie Abbate, Eleanor Blake, Priscilla Stoloff, Alan Strum, Frank Moriondo, the assistant principal, and sometimes Melvin Feil. Bonora also asked about the frequency of these lunches.

"Well, we ate every day, naturally," Lynnor answered, grinning with amusement at her own joke. Just then Mrs. Rosenblatt entered the room.

"Excuse me for interrupting," the older woman said timidly. "I thought Lynnor might like some more ginger ale."

Lynnor's mouth tightened and her eyes narrowed. "Get out of here," she shouted. "Goddammit, can't you see I'm busy."

Mrs. Rosenblatt apologized obsequiously and backed out of the room. And Lynnor, as if nothing had happened, turned back to the detectives and flashed a smile.

"Not everyone came every day," she continued in a soft voice, "but generally the whole group was together."

Surprised by the incident with her mother, Bonora observed the witness with renewed interest, pondering that unexpected Jekyll and Hyde oscillation with the sudden suspicion that "we might be dealing with a schizo." She was sitting back from the table now, her legs crossed, her short dress bunched near the top of her thighs, enumerating once again the list of teachers so that Cardone could record them in his notebook. She shifted her body position and Bonora's eyes, attracted by the movement, inadvertently landed on her now exposed blue underpants. Lynnor caught his gaze, yet she neither blushed nor readjusted her position. Instead she grinned, almost suggestively it seemed. Bonora turned quickly away, confused and somewhat embarrassed but in full agreement with John Arato's earlier assessment: she did have fine legs.

Finished compiling the list of teachers, Cardone asked the witness how they were paired. Lynnor stated that she usually sat next to Holder, Connie Abbate next to Frank Moriondo, and Priscilla Stoloff with Alan Strum.

"Were any of these pairs dating?" Cardone asked.

Lynnor said she didn't know, but insisted that for her it was just a matter of "not wanting to eat lunch alone."

"You never went to a movie or dinner with Holder?" Bonora asked.

"No, never," Lynnor said.

"How about a drink after school?"

"Not that either."

Bonora asked a few more questions pertaining to her marriage and daughter, then instructed Cardone to record her account. An hour later the detectives stood up to leave with a three-and-one-half-page statement completed and signed. They returned first to the living room to thank Mrs. Rosenblatt for her hospitality; then Lynnor showed them to the door, bidding each of them a personal good-bye. Cardone and Karazia departed first, descending quickly to the first floor. But when Bonora left he hesitated at the top of the stairs, his back toward the door. His mind was still consumed by the thought of Lynnor's brutal outburst at her mother and the saccharine smile that followed it. Now in retrospect it made him suspicious of all she had said, of each smile and laugh, of her cheerful good-bye and of the sincere handshake she had just given him.

Suddenly, on nothing more than a hunch, the commander whirled around. The apartment door was still partially open. Sure enough, Lynnor Gershenson was standing there with her face screwed up like a spoiled child, her bright red tongue stuck poisonously out of her mouth.

Bonora winked and blew her a kiss, then turned around and started down the stairs. The door slammed, shaking the old house and echoing through its darkened hallways.

In the days that followed Bonora prompted his men to find and question each of the P. S. 157 teachers that ate lunch daily at Anselmo's Restaurant. Lynnor's strange conduct during the interview and Holder's apparent disingenuousness had made the commander anxious to learn more about each of them and their relationship to one another. This curiosity was further stimulated by three subsequent developments that destroyed, once and for all, the investigation's initial thesis that Joan Holder's death was a burglar's mishap. First, a high school student appeared in headquarters and admitted he had been the one racing a black Chevrolet sedan through the Fulton Street neighborhood that Wednesday night. The youth explained he was dating a girl against her parents' wishes. That evening, after letting her out of the car around the corner from Fulton Street, he had sped past her house, noting the blinking bedroom light that signaled her safe arrival.

The next development came several days later. Howard Holder

telephoned headquarters to inform the detectives he had found the box of jewelry originally reported missing. The third development was most crucial: the completion of Joan Holder's autopsy. While only a trace of chloroform was found in Howard Holder (through a urine test), enough of the anesthesia was present in Joan Holder's brain and lungs to indicate it had been administered for a period of at least five minutes. There was little doubt in the Medical Examiner's mind that she had been purposely murdered.

The Medical Examiner, Dr. Lukash, further offered the opinion that the chloroform had been administered and the victim rendered unconscious before the adhesive tape was applied; otherwise the chloroform would have loosened the bandage. As for the tiny piece of plastic (of the kind used in garbage bags) found attached to the underside of the tape covering Joan Holder's mouth, his assumption was that it had been used in some part of the anesthesia's application.

The Homicide detectives spread out through Brooklyn those first few days of September, looking for the teachers of the Anselmo's luncheon group with considerable persistence and little success. Those teachers not on vacation were either staying away from their own apartments or had moved elsewhere. Once school resumed on September 6, however, headway became rapid and unexpectedly fruitful. Fourth-grade teacher Priscilla Stoloff led detectives to fifth-grade teacher Connie Abbate, who reluctantly pointed them to Frank Vitale, alias "Frankie Rogers," a fifty-seven-year-old former felon who had served more than twenty years in prison for numerous burglary schemes and various other illicit enterprises.

On September 10 Bonora sent Detectives Cardone and Madonia into Brooklyn to fetch Vitale. The commander remained at headquarters in Mineola, directing the other activity of the squad and reviewing not only the statement Connie Abbate had given the detectives but the notes that had been taken during her lengthy interview. He was looking for evidence that could be further documented in the event of a trial, for information that would help in his interrogation of Vitale. Connie Abbate had been Lynnor

Gershenson's closest friend among the teachers at P. S. 157. It was she who first revealed that Lynnor and Howard Holder were having an affair.

A twenty-eight-year-old divorcée with long, bleached blond hair, Connie had been teaching at the school two years when Lynnor arrived in the fall of 1969. Approached by the younger teacher for help and advice, Connie began to see Lynnor at lunch and on weekends. Soon their talk became more intimate. When Lynnor learned that Connie was seeing a married man she disclosed her own interest in Howard Holder, shortly thereafter confessing she was "in love with Howie." Following the Christmas vacation she showed Connie a cocktail ring Holder had given her; a month afterward a gold pendant that was her birthday present. Holder, too, apparently found warm, self-assured Connie a friendly listener. Calling her into his office one day, he confided he'd been considering divorce, though he wasn't sure he "could live without the children with him all the time."

Involved with a married man herself, Connie could ill afford to criticize the affair of her good friend. Yet late in March a conversation with Lynnor had forced her to reconsider her benevolent attitude. Returning from a shopping trip with Connie and their two daughters, Lynnor had started to recount how depressed she had been over the Christmas vacation, how she wished she "could be with Howie all the time."

Weary of this familiar litany, Connie rebuked her friend's childish musings and snapped: "Howie's married and there's nothing you can do about it."

Lynnor smiled mysteriously. "Oh no? Well, I already have." And she proceeded to describe how at her direction Frankie Vitale had hired two men to run over Joan Holder with a car. They had driven out to Valley Stream one evening, Lynnor said, but had apparently been picked up by the police.

Connie had also told detectives of Saturday afternoon rendezvous between Holder and Lynnor in the shopping plazas of Long Island, of dinners in New York at the Camelot Restaurant on Third Avenue and of a summer vacation home on the shore of Suffolk County that some of the teachers had rented where Holder had spent time with Lynnor. In addition, she remembered several other pertinent conversations. In one Lynnor mentioned she had been reading the best-selling novel, *The Godfather.* It made assassination seem so easy to order, she remarked, and wondered out loud whether someone in fact could be hired to kill Joan Holder. A month later Lynnor approached her with a determined expression on her face. "You're an Italian, Connie," she had said. "Don't you know anyone in the Mafia who could help me?"

But one conversation drew Bonora's particular attention that afternoon as he impatiently awaited the arrival of Vitale and the two squeal men. According to the written statement Connie had given the detectives, the two teachers had been discussing divorce over a lunch at Anselmo's. She had ordered quickly, but Lynnor had sat staring at the menu, apparently unable to make up her mind. Finally she had turned to her friend and said, "You know, Connie, I don't want to live on half a principal's salary. I don't ever want to have to look at the right side of a menu again...."

The dull, unsettling sound of a closing door startled Bonora from his reflections and he looked up to find Cardone standing in his office, a playful expression brightening his dark-bearded face.

"We've got the little son of a bitch outside," Cardone said. "Bobby is holding his hand in the Assembly Hall. For a while in the car I thought we might have to stop and change his diaper, but my quick-thinking partner opened the windows and we saved him for you."

Bonora grinned. "I assume then, Detective Cardone, that Mr. Vitale of Brooklyn and Sing Sing on the Hudson hasn't gone for shit."

"Not yet but with a little fatherly advice he may. He seems awfully scared, Matt."

Bonora stood up with a mischievous gleam in his eye.

"Good," he said and, waving, added, "I'll speak with him *out there!*"

The decision to remain in the Assembly Hall was not merely a glib one on Bonora's part. The Hall's isolation and monumental size tended to evoke a "last chance" atmosphere before entry into the Homicide Squad, an atmosphere the commander was planning to dramatize as he spoke with the witness. He walked quickly to the Assembly Hall and found Madonia sitting in the front row with Vitale, a short, stubby man with dark wrinkles of skin underneath his red eyes and a couple of days' growth of beard. On his head, cocked at a slant, was a gray, sweat-stained fedora, creased and twisted like an old piece of chewing gum. Bonora excused Madonia and took his place alongside the witness. In a low confidential voice he began to whisper in Vitale's ear.

"Frankie, we only have a few minutes alone together. Look, I'm Italian and you're Italian. You can trust me. I'll go to bat for you but you've got to level with me. We need the truth, no bullshit. You can count on me if you cooperate with us."

"Cops always fucked me," Vitale blurted out.

"Name a cop that fucked you, Frank."

"Casey from Brooklyn East Burglary."

"He was Irish, right?"

"Yeah."

"So what did you expect. I can't help it if you've been a turkey most of your life."

Vitale farted noisily. "Sergeant, can I go to the bathroom?"

"Sure, Frank, why not."

The two men walked from the auditorium, and as they pushed open the door to the men's room Vitale said, "You know, I didn't think cops had bathrooms."

"No?" Bonora said, vaguely amused. "What the hell did you think they did?"

"I don't know, but I figured that's what made them so mean."

Both men laughed and when they returned to the Homicide squadroom Bonora felt confident the witness was prepared to confess. But he was wrong.

Until nine o'clock that night Vitale denied any knowledge of Joan Holder's murder while proclaiming his innocence. Bonora bullied him ("Frankie, don't try to pull that bullshit") and badgered him ("I guess you must have liked it up the river"). When Bonora grew weary he called in Cardone and Madonia. Cardone was sarcastic and demeaning; Madonia threatening. One at a time, two together, sometimes all three at once, the detectives fired questions at Vitale, showering him with a relentless stream of invectives and threats. But nothing seemed to faze Vitale until Bonora said with quiet matter-of-factness: "It's this simple, Frankie. There's going to be a Grand Jury hearing. All the evidence for the murder of Joan Holder will be presented. Now who do you think those nice people are going to believe? A school principal and a teacher, or Frankie, the twenty-year con. It's really that simple. Either your ass is going up for murder or theirs is."

Vitale's glaring expression softened and for the first time he did not shout back.

"Now you've got good reason to distrust cops with your past experience," Bonora continued, sensing a breakthrough. "But we're different out here in Nassau. We won't fuck you. If you give us the truth we'll help you no matter what the situation. Whatever you've done. You have my word. Give us a chance to—"

"She asked me to but I didn't do nuttin', I swear."

Bonora nodded to the other detectives. "All right, Frankie," he said. "Slowly. Start from the beginning."

"It was that Gershenson broad. She come up to me at Anselmo's back in March," Vitale said, his voice fluttering nervously. "She says she wanted to talk to me about a problem, so I meets her after school and she asks me how much it gonna cost to get a woman killed. And I says, 'Why do you want to kill her for? You could hit her with a bat, you could break her leg.' But no, she says she wants the broad killed. So I tell her it costs twenty grand. She says that's too much and I says, 'Well, if you fuck me, I could get the guys from Detroit to do it for ten.' She says okay, so we go to a hotel."

"You went to a hotel?" Bonora asked, hiding his surprise.

"Yeah."

"Which one?"

"The Franklin Arms."

"Did you use your own name?"

"Nah, this one," Vitale said, picking a calling card off the desk from the pile of things Bonora had ordered him to empty from his pockets. "He's my cousin."

Bonora looked at the card. It read, "Frank Rogers, Farmington Road, Hartford." Then Bonora asked, "When did you speak to the boys in Detroit?"

Vitale shook his head. "I never did. The next day the crazy broad tells me to forget it. So I did."

"Aw c'mon, Frankie, I thought we had an understanding. Mrs. Holder is dead."

"I told yuh, I didn't do nuttin'! You can't frame me," Vitale shouted excitedly. "She asked me and then the next day she said forget it. I swear. I don't know no guys in Detroit, anyways."

"All right, all right," Bonora said, looking at the witness doubtfully. "Let's get back to the hotel. Where is it?"

"Orange Street, Brooklyn."

"And you were there when?"

"I don't know. March sometime."

"What room?"

"I don't fuckin' remember."

"Well you better fuckin' remember. Describe it."

"A double."

"What did you do there?"

"We had a couple a drinks and then had sexuals and all that."

"Cut the crap, Frankie," Bonora said harshly. "What the fuck did you do?"

"I screwed her and then she blew me."

"Blew you?"

"Yeah. She was real good. What a broad," Vitale said, bending his right hand and waving it as if he were strumming a guitar.

"And the next day what happened?"

"She came up to me at Anselmo's. She told me to forget everything."

Bonora was not completely convinced by Vitale's story, four hours of silence seeming singularly odd for an innocent man. Yet through the remainder of the night Vitale continued to insist he had not murdered Joan Holder nor did he know who had. Moreover, a check of all precinct files failed to uncover any substantiation for Lynnor Gershenson's boast to Connie Abbate that the two assassins hired by Vitale to run over Joan Holder had been picked up by the police.

The following morning Madonia and Cardone brought the exhausted witness back to Brooklyn. They dropped him at Anselmo's, then drove to the Franklin Arms Hotel to check the registry. They found Room 304 booked on March 9 in the name of Frank Rogers. It was a double.

CHAPTER

A WEEK AFTER Vitale's admission Bonora awoke with a shooting pain in his knee, his leg bent up like a pothook. It was not a new condition, the commander having awoken with similar spasms on each of the three preceding mornings. But the pain this morning was excruciating, and the fifteen-minute hot shower he had used previously to such considerable effect failed to relax the seized muscles. Leaving the house that day for work, he hobbled like a man twice his age.

The source of this injury was easy to trace. Early in August during the department's annual Practical Pistol Course Bonora had stood up from the kneeling position and wrenched his knee with an audible snap. He deemed it ironic that of all the participants he was the one who injured himself during a shooting refresher program. For unlike most Nassau County policemen, who rarely have cause to lift their guns from their holsters, Bonora was a competitive shooter, honing his skills at least once a week at local ranges and clubs. He had won a gold medal at the New York State Police Olympics and had once captured first prize at the International Police Tournament. Yet it was not merely competition that sustained the commander's interest in target shooting. After a painfully methodical week of trying to outwit suspects and their defense attorneys or after a day of intensive head-to-head interrogation, an hour or two at the range served as the perfect antidote to the agitation and frustration that welled up within him. The intense concentration required to hit a bull's-eye at fifty feet seemed uniquely designed to ease the mind, turning his attention from an equivocal and disquieting landscape to a comforting world of clear and immutable values. There was no mystery or ambiguity in target shooting. Winning was resolved simply. Hit or miss.

When Bonora reached headquarters that September morning a supervisor witnessing his condition ordered him immediately to the police surgeon, who drove him to nearby Nassau Hospital. He lay on a table in the emergency room for several hours until the leg straightened out of its own accord and could be properly examined. The diagnosis was a torn cartilage; the prescription: immediate removal. Yet the commander had too many pressing obligations to enter the hospital right away. The Holder investigation was continuing and Jack Lewis needed him for the preparation of the Pobliner case, which was scheduled to begin trial the following week.

So he persuaded the doctors to postpone his admittance. Instead, they put a cast on the leg, and Bonora left the hospital on crutches. When he returned fifteen days later the Holder investigation was still pending but at least his obligation to the Assistant D.A. had been met. Pobliner would soon be convicted.

Bonora's knee was cut open and the faulty cartilage removed on September 30. The operation left him sore and in continuous pain. In the early period of his convalescence he lay under the covers of his bed heavily sedated, removed from the world and the movement of doctors, his wife and children hazily in the background. For several weeks at home his days were a pastiche of dreams and television shows, of unremembered visitors and newspaper stories. Then, as the knee began its slow healing process and the pain eased, the sedation was discontinued and his days became longer and less dreamlike. His

thoughts turned once again to the Holder investigation and he began
to agonize over it, inviting the men from the squad to his home so he
could become acquainted with its most recent developments.

He learned now of the statement of Pepe diGeronimo, the
headwaiter at La Strada in New York City, whom Lynnor had asked
for an introduction to the Mafia. (The waiter had no such
connections and was deeply offended by the request.) And of the yield
of the wiretap legally secured upon Lynnor Gershenson's telephone.
Though presumably reluctant to converse over the Holder telephone,
the principal and young schoolteacher showed no such diffidence
when Holder called Lynnor at home from a pay phone in Valley
Stream. They talked with the familiarity of old lovers, their
conversation gossipy, gay and affectionate. Lynnor seemed the
aggressor, proudly proclaiming her "love" for Holder, exhorting him
to ignore his melancholy, "We knew it would be like this, my love";
filling the pauses in their talks with tender "I love you's." On one
occasion their remarks led the detectives to the Brooklyn apartment of
Holder's father, where the couple was observed spending the night
together.

Bonora learned too of Vitale's second visit to police headquarters.
During sixteen hours of interrogation the former convict finally
"recalled" that it was Holder who had actually arranged his meeting
with Lynnor in Anselmo's and had canceled the project the following
day. And that Lynnor, in addition to inquiring about an assassination,
had asked whether he could obtain poison pills or chloroform. Bonora
harbored no doubts as to the truth of these assertions even after
hearing the extraordinary circumstances under which they had come
about. It had never seemed quite reasonable to the commander that
Lynnor would approach someone she had never met and baldly ask
him to commit murder. Holder, on the other hand, had known Vitale
for years through his patronage of Anselmo's. As for Vitale's previous
failure to mention the inquiry about chloroform, it seemed at least
understandable when one considered his inherent distrust of the
police and his fear of being implicated in the murder and returned to
prison.

Yet logic aside, the main reason Bonora believed these assertions had not been force-fed to the former convict was the unquestioning trust he held in his men. He was not so naive, however, as to suppose the public carried an equally trusting view of police incorruptibility. He knew Vitale's contention about Holder's involvement would have to be substantiated to prove truly convincing in court, and he was not surprised to discover that a meeting had been arranged to tape-record a conversation between Vitale and Holder.

The planned encounter was set for November 3. That evening Cardone called Bonora to tell him of the results, as the commander had requested. He said early that morning Vitale had been brought to Valley Stream, where he met Holder in the parking lot of a local diner. The two had been photographed together and their conversation recorded and monitored from an unmarked camper bus. Holder recalled and confirmed the alleged meeting at Anselmo's with Vitale, but he denied any responsibility for the death of his wife. "It was a freak," that she had been killed, the principal insisted repeatedly. Sure, he had approached Vitale in March for that purpose. He *was* in love with Lynnor, he had "gone a little ape." But the murder had taken place five months hence in August, and besides, hadn't he told Vitale to "forget the problem"?

Cardone informed the commander that a second meeting between the two had been arranged for November 9. That evening, however, Bonora heard nothing. Only the following morning did he learn what had transpired, and only by means available to the rest of the public. Picking the *Daily News* off his breakfast tray, he was unexpectedly confronted by the stiff, awestruck faces of Howard Holder and Lynnor Gershenson on the front page. The caption underneath Holder's picture read: "Howard Holder, 43, of North Valley Stream, stands before bench at Mineola police headquarters as he is booked on charges of conspiracy to commit first-degree murder. Holder, principal of a Brooklyn school, and a young teacher, were charged in the Aug. 27 death of his wife."

Under the other picture: "Mrs. Lynnor Gershenson, 26, also charged with conspiracy."

Bonora's pulse quickened. *Conspiracy to commit murder?* He ripped open the paper and began to read the story on page three: "Howard

Holder of North Valley Stream, L.I., principal of a Brooklyn school, and a 26-year-old divorcée who taught at his school, were charged by Nassau County police last night with conspiracy to commit first-degree murder in the chloroform killing of Holder's wife. The 43-year-old Holder, principal of P. S. 157 in the Williamsburg section of Brooklyn, was said to be romantically involved with Mrs. Lynnor Gershenson of 1314 46th St., Brooklyn, who won a divorce from her husband, Ira, in Mexico last July. Police said the intensive investigation . . ."

Bonora dropped the paper to his lap. In all his years as a Nassau County detective he had never heard of anyone arrested in the county for a conspiracy to commit murder. The Homicide Squad had always worked until there was sufficient evidence to justify a murder charge. Conspiracy of any sort was for politically motivated investigators who couldn't prove their case but needed something to show for their efforts. By such a charge guilty defendants could end up serving only a few months in jail instead of a punishment commensurate to the crime. The thought that the squad might have given up, settled for less, so infuriated the commander that he could barely contain himself that night when Cardone finally telephoned.

"It was orders, Matt," the detective explained weakly.

"Who gave the fucking orders?" Bonora thundered.

"Archer. It was Archer. He said he wanted to cut the thing short. But don't worry, Matt," Cardone said placatingly, "the case isn't closed yet. You know that."

"I don't know a goddam thing at this point," Bonora replied disgustedly. "Here I am laid up in bed and I read about the squad locking up Holder and Gershenson for conspiracy. What kind of bullshit is that?"

"I know, Matt, but it was orders."

"Well, how did we end up arresting them in Nassau anyway?" Bonora asked. "I thought all the evidence for the conspiracy was in Brooklyn."

"The D.A. wanted them arrested out here," Cardone said. "And besides, we got the evidence for Nassau we needed yesterday."

"What evidence?" Bonora asked, puzzled.

"Holder admitted to me that he and Lynnor had discussed how to get rid of Joan when they met in Green Acres Shopping Center in Valley Stream."

"He did?" Bonora said. "Did you get a signed statement?"

"No. Just an oral one."

"Why not a signed one?"

"He clammed up, but Oehl was there."

"And he heard it?"

"Oh yeah."

A month later Bonora returned to work. He arrived in the Homicide squadroom early Monday morning, December 7, mobile once again and eager to take full charge of the Holder investigation. Fixing himself a cup of tea (a bout of caffeine poisoning after two consecutive fourteen-cup days had sworn him off coffee), he quickly located the Holder files in Cardone's permanent filing drawer. They were stored in three russet-colored envelopes closed with tie strings. Eventually the commander would review all the material, but at the moment he was interested in the note that had been found in Lynnor Gershenson's apartment on the day of her arrest. It was the one piece of evidence he had not yet seen.

Bringing the envelopes to his desk, Bonora began to thumb their contents. He passed the collection of witness statements, the 262 report forms (the official journal of the investigation), the list of property impounded and a brief reference to the out-of-town trip made by a detective to interview Holder's brother. Ian Holder was a chemist in Cleveland who, it turned out, used chloroform in his work. Afterward came the account of the stakeout of the older Holder's apartment, then, stuck between the covers of a manila folder, the curious note found in Lynnor's apartment. The paper was slightly larger than a three-by-five-inch index card, a series of phrases scrawled across its face in the ink of a ballpoint pen.

Already going	*50 seconds*
singing	*2 minutes*
3 minutes	*complaining about trying to make sense*

4 minutes	mumbling
4½ minutes	out cold
5 minutes	bag over face
5 45	very heavy labored breathing
6 – screaming – no resp.	
7 minutes	tried to remove
7½	the end

"Jerry Hunter found that note in the table next to the bed with a piece of brass pipe," Madonia explained later that morning. "I.D. has analyzed the writing and confirmed it to be Lynnor's. We thought the pipe might have been used to club Joan Holder that night in July but the lab hasn't been able to establish anything definite."

Bonora sat listening at his desk, a second cup of tea in his hand.

"What have you been doing on the note?" he asked.

Madonia shook his head, conceding: "Nothing much. I was considering bringing it to my uncle, who's a doctor. I've told him about the note and he thinks it might actually be describing Joan's death."

"He said it might describe her death and you haven't followed it up!" Bonora exclaimed. "What the hell have you been waiting for?" Then, catching himself, he added uncritically, "That's the best lead we've got, isn't it, Bobby?"

Madonia assured him that it was.

"All right then, get going."

The detective jumped to his feet. "I'll photostat it and be on my way," he said, taking the note and leaving the office with a bounce in his step that eased much of the apprehension the commander had brought with him that first day of work.

Returning to headquarters after a ten-week absence, Bonora had entered the squadroom like a soldier returning from the war, anxious and uncertain. He was concerned that he had lost control over the squad, that his leadership had been usurped by others in the department. And he had been relieved to find nothing was changed, that the burnt-out fluorescent light bulbs in the ceiling had not yet been replaced, even that the old typewriters with their broken keys were still around.

Bonora feared too that the conspiracy arrest of Holder and Gershenson had weakened the detectives' interest and resolve. Yet speaking with the other men during the first day, he learned that like Madonia, they also had anxiously awaited the resumption of an unsparing investigation into Joan Holder's murder. When he called them into his office that evening Bonora chided them about their "fantastic arrest. Is that charge still on the books?"

"We just needed some hot-shot like you to lead us on," Cardone replied. The men laughed loudly, but in fact they were hurt. A conspiracy arrest was not their style either. It was an admission of defeat.

In the first few weeks of Bonora's return every bit of evidence collected in the Holder investigation since August was laid out, reexamined, reviewed and when necessary reevaluated. The detectives studied the statements in search of new areas of investigation, and when they deemed it fruitful returned to the witnesses for further interviews. Once more they canvassed the Holder neighborhood around Fulton Street and again questioned the druggists in Valley Stream. They returned to Brooklyn and, by circulating Lynnor Gershenson's photograph around her Borough Park neighborhood, learned of her frequent patronage of Lane's Pharmacy on Thirteenth Avenue. Curiously, Lane's did stock Parke-Davis adhesive tape, the kind used to bind the Holders' mouths. It was the sole drugstore in the neighborhood to do so, according to a store clerk. Yet no one remembered Lynnor purchasing chloroform, though it was available to customers by special order.

It was no surprise that the reinterviewing of witnesses in early December produced scant new evidence. Witnesses tend to lose interest in a case once a suspect has been arrested. Despite detectives' exhortations to the contrary, they assume all necessary information has been supplied—an assumption that can prove devastating. For often a witness's best information emerges only after his memory has been stimulated by three or four previous interviews. Thus normal investigative procedure urges the compilation of necessary evidence *prior* to making an arrest, unless of course there is a possibility the suspect might endanger other people or take flight.

Bonora nevertheless maintained faith in his squad's ability to solve the case, given the time and opportunity. But after ten days had passed he realized the department's attitude did not mirror his own. Already he felt the pressure to succeed at once or dispense with the investigation entirely. Except for the squeal man, all the Fifth Squad detectives had been returned to Valley Stream. Oehl had been reassigned to Burglary. Now Fifth Squad commander Lt. Tracy Smith was making pointed demands for Madonia's prompt return.

It was virtually impossible for a detective leaving an investigation after any length of time to transfer all his information. There were remarks and facial expressions that stayed with him, that he might not remember to record but that could tie things together if combined with new information. And there was his intimate knowledge of the witnesses he had dealt with, a knowledge that allowed him, for example, to recognize that a specific witness's smile was actually a sign of deep concern. Or that her characterization of a man as "worrisome" was really a description of his moral character, not his ability to harm someone. As any psychiatrist will agree, this kind of information can take much time and talk to acquire and may not be readily transferable.

Bonora tried to impress these observations upon Lieutenant Smith and the other ranking officers who paid him cordial visits "just wondering" when Madonia might return to regular duty. But sensing that those concerned with "administrative order instead of solving a goddam murder case" would prevail, he pushed his men hard through the Christmas and New Year holidays until finally a meeting on January 8, 1971, proved significant enough to silence, at least temporarily, Smith's grumblings.

That day Bonora, Cardone and Madonia spent two hours at South Nassau Community Hospital in Oceanside with Dr. Jesse Edwards, the chief anesthesiologist. Dr. Edwards had been recommended by the

Nassau County Medical Society as preeminent in his field. He was a grave, calm, soft-spoken man, whose pallid eyes showed the fatigue of a full morning spent in the operating room. Presented with a copy of Lynnor's note, Dr. Edwards left no room for equivocation in his conclusions. Someone, he said, had watched a person expire of chloroform asphyxiation.

Dr. Edwards went on to explain to the detectives that all anesthesias affect a person similarly, taking him through four distinct stages at a pace determined by the particular drug. The first stage precipitates a loss in consciousness, what in medical terms is called the state of "analgesia." There is a loss of pain sensation, but the patient is awake and aware of what is happening, though his perception is somewhat diminished. In the second stage of "delirium" or "excitement" the patient loses control of his actions and is liable to shout or scream or thrash about. In the third stage of "surgical anesthesia" the patient is completely unconscious and perfectly calm. This is the time during which a surgeon can do his work. The fourth stage, "respiratory arrest," is death.

All these stages, the doctor stated, were clearly identifiable in the note. "Already going 50 seconds" described the victim succumbing to the anesthesia's sedative effects, entering analgesia. "Singing 2 minutes" and "3 minutes complaining about trying to make sense" evidenced her passage into delirium, the second stage; "4 minutes mumbling" showed her going further under sedation until at "4½ minutes out cold" surgical anesthesia was reached.

Dr. Edwards puzzled over "5 minutes bag over face" until the detectives remembered the piece of plastic that had been found attached to the adhesive tape sealing Joan Holder's mouth. Presumably a plastic bag had been placed over her head after five minutes.

Continuing his analysis, the doctor said that "5 45 very heavy labored breathing" was the result of failing to raise the victim's chin to let air in the windpipe. "It's one of the first things you're taught in medical school," he remarked. "Otherwise the patient starts to heave, trying to suck in air."

The apparent inexperience on the part of the anesthesia's dispensers was also reflected, he said, in "screaming—no resp." and "tried to remove," evidence of a return to the delirium stage that should not have occurred with proper administration. Nevertheless at seven and one-half minutes the victim did reach "the end," respiratory arrest.

Though Dr. Edwards conceded to the detectives that a number of different kinds of drugs could conceivably kill a person in the seven-and-one-half-minute time limit, only anesthesias would display such clear gradations of the four stages. And of all the anesthesias known to man, only one, he said, worked in the time ranges described—chloroform.

Dr. Edwards' statement produced an unofficial moratorium at police headquarters on interfering with the Homicide Squad. For two weeks Bonora and his detectives worked unhampered, buoyed by the Edwards meeting and a statement taken five days later from Ronnie Sandler. Miss Sandler, a resident in the Brooklyn apartment house of Joan Holder's father, had witnessed Howard Holder and Lynnor entering the old man's apartment on four separate occasions in the month he vacationed in Florida during the previous winter. This was the first independent proof that their secret liaison existed prior to Joan Holder's murder.

At the end of that two-week period, almost as if by prearrangement, Bonora heard from Archer and Lieutenant Smith on the same day. Archer visited him to discuss "wrapping up" the investigation, and Smith in a telephone call demanded a date for Madonia's return. An appeal to Bonora's immediate superior brought the warning that "time is growing short."

The realization that the investigation might be finally abandoned was all the more difficult for the detectives to accept in light of Dr. Edwards' conclusion. The evidence incriminating Holder and Gershenson now seemed indisputable. Lynnor had documented the death in her own handwriting, which meant she must have witnessed it. And it was inconceivable to think she had committed the murder on her own without Holder's foreknowledge and assistance. A detective's partisan conviction, however, is not the same as what an independent jury will believe "beyond a reasonable doubt." Clearly, more evidence was needed.

The detectives continued to investigate. Cardone and Madonia started out early in the morning and finished late, often after midnight. With the help of the other squad members they reviewed the entire investigation again, then interviewed more witnesses and took another canvass of the drugstores in both Borough Park and Valley Stream. Yet two weeks later, when Bonora was questioned about the present direction of the investigation, he could only speak of "retracing our steps." The following day, despite the commander's assurances that fresh leads were coming in all the time and there was still a "good chance for a break," Madonia was abruptly transferred back to the Fifth Squad. At the end of the week Bonora received orders to return Detective Cardone to "the chart," the duty roster scheduling the squeal tours of each detective in the squad.

This last order was a critical blow to the investigation. It meant that Cardone would now be picking up new cases as his turn arose to answer the incoming requests for assistance. Yet Bonora was determined it should not prove fatal. When apprising the detective of his new schedule he urged Cardone to maintain his interest in the Holder case and to pursue the investigation in all of his spare time. He promised there would be detectives available to substitute for him in the event of an important interview.

Fortunately the weather on Long Island turned wet and bitter at the end of January with a snow storm that blew south from the Great Lakes. The temperature rose and then fell; the fallen snow hardened into ice, leaving most of the county covered in a shiny but threadbare garment of gray. The activity at the Homicide Squad slowed as it normally does during such frigid weather, when street-corner gatherings cease and automobile drivers fear the treachery of the roads. With the general languor Cardone was able to perform his regular duties as well as maintain an active involvement in the Holder case. He drove into Brooklyn several times to speak with Connie Abbate and Priscilla

Stoloff; he returned to P. S. 157 for further interviews with faculty members and he stopped into Anselmo's to talk with Frank Vitale.

None of these interviews advanced the state of the investigation, as far as anyone could tell. Still, the resolution of a homicide case has often come about from the most unforeseen of circumstances. To an incalculable degree accident has always played a key role. Not accident in the pure sense that Pascal described when he remarked how the length of Cleopatra's nose could have changed history. But rather in the sense of an unwitting result, such as the unexpected legacy bequeathed the delivery boy whose affability made him a favorite of the wealthy widow on his route. In the Holder case it was Cardone's relentless dedication during those end weeks in January that actually brought about the accident, or "break," as policemen prefer to call it: a phone call from an eighth-grade science teacher at P. S. 157.

The teacher was Al Davis, director of the school laboratory. He had been interviewed in the fall about the laboratory's use of chloroform (it didn't stock any). In a desperate attempt for new leads Cardone had sought him out again in January. Though once more the science teacher had nothing remarkable to report, he did express his amazement that the investigation was still continuing. Having read the newspaper accounts of the arrests in November, he just assumed the detectives had completed their work. Cardone assured him they had not.

A week later on Saturday, February 6, Davis called Cardone from the Brooklyn drugstore where he worked part time. He had just heard through a third party that a pharmacist now employed elsewhere, Louis Weissen, claimed to have sold Lynnor Gershenson chloroform when he worked at Lane's Pharmacy the previous August. He was boasting he could prove "this is Murder One."

Monday afternoon the detectives located Weissen in another Brooklyn drugstore and brought him to headquarters. He was a tall, stoop-shouldered young man with loose glabrous cheeks, large ears and soft, blinking eyes. A twenty-nine-year-old pharmacist with a degree from Columbia University, Weissen sounded like a vaudevillian double-talk artist, the words spewing forth in the garble of a tape recording played backward. It took most of Bonora's patience as well as a continual barrage of injunctions to "slow down, Louie," to plod through the witness's recollections. And with all that effort the story fell significantly short of the detectives' expectations. While Weissen claimed to have taken an order for chloroform from Lynnor Gershenson, he denied ever delivering it to her.

This curious transaction reportedly occurred on the first Sunday in August, a blistery, hot day that had taken its toll on Lane's normally active clientele. Lynnor entered the shop in the early afternoon and approached Weissen directly at the back counter. She was a regular customer, a young, attractive woman whom the pharmacist had always found affable and flirtatious. With the drugstore nearly empty he had time to kid her about her recent divorce as he went about refilling her prescription for birth control pills. Then, as he was writing up the charge slip, Lynnor mentioned needing "a few other things," and produced a sheet of paper with a list of four items: chloroform, ether, amyl nitrate and carbon tetrachloride. Weissen agreed to order them after she explained the supplies were necessary to teach her class about dangerous drugs. He warned her, however, that a prescription would be required to actually purchase the chloroform, the ether and the amyl nitrate. Lynnor promised to bring one when she picked them up.

The following morning Weissen ordered the drugs from a wholesaler, and that, in his words, "was the last thought I gave to Lynnor until her picture appeared on the front page of the New York Post." Weissen was eating lunch then, reading an account of the conspiracy arrest in the afternoon paper when Al Fromme, Lane's owner, entered the delicatessen and approached his table.

"Boy, are we in trouble," Weissen said, pointing to the photograph. "We sold Lynnor the chloroform."

The elderly owner appeared stunned. He listened to Weissen recount his meeting with Lynnor then warned him to say nothing further. To anyone.

In spite of the explicitness of Weissen's account Bonora was left with some doubts about his innocence. Indeed, the commander strongly suspected he might have sold Lynnor the chloroform without a prescription and was presently withholding disclosure of his role for fear of losing his license. Weissen himself reinforced this suspicion when he exploded angrily at Bonora's offer to seek immunity for him with the District Attorney. ("Fuck the D.A.! I don't trust that scene.") Yet under four hours of intensive interrogation Weissen refused to amend his story. He continued to maintain that he had not given chloroform to Lynnor and was unaware if anyone ever had. Moreover, his dislike of the District Attorney, it seemed, stemmed not from any present anxiety, but from a previous experience with a Queens Assistant District Attorney who had investigated his alleged role in a horse-doping scandal.

Believing further questioning futile at this time, Bonora took Weissen back into Brooklyn. Then, together with Cardone and Madonia, who had been reassigned to Homicide with Davis's phone call, the commander drove to Lane's Pharmacy, a modern, brightly illumined retail drugstore with a clutter of discount signs plastered across its front windows. The three detectives entered unobtrusively through the front door and approached Al Fromme at the rear counter. He was bent over the cash register, appearing frail and spent like a man whose illness had taken him close to death.

Bonora waited until he finished with a customer, then presented his shield and suggested in a soft voice they talk privately. When Fromme asked why, the commander immediately sensed trouble. After all, how many different cases would the Nassau Homicide Squad be interested in discussing with the owner of Lane's Pharmacy in Brooklyn? Yet at Bonora's urging Fromme agreed to take the men to his private office underneath the basement stairs. There amid a jumble of filing cabinets, catalogs and notebooks Bonora gave a detailed account of Joan Holder's death and the findings of the Medical Examiner. When he finished, he asked for the pharmacist's "help," cautioning him not to mislead them "because it would create an awful lot of problems for us, and incidentally for you too."

With that admonition Fromme's sallow complexion began to color in the most extraordinary manner. It flushed pink, darkening immediately to scarlet, which soon had turned vermilion. Then the colors passed swiftly through the wheel of purples until the gaunt, hawklike features were toned a grayish green. Or so the commander recalled. By then Fromme was visibly shaking. Bonora, fearful for the old man's health, quickly assured him the police were interested only in solving the murder. He avoided posing the crucial inquiry of who had sold Lynnor the chloroform, instead asking easy, general questions about the pharmacy and its methods of operation. The detectives learned from Fromme that a notebook kept on the rear counter of the store was used for maintaining the list of needed supplies and that the order for these supplies was placed each morning and usually received in the evening. They learned further that the staff was instructed to reorder an item automatically when the last one was taken from stock.

When Bonora eventually returned to the crucial inquiry Fromme denied knowledge of the chloroform sale. But before the detectives could question him further, a thick-chested man wearing a well-tailored black overcoat and black fedora appeared at the office door. He identified himself as "Rappaport, Mr. Fromme's attorney." He asked, "Who are you men? Why are you bothering my client?"

It was an uphill battle from then on. Rappaport wanted to protect his client from all police inquiries. "Lane's is a very busy place, and Mr. Fromme has all the responsibility," he asserted. "He doesn't have time for this sort of thing. Now you'll just have to understand."

Bonora was not to be put off. "Mr. Rappaport, I'm sure I don't have to tell you about the powers of the law—"

"No, you don't," the attorney cut him off. "I've been practicing law, successfully, I might add, since before that young man over there"—gesturing toward Madonia—"was born."

Bonora said, "Okay, then let me make it simple. We're going to interview everyone in the store. We can do it here, where it will be easy for everyone, including your client, Mr. Fromme, who we all know is a busy man. Or we can issue subpoenas and have everyone come out to Nassau County to appear before the Grand Jury.

Personally, I'd like to do it here. I don't want to inconvenience anyone. But of course, counselor, that's your decision."

Rappaport angrily eyed the commander. "I want to speak with my client alone," he said, and the detectives left the office. A few minutes later Fromme had agreed to "cooperate."

That night the three detectives interviewed the available staff and inspected the notebooks used for ordering supplies beginning from the end of July. None of the employees remembered a chloroform sale, but there were two chloroform orders in the notebooks. On Monday, August 3, chloroform was ordered in conjunction with ether, amyl nitrate and carbon tetrachloride. Then again on August 4. And on the back shelves behind the drug counter was a pint bottle of chloroform–the bottle, the detectives concluded, that was automatically reordered when the first bottle had been collected. Before leaving for the evening Madonia also checked the prescription file under Lynnor Gershenson's name. Only the birth control prescription was listed.

In the days that followed, the detectives worked to document the sale even more conclusively. They checked with the S and P Distributing Company in Brooklyn and learned that two orders of chloroform had been sent to Lane's Pharmacy in the past six months. One pint bottle on August 3, another the following day. They also interviewed the remainder of the store's sales personnel. Ted Pickwith, a salesman and stock clerk for two decades, remembered checking in the August 3 S and P order because two items were missing from the already opened box–after-shave lotion and a pint bottle of chloroform. He had placed circles after each missing item on the store receipt. Yet upon retrieving the receipt from the store files, the detectives found a check inside the circle following the chloroform. This sign, according to the shop's operating procedures, indicated that the chloroform had been taken by whoever had opened the box. Pickwith was certain the check looked "like the kind Al Fromme makes," but the owner continued to insist he knew nothing of the chloroform sale. And so by the end of the week the detectives were stymied. Still unable to identify the person who had sold Lynnor chloroform, they had no witness to testify she had actually received it.

The polygraph machine, or lie detector as it is popularly known ("the box" in the policeman's vernacular), helps predict the truth or falsity of a witness's statements by measuring his physical reactions when answering questions. Varying in size from a small typewriter case to a full office desk, each unit is equipped with recording pens that measure three different physical conditions: blood pressure, breathing patterns and galvanic skin response. The galvanic skin response is the amount of electric resistance in the skin, and changes under stress. No one knows exactly what it is or why it changes, but as a guide to tension it has shown a remarkable consistency. Blood pressure and the rhythm of breathing are measured in much the same way that they are by a doctor. When a person is hooked up to the machine, shifts in his tension levels will be registered by the three pens. The examiner does not look for specific reactions, such as surging blood pressure; what he watches for instead is change. Thus it doesn't matter whether the blood pressure increases or decreases; the fact of change is what counts.

In giving an exam, the polygraphist tries to establish norms to measure against. He does this by asking three types of questions: relevant questions ("Did you kill your wife?"), irrelevant questions which the examinee will answer truthfully ("Is your name Howard?"), and control questions ("Have you ever in your life stolen anything?"), which will normally provoke a lie. If properly posed, the control and irrelevant questions will establish norms on the graph paper for both prevarication and truth-telling that the examiner can then use as indices to compare the results of the relevant questions.

Unlike fingerprint identification, lie detection is by no means an exact science. The polygraph machine does not determine truth-telling, only bodily reactions. The examiner, interpreting these reactions, actually makes the judgment. Precisely because of the significant human element involved in this judgment the results of the polygraph examination are not admissible in the nation's courts.

Yet the preponderance of police departments across the country have found the polygraph an indispensable tool in criminal investigation. Over the years that Bonora himself had served in the Nassau County department he had never known it to falsely accuse a suspect. Moreover, on countless occasions it had worked to lift the veil of suspicion from one man, thus releasing the detectives to pursue other leads. In so many different instances it had proven itself worthy that it was only natural the commander should turn to it now, faced as he was by the difficult task of sorting through so much unsubstantiated testimony.

In the following week five witnesses who were in the position to sell Lynnor Gershenson the chloroform were brought out to Nassau County to be examined on the polygraph machine: Louis Weissen and his brother, who worked part time in the store; Robert Himmelfarb, a student and part-time clerk, Al Fromme and his son Richard. All but Al Fromme passed the test.

The afternoon of Al Fromme's examination Bonora called the pharmacist into his office and confronted him with his failure. Normally the psychological effect of the polygraph's accusatory judgment is sufficient to prompt a confession, even from a hardened criminal. But Fromme, frail and debilitated as he appeared, continued to proclaim his innocence. And when Bonora (believing the pharmacist's reluctance to testify stemmed from a fear of losing his license), mentioned that the District Attorney was prepared to grant immunity, Fromme jumped to his feet and began to shout at the top of his lungs. He blamed the results of his polygraph exam on his "heart condition," which he accused the commander of aggravating by the welter of police activity about his store.

Instead of pressing for an admission, Bonora suggested the pharmacist take another examination after a few days' rest, conceding that fatigue and nervousness might affect the readings. Fromme quickly agreed. He promised to notify the commander when he felt rested, but the following afternoon it was his attorney who telephoned headquarters. "My client has helped you all he can and now you are beginning to jeopardize his health," Rappaport said. "He has a heart condition. Another attack will probably kill him. Mr. Fromme is through cooperating."

The attorney's declaration was unchallengeable. There was absolutely no way the police could compel the pharmacist to take a polygraph examination. And with the presence of so protective an attorney, no chance now of even talking to Fromme again.

Bonora called Cardone into his office to discuss the situation. It was not a pleasant predicament to consider, the squad having probed as far as it could and now its last open path irrevocably blocked. Nevertheless, the two-hour meeting did not end on a hopeless note. Both men concluded they had done all the law deemed necessary: they had collected sufficient evidence to persuade a jury Holder and Gershenson were guilty of murder.

"We've got the motive—the eternal triangle—the conflicts and lies in their stories, the Vitale testimony, the chloroform order by Lynnor and the note," Cardone said. "What more do we need?"

Bonora's years of experience as well as his instincts answered *nothing*. Yet he wondered after six months whether he might not have lost his perspective, whether he might be too involved to make an objective evaluation of the case. He decided Cardone should review the entire case with the District Attorney's office.

"Don't tell them what I think," he instructed. "See what they have to say. I don't care how long the review takes. Just make damn certain you've told them everything we've got."

Cardone left Homicide that evening and for the next two weeks he spent every day on the second floor of the Nassau County courthouse in the offices of the District Attorney, rehashing the Holder case with Stephan Scaring, a member of the District Attorney's Homicide Bureau; Frank Dillon, acting chief of the Bureau while Jack Lewis was away; and Henry DeVine, head of the Appeals Bureau. He telephoned Bonora on Wednesday, March 3, with the approving judgment of the three attorneys. They could forget the conspiracy charge. The evidence was strong enough to try Holder and Gershenson for murder!

Bonora was thoroughly pleased. He asked Cardone when the case would be taken before the Grand Jury.

"We've got the presentation set up for next Tuesday," the detective replied, explaining that the decision to indict for murder still needed the final approval of William Cahn, the District Attorney. Such approval was ordinarily a formality, but Cardone promised to call Bonora when Cahn returned on Friday from an out-of-town conference.

Two days later the expected phone call brought unexpected news.

"You won't believe it, Matt," Cardone said bitterly. "Scaring just got thrown out of Bill Cahn's office."

"What do you mean, got thrown out of his office?"

"Just that. He wasn't there two minutes. Cahn won't let him call the Grand Jury. He says we don't have a case."

Bonora felt the rage rising within him, and when Scaring picked up the phone he exploded. "Steve, what the hell is going on over there?"

"I don't know, Matt," Scaring said. "He's probably in one of his moods."

"Well, what are you going to do?"

"Let's wait a few days," Scaring suggested. "I'll go see him again."

But the passage of time did nothing.

"I just don't understand this bullshit," Bonora agonized several days hence when informed of Cahn's continued intransigence. "We've got you, Dillon and DeVine convinced we have a murder case. And he says no. Since when did Bill Cahn become such a great legal brain? He's just a politician."

"Matt, Matt," Scaring implored, "you know I agree with you. I think we've got sufficient evidence for the murder case, but I'm not the D.A. What do you want me to do?"

"I don't know. But Christ, even if we were to lose the murder case, we could always hit them with a solid conspiracy charge in Brooklyn. But you can't do that vice versa. We've got the cart before the horse. Besides, our conspiracy in Nassau is weak. All we have is Holder's oral statement to Cardone and Oehl."

"I know that, Matt. We're agreed about that."

"I just can't believe that we've got the bomb and we're not going to use it. This whole thing is as insane as our war in Vietnam. Either we should get in all the way or get out. Goddam it, we've got to do something, Steve."

"Okay, Matt," Scaring said placatingly. "I'll tell you what I'll do. I'm sending Bill a memo in writing today for the record. Maybe that will get him to reconsider."

Bonora hung up and during the next few days tried to fully involve himself in the day-to-day operations of the squad. He avoided discussing the Holder case both at home and in the squadroom, but this pretended apathy succeeded only on the surface. Arriving momentarily would be a decision determining the merit of an entire six months' work. And if the plain frustration of waiting were not enough to distress the commander, every so often a conversation overheard several months before on the wiretap would return to him, challenging and mocking. Holder, deriding the detectives' chances of ever solving his wife's murder, had said smugly to Lynnor, "What do you expect? Look who's heading the investigation. A Bonora, a Cardone, a Madonia." And the two had laughed giddily at his Italianized pronunciation of the names.

Scaring finally called Bonora on Thursday, March 18.

"No go, Matt," he said. "Cahn says put the chloroform in Lynnor's hand and he'll call the Grand Jury."

Bonora was stunned. "That's it. You mean that's really it?"

"I'm afraid so. Unless you can find out who actually sold her the chloroform."

Bonora set the phone down without another word, his thoughts spinning through the months of investigation and the incriminating evidence that now filled two voluminous filing drawers. He was convinced Howard Holder and Lynnor Gershenson were guilty—a belief, he knew, that meant nothing without the support of the District Attorney. Yet what could he do to prove the identity of the chloroform seller? Surely Cahn recognized the impossibility of his demand. Why then even make it? What was the D.A. really trying to prove?

Try as he might, the commander couldn't deal with the questions his inner voice asked him. He could only think one thing: Holder and

Gershenson had succeeded, they had gotten away with murder (though their eventual conviction for conspiracy would require a prison term of from one to twelve years).

For a moment Bonora allowed that defeat to weigh upon him, hurt and outraged. Then, rising from his chair, he approached the squad deputy commander aware of his duty. All homicide cases theoretically remain open until solved, but Bonora had been a member of the department long enough to recognize where things stood. His command conveyed that recognition.

He said, "Put Cardone back into the chart."

But there was more to be heard from the Holder case.

CHAPTER

Thus far it would seem a detective pursues only one case at a time to its ultimate conclusion, his thoughts and days consumed by little else. In truth, the commander of a detective squad, and in particular the Nassau County Homicide Squad, is never afforded the luxury of attacking one investigation individually. He may become tantalized by a specific case, but his efforts are spread through many: suicides, drug overdoses, automobile fatalities, felonious murders—at a rate of more than 2,400 a year. This incessant turmoil places great demands on a commander's administrative skill. Like the circus juggler, he must be a continual manipulator, pushing his small staff from one homicide to the next while weighing the particular needs of an investigation against the peculiar skills and work schedules of his men; pursuing an investigation at full steam, then holding it in abeyance while another with more rapidly deteriorating evidence is begun.

Bonora much preferred investigating to administrating. Yet he did not neglect those managerial duties that were a fundamental part of his stewardship of the squad. Studying the crime statistics as he had twice before in an attempt to improve squad performance (first as deputy commander of the Seventh Squad, then as commander of the First Squad), he discovered that the preponderance of homicides occurred at night, particularly between 9 and 11 P.M. Curiously, the schedule of the Homicide Squad, like that of the other special squads, encompassed only the daytime hours. A nocturnal murder forced the detectives out from their homes, a procedure creating a considerable lapse in time before a professional was on the scene to preserve the evidence and begin interviewing local witnesses—actually get the investigation started.

The solution would have been simple had tradition not reigned like divine right in the department. As it was, several months of protracted negotiations passed before Bonora was finally given permission to divide the squad into a day and a nighttime shift. Once granted, the squad's response time to the crime scene was cut from an average one hour to fifteen minutes.

There were other benefits besides. With only half the detectives working at one time, the small quarters no longer seemed crowded and there were enough squad cars and typewriters. Moreover, suburban witnesses, often at business in New York City during the day or out shopping or visiting, were now accessible for interviews when the detectives called at night. In less than six months' time the two-platoon system managed to eliminate the backlog of cases that had built up during the tenure of Bonora's predecessor, Captain Archer.

Naturally, the day-to-day operation of the Homicide Squad was never completely routine. Still, when the investigations were mostly conventional, Bonora was less compulsive. He took an occasional afternoon off to play golf, spent hours refurbishing his new home—a Dutch colonial Hazel had purchased on her own initiative during his hospitalization. And when away from the squad he considered his own private whims and inclinations, thought of his own family's needs.

In the final month of his first year as Homicide commander, May,

1971, there was ample opportunity for such introspection. Squad activity was hectic—the men were investigating more than ten deaths a day—but nothing was so intriguing that the commander's attention became monopolized. Indeed, on the morning following the long Memorial Day weekend he sat at his desk thumbing absent-mindedly through the completed Homicide reports he was supposed to review and approve, reflecting not on squad work but on the time he had spent with his son over the holiday weekend. He was alone in his office, the squadroom empty and still except for the occasional ring of a telephone promptly answered by the receptionist. Most of the detectives were following up automobile accidents which had soared over the weekend. Even the squeal man for the day, Det. Jack Wichmann, had departed. He had been called to the county's North Shore to investigate a "dead one"—detective terminology for a corpse, the nature of whose death, whether natural or unnatural, had yet to be determined.

Bonora's thoughts were at once bright and reassuring. Over the holiday weekend it had become clear that the estrangement from his son had finally dissolved. For the first time since September they had laughed and joked with one another, spoken openly of thoughts and feelings without caution or an unnatural courteousness. Bonora felt the renewal of their once respecting and protective relationship, felt once more a general optimism about things.

The commander's life had not been easy during the past eight months. In addition to the quiet conflict with his son, he had had to deal with Captain Archer, who was still attempting to usurp the leadership of the Homicide Squad; with his painful operation and absence from work; with the conspiracy arrest of Holder and Gershenson; and with the ultimate failure of the Homicide investigation itself. Bonora could remember taking a hard look at himself in the mirror one recent morning, shocked by the unaccountable aging in his face. The skin was puffy and dull, the smile lines around his eyes and mouth, the cleft in his chin more sharply etched. His hairline had ebbed in front and now an unmistakable bald spot crowned the top of his head. All of his difficulties contributed to these changes in his physiognomy, but clearly it was the coolness his son had continued to express toward him that cut Bonora most deeply.

Its genesis could be traced to the previous June when John returned home from his first year at Tufts College. The school was a small, highly selective liberal arts institution located just outside of Boston. John's attendance there (on partial scholarship) was a great source of pride to Bonora, who each year grew increasingly regretful of his own failure to attend college. Yet when John returned home for the summer vacation he was a changed person, no longer the timid, docile young boy the Bonoras had driven to the New England campus in the fall and helped install in his new lodgings. Confident and outspoken at age eighteen, he had decided he no longer cared for the stringent rules that governed behavior in the Bonora household. After spending a year in a college dormitory coming and going as he pleased, John was outraged at his parents' attempts to treat him "like a child," telling him what to do and when to do it. A quiet, moon-faced youth, sturdily built and with the soft eyes of his father, he reacted bitterly when Hazel inquired into his evening plans. "You don't know where I've been all year, so what difference does it make now?" he would ask. He particularly resented Bonora's imposition of a one o'clock evening curfew, and as the summer wore on, he broke it frequently and with increasing boldness.

These acts of rebellion were just part of a more rudimentary change in John's attitude toward his father. He had left Wantagh, Long Island, in awe of Bonora, proud of his work and reputation. He returned less deferential, neither excited by police work nor particularly impressed by his father's skills. The decided liberalness of the student body at Tufts with its concomitant anticop dogma was by no means responsible for this transformation. (John still considered himself a conservative on most matters and took pleasure in the verbal sparring that often erupted between his classmates and himself over topical political matters, particularly the Vietnam War.) Rather, it was the year spent with sons of some of America's wealthiest families that had shaped his new perspective. Having grown up under the straitened circumstances that a policeman's salary demanded (after twenty-one years' service Bonora's salary was finally a respectable $19,000 a year), John now looked with disdain upon a career whose rewards were mostly intangible. Big business was his ambition (he would eventually attend the Harvard Business School), his heroes the American business executives who traveled and lived with financial ease. John remembered his father's feeble attempts at business and saw a man unable to deal with the hard realities of the world outside the protective womb of the police department, an idealist more concerned with solving a crime than making money. (Bonora had once owned a gun-and-sport shop that was unsuccessful, and the company set up to manufacture his fingerprint spray failed to market it properly.)

Aware of this change in attitude, Bonora was less troubled by his son's aspirations than his specific acts of defiance. He didn't especially want John to become a policeman either, though whatever career his son pursued he would never abide his disobedience or disrespect.

Often during that summer as John's challenge to Bonora's authority grew more intense, he thought to sit down with his son and talk things through. But his first months as Homicide commander had left him few free moments. When he came home late at night John was either asleep or out. When they were together on the weekends Bonora was generally too exhausted to offer more than curt reprimands. Then one evening in the middle of August it all came to a head.

It began with an automobile accident in which three young college students were killed. Supervising the investigation, Bonora had returned home past one o'clock, deeply disturbed by the memory of their young mangled bodies. He checked his children's bedrooms as he often did after a gruesome homicide, needing the reassurance that they were home and safely asleep. Much to his surprise, Nancy's bed was empty. He found Hazel and she quickly explained that their seventeen-year-old daughter was spending the evening at a girlfriend's pajama party. John, however, had left the house after dinner without a word and had not yet returned.

Finishing off the Scotch he had brought from the kitchen, Bonora settled into bed and was soon asleep, wrestling with the hideous memory of the accident. Then he heard Hazel's troubled whisper and his eyes snapped open. It was 2:30 A.M. and still no sign of John. Bonora stalked into his son's room and seeing the empty bed grew angry, thinking only that the boy's defiance had gone too far. But by 3 A.M. he was telephoning the Seventh Precinct desk to leave John's description and that of his car. Another half hour passed and Hazel was beside herself with fear. Bonora telephoned the pajama party, hoping Nancy might give him a clue to her brother's whereabouts. The hostess's mother, awakened from her sleep, searched the house and returned to the phone in disbelief. Nancy was nowhere to be found!

Bonora dressed at once and drove to the house, questioning the girls brusquely and with impatience. He was able to learn only that John had come by three hours before and picked up Nancy and a friend. No one seemed to know where they had gone.

He left the house with his pulse jumping, gripped by anger and dread as he began to cruise Wantagh's quiet residential streets, shining his flashlight into the driveways belonging to John's friends in a vain search for his small blue Morris car. He canvassed the local pubs and bars that John frequented and failing to locate him thought only the worst. What if he had gotten drunk and run off the road with the girls? Or had picked up a hitchhiker and had been beaten and robbed or was now being held under gunpoint?

The commander widened his search, driving south toward Jones Beach, passing through the vast black emptiness of the parking lots. The three mutilated bodies he had seen that evening reappeared before him. They turned over and over in his mind like some child's kaleidoscope run amuck, torturing him with visions of riven flesh until he thought he was about to go mad. Then suddenly he was aware he had reached the Seaford Channel and was pulling into the parking lot of Mabel's Room. Parked next to the white Victorian house that had been converted into a young singles' bar was the small blue Morris car.

Bonora's first reaction was relief. Drawing closer, resentment began to well up inside him, aggravated by the grating sound of the jukebox drifting from the bar's open windows. He pulled his car to the curb, waving down a white Nassau County Highway Patrol car as it passed by. Minutes later Bonora and the young highway patrolman were standing on the porch of the old house, the commander poised at the side of the door as the patrolman knocked.

When the door opened slightly Bonora could see that it was his son who had answered. John turned away unaware, heading back inside. Without a warning Bonora barreled through the door, catching John by the shoulder and spinning him about. He saw the pale slackened face and the bloodshot eyes, and all the emotion that had been caught inside him, all the fear and the anxiety, exploded. He lay his right hand back and smacked his son harshly across the face. Nancy was seated several feet away at the bar. Grabbing the glass from her hand, Bonora smashed it to the floor. Then as he slapped her face, his eyes settled on Glen, standing behind the bar. Glen was several years older than John, and in the commander's opinion, a corrupting influence. Leaning over the wooden counter, he seized his shirt, pulling the stocky young man off his feet. With all his might he slashed the back of his hand across Glen's face, opening a wound on the nose that sent blood spurting forth.

"What the hell are you doing letting these young kids drink in here after hours?" Bonora screamed, now turning toward the bartender. "I could close this goddam place up for good. Do you know how old these girls are?"

He started for the bartender, but the uniformed patrolman restrained him, pulling him down off the counter. Bonora turned away and grabbed at his son, latching onto his arm, tugging and pushing him toward the front door. He ordered the two girls to follow. Nancy and her friend, Sue Guando, came quickly, frightened and shaking, trailing Bonora to his car, then climbing swiftly into the back seat. John stood defiantly by the front door.

"I'm driving my own car home," he announced drunkenly.

Bonora pushed him into the front seat and closed the door. He went around to the driver's side and climbed in. As he started the car and it began to move, John opened his own door.

"I'm driving myself home," he declared. "I don't need you."

Bonora jammed on the brakes and leaning across the front seat, slammed the door shut. "Touch that again and I'll knock your goddam head off."

John glared at him. "Go ahead if you think that will prove anything."

Bonora floored the accelerator, staring straight ahead.

"C'mon," John urged. "Aren't cops always big for fights? You obviously want to prove who's tougher so let's go." It was a young man's dare. John was almost his father's height, but his one-hundred-and-fifty-pound frame was still that of an adolescent.

"How could you bring your sister into a place like that at three in the morning?" Bonora asked.

"We got there at midnight," John corrected him.

"Don't push me, John. Your mother and I have been worried sick not knowing where you were or what may have happened to you."

"That's tough shit."

Without removing his eyes from the road Bonora slapped John with the back of his hand. The boy stiffened but didn't move. After a while he said, "Sure, that's the way cops always handle things."

Bonora ignored the taunt and the car fell silent as he dropped Sue Guando home, then a few minutes later arrived at his own house. Pulling into the driveway, he saw lights on in all the downstairs rooms and Hazel in the kitchen, dutifully boiling water for coffee and tea. He let John out in the back yard and the boy clambered boisterously up the porch steps, banging open the kitchen door. Hazel, standing by the stove, turned ashen at the sight of her son. She rushed to his side trying to settle him into a chair, the beer smell of his breath and clothes making her nauseated and frightened. Finally he was seated and she brought him a cup of steaming coffee. John took one sip before slamming the cup down.

"I'm going to get my car," he announced, pushing his mother aside as he stood up and strode toward the front door. Bonora caught him as he reached the living room; John turned around and swung wildly. A trained police fighter, the commander instinctively ducked and grabbed the boy's hand, twisting his son to the floor.

"Goddammit, I'm going for my car," John shouted, struggling to stand. Bonora let him go and when John reached his feet, he swung again. This time the punch glanced off Bonora's chin. The detective reacted by flailing out, slapping his son hard in the face, then punching him in the chest.

John threw another punch, this time wide of his father. And then another. Bonora was alternately trying to grab his son's hands, and jab back at him in an attempt to end the fight before either of them became seriously injured.

Awakened by the commotion downstairs, Betty and Jeanne now came racing into the living room, screaming at the sight of their father and brother battling.

"Stop, stop it," Hazel pleaded desperately as John grabbed his father around the chest and the two wrestled to the floor, overturning the coffee table and breaking a glass lamp.

Hazel ran sobbing from the room. A moment later she returned with a hysterical pitch to her voice. "All right," she shouted. "Stop it, both of you. Stop it or I'll shoot."

Bonora froze. Peering up from the floor, he saw the three-inch barrel of his Colt .38 pointed at him, the lead tips of bullets visible in the revolver's cylinder. He relaxed the grip on his son and began talking. "It's all right, Mom. It's all over now. There's nothing to worry about."

He stood up cautiously, his eyes glued to Hazel's face. "We've got everything under control. No need to worry. It's all right." He began to walk hesitantly forward. "It's all over now. Relax. All right . . ."

He took two last steps and, certain Hazel's finger was not on the trigger, reached for the pistol. Her grip was loose. He lifted the gun neatly out of it, turned quickly away and emptied the pistol of its six bullets. He dumped the cartridges into one pocket and placed the pistol out of sight in another. Then he turned back to John, who was still sitting on the floor, stunned. Bonora extended his hand, which the boy accepted after a moment's consideration, pulling himself up. Neither uttered a word, the sobbing of the two young girls filling the silence as they restored the overturned furniture to its proper place, swept the broken glass off the floor into a brown paper bag.

When the cleanup ended, the Bonoras sat down together over coffee and cake, trying vainly to repair the damage. Yet it was days before they dared confront one another without undue caution, before the initial shock wore off. Afterward John had returned to school, never once mentioning the incident to his father though they were both aware of the distance it had created between them.

Through the fall and winter months Bonora's work kept him from the time he so desperately needed to spend with his son. That was why finally in May, freed of investigative compulsions, he had taken two extra days off over the Memorial Day weekend. John and his father had worked together on the new house during the holiday, fitting the porch windows for screens and cleaning out the garage. And as they worked they talked. For the first time they were able to discuss "Mabel's Room," as the incident would thereafter be known in the Bonora family. Even joke about their free-for-all. Bonora regretted the severity of his actions that night but insisted that John had left him no other recourse. John readily agreed. From eight months' perspective he could appreciate the thoughtlessness of his behavior.

Thinking about the weekend now in the squadroom, Bonora was profoundly grateful for the way things had turned out. John's rebellion had not cost them their friendship. If anything, the bond between them had become stronger. He understood John a little better and John respected him a little more. The experience had matured them.

CHAPTER

10

In 1972 Bonora was a stranger to the Upper East Side of Manhattan, that small pocket of New York City containing some of the world's most glamorous shops, restaurants, offices and personalities. Like most Long Islanders, he was content in his suburban life and saw little justification for the forty-mile trek into the city. When not working during the day in Nassau County he could use the well-kept public golf courses or the broad sandy beaches; at night he could find sufficient amusement in the local clubs and restaurants with their wholesome but unremarkable fare or in the new shopping plaza cinemas that showed the top commercial films. Other than an occasional shopping venture with his wife or a rare holiday dinner, he had done his best in recent years to avoid Manhattan completely, disliking the traffic, the exorbitant prices, and the city's cold, patronizing face. Yet in February, 1972, a murder in Nassau County suddenly directed him there, and for more than a month he was forced to spend his days and nights exploring the diversified world of the Upper East Side. The ordeal, surprisingly, proved much to his liking.

The Upper East Side is only a few square miles in total—that area generally considered bounded by Fifth and York avenues, by Fiftieth and Ninetieth streets—but for most visitors it is all that remains of the "Big Apple" Walter Winchell once so eagerly publicized, the place where everything is happening, where everything seems shimmering and new. It is a distinctively attractive community with dark, stately apartment houses along Park Avenue, Gothic revival limestone mansions on Fifth Avenue and tree-lined cross streets with brownstone townhouses, small antique shops and chic restaurants and clubs. Each year thousands of new faces appear there: young college graduates, high school dropouts, lawyers, would-be actors and account executives, models and single working girls. They come from all parts of the country, hopeful and ambitious, lured by the bright lights and the pace of the city, charmed by the beauty of the Upper East Side, by its polish and bluster.

Among these youthful aspirants was a thirty-year-old former model named Patricia Parks, the daughter of a wealthy Midwestern business executive. On the evening of February 3, 1972, she was at home at the Newport East, a towering white apartment house at 370 East Seventy-sixth Street, a "luxury" building with twenty-four-hour-a-day doormen, a decorated lobby and an expansive penthouse suite occupied by the professional football star Joe Namath. Patsy's roommate, a United Airlines stewardess, had arrived home late from a California flight, and at ten o'clock the two girls were still seated about the small round table in the living room of their four-and-one-half room apartment. They were sharing a Chinese meal out of white cardboard cartons.

Suddenly, without announcement from the doorman downstairs, there was a brusque knock on the door. The ominous noise stilled the girls' animated voices, its insistent repetition stiffening them momentarily in fright. At Patsy Parks's silent urgings Pat Quinn tiptoed to the door and peered cautiously through the peephole. Two strange men stood in the hallway, both dressed in dark overcoats and fedoras.

"We've got a federal subpoena for Miss Patricia Parks," the

younger of the two men announced loudly, brandishing a piece of paper toward the peephole.

Patsy had begun to creep toward her bedroom, motioning frantically to her roommate not to reveal her presence. Pat understood.

"Patricia Parks has left town for a few days," she responded in a controlled voice. The men thanked her and departed.

For a moment the red-haired stewardess remained by the door, terrified and uncertain what to do. Then hearing her roommate's bedroom door lock, she grabbed her coat and rushed out senselessly into the winter night, into the cold dark corridor of Seventy-sixth Street between First and Second avenues. She drifted toward the lights and noise on First Avenue, stopping before Gobbler's Nob, the corner pub. When the front door opened, she entered impulsively. She pushed through the crowded bar area to an empty table in the rear of the dusky, low-ceilinged room, and ordered a glass of wine.

The incident had totally unnerved her. When her drink came she began to sip at it fretfully, feeling herself tremble. In her eight years as a stewardess Pat Quinn had traveled all over the world. She had seen and done countless things that others from her small hometown outside of Minneapolis would never dream of. Yet nothing in all those experiences had prepared her for the past ten minutes. What had just transpired seemed lifted from some old Hollywood crime movie, a nightmarish fantasy where innocent people are inexplicably murdered, where tortured bodies are found floating in the river. She ordered a second glass of wine. Finishing it, she thought to use the telephone.

"What's it all about?" she demanded in a frightened voice when Patsy answered her call. "Who are those two men whose names I saw on the subpoena, Pacelli and Papadakos?"

Her roommate seemed hesitant to talk over the phone, but after a long pause indicated she would come to the bar. Moments later she arrived, pale and trembling. She ordered a triple martini and drained the glass in two gulps. Then as if their telephone conversation had never been interrupted Patsy began to talk, her voice flat and remote.

"Vincent Pacelli and Demetrios Papadakos are drug dealers. Last May, Jimmy—that's Papadakos—stored a box of heroin in the apartment."

Pat Quinn's eyes and mouth gaped.

"He lived on the floor above us," Patsy continued. "I didn't do anything wrong. He just left the box in the living room for a few days. Then picked it up. Somehow the federal agents found out about the box. They forced me to testify before a Grand Jury. A couple of months later Jimmy and Vinnie were arrested."

"What's the subpoena all about?" Pat asked in a tremulous voice.

"They obviously want me to testify in the trial." Patsy took a sip from her second drink, then shook her head. "I just can't do it. I can't."

These revelations stunned Pat Quinn, as well they might. The two girls had met only a few months before at an elegant society ball. Pat knew of her roommate's moneyed background and had been introduced to Patsy's father, F. Newton Parks, a handsome, urbane gentleman who directed the European operations of the management consultant firm, Booz, Allen and Hamilton International of Chicago. But this was only one part of Patsy Parks's existence. And a small part at that.

Ten years before, Patsy had arrived in New York, a patrician-looking girl who had found Cleveland, Ohio, stifling, and a year at a finishing school in Switzerland hardly less restrictive. Tall and slender with a thick cascade of black hair, she had come to Manhattan with no immediate goal but with a general, undefined and restless ambition to find a career or a way to exist that would fully satisfy her—a search that had proved mostly futile.

She began by attending the Parsons School of Design. After flunking out, she married a well-to-do South American student and for five years felt restrained and unhappy. She divorced her husband and received custody of their son. Then with an abandon reminiscent of her late adolescent years in Cleveland, when she spent her weekends dancing and drinking, Patsy discarded her domestic role and ventured forth into New York City's night life. She danced into the early morning, hopping from one discotheque to the next, mixing with some of the city's wealthiest residents in addition to gamblers and criminals—that strange amalgam populating the "in" discotheques of the 1960's such as the Salvation in Greenwich Village and Arthur on the Upper East Side. Patsy smoked marijuana and hashish, then snorted cocaine. She began dating a man who was later indicted for illegal drug sales, and those who knew her well suspected she was intimately involved with these illicit dealings. It was a wild and unreal existence for a young girl who had been schooled in private academies and debutante parties, yet her family seemed to know nothing about it. Her divorced parents lived in Europe by then; her father in London, her mother in Greece. Her four brothers and sisters were scattered across the country in different prep schools and colleges.

In early 1971 Patsy's life underwent an abrupt transformation. Arriving home one afternoon she found that her former husband had abducted their son, flying him to South America to live with his family where he would receive a more conventional upbringing. From that moment on, the frenzy that had characterized Patsy's daily world subsided. She purposely avoided both the discotheques and her drug acquaintances. She started dating a hospital administrator and eventually acquired twenty-nine-year-old Patricia Quinn for a room-mate. She began seeing a psychiatrist and directed all her efforts (and forty thousand dollars of her father's money in legal fees) toward the recovery of her son.

These tumultuous ten years had left their scars. Patsy's once moist eyes were flat now and untrusting; her mouth petulant. In the past six months she had lost twenty-five pounds, and the soft curve of her high-boned cheeks had hardened so that she appeared tough and jaded. Looking at her with new perspective, Pat Quinn felt suddenly removed and distant from her roommate. Sipping at her wine, her eyes fell mesmerized onto the flickering yellow candle in the center of the table, and for the next half hour her thoughts ran in different directions. The two women said little.

During this quiet interlude Patsy left the table to call her boyfriend. At a few minutes after eleven o'clock John Manzi arrived, a professional gambler who was an apparent throwback to her past. He was forty years old and affected a curiously mod look, wearing his hair to his shoulders, shading his eyes in dark blue aviator glasses. Dressed in a smartly tailored suit, his boots and fingernails polished, he appeared the picture of affluence, though he had not discarded the cool street sense of survival that had been his legacy from a childhood spent on the Lower East Side. Hearing of the evening's events, he recommended that Patsy immediately call the federal agents to see what they wanted. Since a subpoena had to be delivered personally, she would still be free to avoid it should the demand prove untenable.

Patsy disagreed. "No," she said with a decisive shake of her head. "I've got to see some people."

Through three more rounds of drinks both Manzi and Pat Quinn endeavored to change Patsy's mind, but to no avail. Eventually they returned to the apartment. Then at about 1 A.M. Manzi drove Patsy downtown in his bronze Eldorado Cadillac and left her at the Hippopotamus on East Fifty-fourth Street, the discotheque that had formerly been Arthur.

The following morning, Friday, February 4, 1972, Bonora was in Suffolk County at the end of Long Island, closing out a joint homicide investigation with the local police. At 10 A.M. he received a phone call from Sgt. Jim Short, the Seventh Squad detective he had recently appointed his deputy.

"We're out here in Massapequa on a dead one," Short said. "One of the employees of the Oyster Bay Highway Department found the body about seven this morning in that wooded lot across from their garage. The guy said he thought it was a log at first because it was smoldering. He got suspicious when he saw some dogs tugging on one end. It looks like she's been stabbed quite a number of times. Then burned. I've got the men searching the entire area."

Bonora's anxiety started to grow. The search of the crime scene was crucial to a homicide investigation; it was a process no different from an operation where efficiency is essential and the slightest mistake can prove fatal to a case. Yet here he was twenty-five miles away, stuck in

Suffolk County for the remainder of the morning. He remembered the McKie investigation where his curiosity alone was responsible for the recovery of the murder weapon and more recently another case where his insistence had insured that a proper time of death was determined *before* the body was moved. Then abruptly, before his deputy could proceed further with his narration, Bonora interrupted.

"Jim, I don't give a damn how long you keep the men there today. We've got to get a good scene search. You can't miss a thing. You understand?"

"Sure, Matt."

"Now what about I.D.?"

"They've been here since nine helping us," Short said. "We've got extensive photographs."

"How about the girl?"

"The body's burned beyond recognition. The clothing doesn't look usable, but there's a chance we might do something with the shoes. I don't think—"

Bonora, who had been hovering restlessly about the phone, plumped himself down on a nearby desk as he cut in. "Well, what the hell do you have to work on? What about tire tracks?"

"No good," Short answered. "It's a dirt road and there're hundreds. There is some jewelry, though. The girl was wearing rings on every finger and some pendants around her neck. And five crucifixes."

"Five crucifixes?"

The unexpectedness of Short's statement halted the commander's line of questioning.

"You know, Jim," he said, "maybe this is one of those cult murders. What does she look like to you?"

"I'd say she's probably a fuckin' hippie with all that jewelry. She isn't wearing a bra either."

At that moment Bonora thought of Olson's, a motel less than a quarter mile away. If the girl had been a guest there, her jewelry would certainly have attracted attention. Massapequa is an archly conservative community even by Long Island standards, notorious for the hostility with which its citizens have greeted those who overstep the norm. It was here that three volunteer firemen had been dismissed from the department for failing to trim their sideburns, that crosses had been burned on the front lawns of several homes with prospective black tenants and that a number of schoolteachers with antiwar sentiments had been censured for speaking out. If the girl had been at the motel, someone would remember her.

"The men are already interviewing guests at Olson's," Short said proudly, having anticipated the commander's order. "I had them measure the body first so we could get a general description."

Tentatively satisfied, Bonora returned his attention to the jewelry. Short said there was a ring with the initials GRP and a bone pendant with some inscription on the face.

"Send them all over to I.D.," Bonora directed. "We'll photograph them. You'd better take some footprints too, just in case the fingerprints don't check out. Now what about the M.E., has he arrived?"

Short acknowledged that the county Medical Examiner had been on the scene for more than an hour and was now leaving with the body.

"Okay," Bonora said. "Get back to me after the post [the autopsy]." Then, before hanging up, the commander made a final attempt to emphasize the critical nature of the crime-scene search.

"Damn it, Jim," he said. "Make sure the men get everything."

At four o'clock that afternoon Bonora returned to the Homicide squadroom and lost no time assuming command of the investigation. He gave out a full description of the body to the press, distributed photographs of the girl's jewelry so they could be published, and announced the establishment of a special telephone line that would be manned at all hours to accept information regarding the murder. He made certain that the Property Bureau had begun to disseminate information about the recovered jewelry and that the girl's fingerprints were en route to the national office of the FBI in Washington, D.C. In addition, for the next several nights he assigned detectives to patrol the area surrounding the wooded lot in

Massapequa where the body had been discovered. The men were to stop all cars and interview the drivers in the hope that those who passed there regularly during the hours of the murder might have noticed some unusual activity that Friday morning.

The entire Homicide Squad worked the weekend. Yet despite their efforts and the range of investigative measures employed, by Monday morning, three days following the discovery of the dead girl, her identity remained an enigma. There had been no public response to the murder's publicity, nor did the FBI have a record of the girl's fingerprints. This latter failure particularly nettled Bonora, for the commander had long decried the absence of a federal statute requiring the fingerprinting of all U. S. residents. Such a statute, he believed, would significantly facilitate the identification of unknown bodies and might reduce crime as well. So often, following fires, floods, automobile and airplane accidents the police spend days trying to identify victims, additional time that brings extra pain to waiting relatives and friends and that might be better spent trapping criminals. Bonora recalled reading only recently the poignant newspaper account of a teen-age boy who had wandered aimlessly through Florida for weeks on end, unaware of his name or hometown. With no fingerprints on record the police were able to do little more than advertise his plight; almost three weeks passed before a Michigan mother could fly to Florida and identify the boy as her own.

Fortunately the girl found in Massapequa was wearing jewelry, a circumstance that would prove decisive in determining her identity. A full description of the jewelry had been sent out by teletype across the country so that detectives from as far away as California and Hawaii could search through their records of lost property. Not only do local police agencies make a practice of listing each piece of jewelry that is reported stolen, with a complete description and photograph if available, but most states require that pawnshops submit to the local police a daily record of merchandise acquired. The Nassau Property Recovery Squad had begun receiving responses to its inquiry over the weekend, but it was not until Tuesday that a positive match of a piece of jewelry was made. At noon the New York City police reported that a Manhattan pawnshop had recently sold one of the long pendants found around the victim's neck.

Bonora promptly dispatched two Homicide detectives into Manhattan, Leonard Karwowski and Albert Vincinere. They returned late that night, stalled in their efforts to determine the provenance of the jewelry. From the pawnshop the two detectives had traveled to the New York City prison on Riker's Island to interview an inmate who had bought the pendant; from there to an address in White Plains where the present owner of the jewelry was said to reside, a man by the name of John Manzi. Manzi was not at home. However, the detectives found his aunt, a pinched, nervous woman with a decidedly inimical attitude. She answered the men's questions in monosyllables, even after they flashed their badges and identified themselves as New York City plainclothesmen seeking to make a "deal" with Manzi over his unpaid parking tickets. The woman stated she had not seen her nephew in months, nor did she expect to—a disappointing visit, though effective, as the detectives would soon learn.

In the meantime Bonora had become engrossed in a matter of another sort and perhaps of graver consequence: a new and unexpected Detective Division ruling that threatened to cripple the Homicide Squad. Procedural Order #3-1972 had come down that Tuesday morning without forewarning, though it was not difficult for Bonora to attribute its source. Since the Holder investigation Deputy Inspector Archer (he had been promoted from captain) had led an unrelenting campaign to undermine the position of the Homicide Squad. At departmental meetings he was quick to voice the opinion that local squads were better staffed and equipped to handle homicide investigations, and he had been working diligently to enlarge the ring of his supporters. Just a month before, one of these supporters, Capt. Robert Edwards, had stunned Bonora by appearing at the scene of a murder and without provocation remarking: "I hope I'm not going to have trouble with you, Bonora, as far as supervision is concerned." Edwards implied that he would be taking direct control over the investigation, though after the first day he had gracefully bowed out.

Procedural Order #3-1972 transferred the ultimate responsibility for homicide investigations to the commander of the local precinct squad in which the crime had been committed. After fully studying its implications, Bonora appealed directly to its author, Chief of Detectives Edward Curran. Bonora was gravely concerned about the viability of the Homicide Squad, whose specialized training and experience would be foolishly wasted, he believed, should the precinct squads be given priority investigating murders. He met with Curran that afternoon and several more times in the ensuing few days. He spoke with other supervisors as well, trying to marshal forces to support his position. He talked about the need for specialization in modern police investigation and cited the record of the Homicide Squad as evidence. (In 1971 the Homicide Squad had "closed out," that is, resolved, 2,479 of 2,480 cases, a 99.9 percent completion rate that among major police forces was the highest in the country.) Ultimately the campaign was successful. The former Homicide commanders in the upper level of the department's hierarchy rose to Bonora's defense. And by the end of the week Curran, a cautious department politician, agreed to reconsider the order. Bonora's authority over the county's homicide investigations remained in force, however tenuously.

Wednesday morning, five days after the discovery of the body, the special red telephone rang for the first time. Bonora, who happened to be standing nearby, answered.

"My name is Spanakos," said a well-articulated voice on the other end. "I'm an attorney. I understand you're looking for my client John Manzi."

Bonora's hand tightened around the receiver. Karwowski and Vincinere had never mentioned they were Nassau County cops!

"I want to thank you very much for calling, Mr. Spanakos," the commander responded, speaking very slowly in an effort to stall. "Do I have the name right, Spa-na-kos?"

"Yes, that's correct. William Spanakos."

"Hmmn ..." Bonora said casually. "Well, what can I do for you, sir?"

"Listen, don't try any games with me," the attorney shot back. "I know you're looking for Manzi."

"All right," Bonora hastily conceded, fearful the attorney might hang up. "That's true. We would like to talk with him."

"You want to talk to him about Patsy Parks, right?"

"Patsy Parks?" Bonora said hesitantly, wondering whether he was speaking of the dead girl. He decided to bluff. "I'm not sure I quite know what you're talking about. Could you be more specific?"

"Now don't get cute," Spanakos warned. "You know damn well I'm talking about the girl found in Massapequa. I called to be helpful, but if you men don't want any help, that's fine with me. I'll hang up right now."

"No, hold on," Bonora said, soft-pedaling. "It's not that we don't want your help. But we're talking about a very serious matter over the telephone, and quite frankly, Mr. Spanakos, I don't even know who you are or what you represent."

"I just told you all that," replied the lawyer, indignant.

Bonora's heart started to race; the crucial moment had arrived. "All right," he challenged. "If you know about Patsy, what address do you have on her?"

"Three seventy East Seventy-sixth Street," Spanakos snapped.

Bonora's grip relaxed around the phone and he exhaled a soft rush of air. "That's a starter," he said. "Now when can I see your client?"

The lawyer suggested the following morning.

That evening Bonora sent two detectives into Manhattan's Upper East Side. The doorman at the Newport East confirmed for them that a Patsy Parks did live in the building, though he declared neither she nor her roommate, Patricia Quinn, had been home since the night of February 3. On that evening, he recalled, two federal agents had tried unsuccessfully to serve Miss Parks with a subpoena. After the agents had departed, both girls left the building. As far as the doorman knew, they had not returned.

The following morning William Spanakos arrived at the Homicide Squad as promised. With him was John Manzi. The lawyer immediately stipulated that his client was prepared to discuss only the killing, nothing of his own work or private dealings. Puzzled by what the witness might want to conceal, Bonora nevertheless agreed to the conditions and Manzi promptly summarized the events of the evening of February 3. He recounted the attempt to serve the subpoena and explained the circumstances under which Patsy might be involved in the narcotics trial of Vincent Pacelli and Demetrios Papadakos. He related the discussion at the Gobbler's Nob bar as well as the trip downtown to the Hippopotamus where he had let Patsy off at the front door. He swore to Bonora that he did not know whom his girlfriend planned to see nor what eventually happened that evening. Patsy, he said, had promised to call him later but never had.

Bonora took no issue with any of Manzi's statements, at least not openly. He had no information from countersources to challenge them with any degree of authority nor did he see any reason at this point to risk losing the boyfriend's cooperation. Nevertheless, before the interview ended, he did manage to elicit two items of significance: Manzi's consent to take a polygraph examination and the address of Pat Quinn, who had fled to Denver after her roommate failed to return home.

Bonora contacted the Federal Bureau of Narcotics and Dangerous Drugs in Denver and requested they bring the stewardess to New York. Later that evening he sent ten detectives into the Hippopotamus to find witnesses who might be able to describe Patsy Parks's final movements. He remained in Mineola during that time, directing the other activity of the squad, which was busy with three fresh felonious homicides. He answered phone calls and offered advice to his men in the field, oblivious to the dreary atmosphere of the empty squadroom, to the sterile white glare of the fluorescent lights that shone down on ashtrays overrun by cigarette butts and half-empty styrofoam coffee cups. For five hours he worked alone. Finally at 1 A.M. a stranger in a gray suit poked his head into the back office.

"She's here, Sarge," he said.

Bonora needed no further explanation. He jumped to his feet and hurried into the reception room where Pat Quinn was sitting with another federal agent, her two suitcases beside her. She was playing nervously with a gold locket on a chain around her neck, one of her long legs draped languidly over the other. Slim, with shoulder-length red hair and bright green eyes, she was smart-looking in her elegantly hip clothes, and for a moment Bonora wished he hadn't abandoned his sport jacket and tie hours before and that his shirt sleeves were not rolled to the elbow. Pat was wearing a profusion of jewelry, a red suede sport jacket, a sparkling white satin shirt and black wool trousers that stretched snugly around her thighs as she walked to the commander's office and seated herself next to his desk.

In the past eight hours the young stewardess had been whisked from a ski-house in the Rocky Mountains to the Denver airport, flown to New York, then raced out by car to Long Island. Upset and frightened, she complained bitterly of her ordeal. Bonora apologized, nodding sympathetically. But the witness went on, criticizing the federal agents for appearing at the ski-house unannounced, then ordering her to accompany them without explanation or much time to pack. Suddenly she stopped.

"Say, how did you find out where I was staying?"

"From John Manzi," Bonora answered.

"Oh . . ." Pat looked at the commander anxiously. "Is Patsy dead?"

Bonora reached into his desk drawer and withdrew some of the jewelry that had been recovered from the victim's body.

"We haven't made a positive identification yet," he said, "but it—"

Pat gasped. "That was her ring with the GRP."

Bonora nodded.

"It stands for George Randolph Pino. Her son, Georgie."

"She was married?"

Pat's eyes began to blink. "Divorced. Her son is in South America with his grandparents," she said haltingly.

Bonora suggested a cigarette and the witness eagerly accepted. The commander left the office, returning a few minutes later with several unfiltered Camels—all he could find. The witness had been weeping in the interim. Her cheeks were tear-streaked.

"What am I going to do?" she cried out. "What am I going to do? I could be next. I—"

Bonora handed her one of the cigarettes and lit it. He told her to relax, that the police would take care of her now.

"Maybe I should move to California," Pat said. "I have friends there."

"You have nothing to worry about," Bonora said, smiling warmly. "I told you, Patty, we'll watch out for you. You have my word."

She drew deeply on the cigarette, straightening up in the chair and smoothing her hair into place. Bonora watched her smoke for a while, then began to talk in a low gentle voice, a voice that was almost a whisper and that required her to lean forward, straining to hear him. It was an interrogation technique Bonora had long ago perfected and that he now used unwittingly. Soon he was talking directly into the witness's ear, giving her the impression he was confiding only in her. The soothing, rhythmic quality of the commander's voice had a kind of hypnotizing effect, so that one began agreeing with his assertions without knowing exactly why.

Pat Quinn began talking about her family and her work, slowly bringing in aspects of her relationship with Patsy Parks until finally she discussed their last evening together. By then her voice had lost its tenseness, the terror had faded from her eyes; she recounted the events of February 3 almost as if they were part of just another evening in her life. When she mentioned Patsy's part in storing drugs in the apartment, however—that ten-day period in May when more than $100,000 of pure heroin had rested in a small wooden box on a bookshelf in the corner of the living room—her composure underwent a radical change. Her face flushed and she stiffened defensively.

"I wasn't living there then," she said emotionally. "I didn't know a thing about it. I only moved in with Patsy last September."

Bonora quickly assured her she was not under suspicion, a slightly disingenuous remark that had the proper effect of settling the witness and inducing her to continue her account of her last evening with Patsy.

"Pretty soon John came to the bar and Patsy told him the entire story. John told her to call the federal agents and see what they wanted. But Patsy said no. She said she had to talk to someone. She asked John to take her to the Hippo."

"Who did she say she had to see?" Bonora asked.

"Oh, she didn't," Pat answered with a furtive casualness that made the commander suspicious. He held her gaze for a moment until she turned away.

"We stayed at Gobbler's for a while drinking and talking about the situation and then about twelve thirty went back to the apartment. Patsy got dressed all in black. It didn't occur to me then, but it must have been symbolic of something. She put on black pants, boots, a shirt, a black pocketbook and took my black fur jacket. She also put on all her crucifixes and then left with John."

"Crucifixes?" Bonora said, puzzled. "Why all the crucifixes?"

Pat smiled and pushed forward a cross hanging from her neck. "It's the style."

Bonora shook his head, frowning.

"Do you remember anything else about that evening, Pat, anything at all that might be helpful to us?"

The witness began polishing the darkened silver cross with her fingertips, turning it over and over. She looked up. "You know, there was something else, though I'm not sure if it's important or not. At about four o'clock that morning I thought I heard John Manzi come into the apartment. I was asleep, so I can't be sure of the time. Maybe it was earlier. He made a telephone call. Lasted only a minute or so. I didn't hear what he said and he must have gone after that, because I went back to sleep."

Bonora started to consider the significance of her revelation, when the telephone rang. It was Short from the Hippopotamus. He put the call on hold and turned toward the witness.

"Would you mind repeating your story to another detective so it can be recorded?" He explained that he needed to speak privately with his deputy.

The stewardess nodded, but before Bonora could call for another man she had collapsed into tears, blurting out her confusions and fears. Bonora put his arm around her shoulder, handing her one of the two linen handkerchiefs he always carried for just such occasions. While she dabbed her eyes he talked to her soothingly until the tears stopped and she had collected herself. Then he delivered her to one of the younger detectives and raced back to the office, picking up the telephone.

"Where the hell have you been?" Short said tersely. "I've been hanging on this phone ten minutes."

"What the hell are you worried about, Jimmy, a few dimes? If you're running out of change, give me your number and I'll call you back."

"Don't bother. We spoke with the manager of the club, Ralph Lee, and he remembered Parks being in here Thursday night. Said she was a regular. He told us a waitress by the name of Aaron Keefe took care of the table she was at."

Bonora was standing by his desk making notes on a legal-size yellow pad already well filled with the day's work.

"Aaron, a girl, like the Bible name?" he asked.

"That's what she says. We spoke with her and she remembered Parks too. Said she was sitting at a table with a guy named Benny Febre. He's supposed to be the big shot around here."

"Have you talked to him?"

"The bastard just walked in about an hour ago. Acted real tough with us until I read him the riot act. I told him it was gonna be his ass on this murder unless he talked. That just about made him cream. We're taking his statement now."

"Good," Bonora said approvingly. "You take statements from the manager and waitress?"

"Yeah."

"Okay. Make sure you get a complete rundown on everyone who was sitting at that table."

"That's what we're trying to do now. We'll be in as soon as we finish."

Bonora hung up and slumped into his desk chair, burying his head in his hands. He had started work before 8 A.M. the day before and now at two o'clock the next morning he was beginning, finally, to feel the strain. His legs were stiff, as if he had been walking for days;

the muscles in his back throbbed. When he leaned back in his chair his swollen eyes fell heavily closed. The next time they opened—about a half hour later—Pat Quinn was standing before him, a cross look on her face.

"How am I going to get home?" she demanded.

Bonora started awake, smiling with embarrassment. "I'll get one of the men," he said, rubbing his eyes with his fists, then stretching his arms luxuriantly above his head. "There's no need to get upset. It'll only be a few minutes."

Pat sat down in the chair, her upper lip trembling visibly.

"I'm terrified. I don't know what to do," she said. "Should I get out of that apartment?"

Bonora shook his head. "There's no rush, though it wouldn't be a bad idea to find some other place to live, in another building, perhaps."

"Maybe it would be better if I went to Europe. Or California. I've got very good friends in California," she repeated.

"No, it's not necessary," Bonora insisted, though once again he was being less than candid. Pat would have to be careful in New York City, but it was important that she remain nearby. As Patsy Parks's roommate—privy, no doubt, to much that had gone on in the victim's life—she could prove an extremely helpful aide to the investigation.

"We'll notify your doorman to be on his toes and we'll have the city cops watch the apartment building," he said.

"Will that be enough?" Her eyes were shadowed in doubt.

Bonora nodded matter-of-factly. "Now I'm going to send you home to get some rest," he said, rising out of his chair and escorting the stewardess to the coffee room where two detectives were seated. He directed them to take Pat home and returned to his office to await the arrival of the other men. It was almost 5 A.M. before they appeared.

Marching into the commander's office, Short began at once to recount what they had learned. Bonora listened carefully, asked a few questions, then sent the entire crew home. Their findings could be reviewed at the 9 A.M. strategy session, he told them, seeing the fatigue on their faces. They gratefully accepted the suggestion.

Alone once again in his office, Bonora remained a few minutes longer, making some final notes on the day's work. Then he grabbed his sport jacket and coat and headed out of the squadroom on the way to his car. When he opened the rear door to the parking lot he found a thick blanket of snow stretched out before him, clean and untouched, glistening white under the glow of the mercury vapor lamps. It came as something of a shock. Twenty-one hours earlier, when he had first entered headquarters, the sun was shining brightly in a cloudless sky.

CHAPTER

11

THE "STRATEGY SESSION" was an innovation Bonora brought to the Homicide Squad when he took command in May, 1970. For the first time members of the squad met each morning on a regular basis to discuss their investigations, communication that became especially important with the advent of separate day and night shifts. By familiarizing each detective with all the squad's activity, it became possible to substitute one man for another during an emergency or to assign detectives to a specific aspect of a fast-breaking investigation without having to waste crucial time briefing them. In most other police departments the individual detectives working a case or in some instances the supervisor, after reviewing their reports, decided which leads to pursue. Bonora, however, envisioning these sessions as think-tanks, encouraged everyone present to suggest subsequent moves. Such license often produced full-voiced encounters, but the discussions generated a broad range of ideas and a sense of teamwork among the squad members that was vital in motivating a lengthy and inevitably frustrating investigation.

The concept of daily meetings had rested in the back of Bonora's mind since 1956 when he was first assigned to the Weinberger case. The investigation into the kidnapping of month-old Peter Weinberger had brought more than one hundred FBI agents to Long Island, an experience that left Bonora as well as most of his comrades with a highly unflattering view of the federal agency and its public image as a dedicated and selfless law enforcement office. For fifty-seven days the FBI and the Nassau County detectives worked together until they recovered the dead baby and arrested Angelo LaMarca, an unemployed truck driver who had been imprisoned for bootlegging two years before. But following the arrest the federal agents double-crossed the unsuspecting county police department. Under orders from J. Edgar Hoover they stole off with LaMarca, taking the suspect into their New York City offices and refusing the Nassau detectives further admittance. The following day the newspapers published an account of the FBI "success" without a word of the Nassau County participation.

Incensed by their deceit, Nassau County Chief of Detectives Stuyvesant Pinnell, ordered his men into the New York FBI office with the warning not to return without the suspect "even if you have to shoot your way out." Bonora helped bring LaMarca back to Mineola that day and it was only then that the case was actually resolved. Within three hours LaMarca, who had heretofore refused to admit his role in the crime, confessed to then Det.-Lt. Edward Curran.

Politics aside, the nearly two-month investigation was perhaps the most instructive in Bonora's entire career. Paired always with members of the FBI, the young detective had the opportunity to observe the coolness and detachment with which the agents carried out their business, the detail and persuasiveness of their interrogation techniques, the emphasis they placed on the crime lab and other "scientific" approaches. Yet one aspect in particular had etched itself indelibly on his memory: the daily meeting held in the Assembly Hall of the Nassau County Police Department headquarters. Each after-noon at five o'clock two hundred investigators gathered in the green, school-like auditorium to present their findings so that each man would have at his disposal all the pertinent evidence. With the inclusion of another detective's information the pieces of the case could then be put together in new and different constructs until those elements which had seemed inexplicable finally made sense. Just as important, these lengthy sessions had the harmonizing effect of old-fashioned prayer meetings. When they ended, the men felt closer, filled with an exhilarating rapport that motivated them in the face of the dimmest of prospects.

Bonora could not forget observing the men during those sessions, seeing their drawn faces, their reddened eyes, their shoulders bent by fatigue (four agents and two county detectives were hospitalized for exhaustion during the two-month investigation). It was then that he was certain he had chosen the right calling, that he felt proudest of being a cop.

This Friday morning as the Nassau County detectives gathered for their own strategy session they were joined by a visitor from New York, Agent John LePore of the Federal Bureau of Narcotics and Dangerous Drugs. A short, chunky man in his midthirties, LePore had been contacted the day before and had confirmed that Patsy Parks was to testify in the trial of Vincent Pacelli, Jr., and Demetrios Papadakos. Seeing him for the first time as he marched about the office introducing himself, Bonora mused wryly that the Bureau had sent them a caricature of the Hollywood G-man. The agent had a baby face, wore his hair in a crew cut and was dressed in a dark narrow-lapel suit, white shirt and thin tie.

LePore had been invited to Mineola to supply further details about Patsy Parks. He prefaced his briefing that morning with the declaration that Patsy's "playmates" were part of one of the largest and most pernicious drug rings in the country. Surrounded by detectives with cups of steaming coffee in their hands, he went on to explain that Papadakos had already been convicted of drug possession and conspiracy to distribute and was now incarcerated in Connecticut at the federal prison in Danbury. Pacelli's father was Vincent Pacelli, Sr., a powerful lieutenant in the Vito Genovese crime family; his wife was Beverly Jalabar, whose family reputedly controlled most of the French and Turkish drug contracts. Recently this syndicate had arranged to bring through Canada a shipment of 218 kilos of heroin worth nearly six million dollars on the street. The entire bureau had been set to bust the ring, LePore said, but for some reason the ship carrying the drugs never left Marseilles. A month later Pacelli and Papadakos were arrested for other violations.

Patsy's relationship to the syndicate was problematical. LePore assumed she had become involved through Papadakos's younger cousin, Peter Papadakos, who was her lover for two years. He too had been indicted for narcotics violations, but after two hung juries was acquitted in the third trial. While Patsy was not familiar with the inner workings of the ring, she knew enough to support a conspiracy charge against Pacelli, Papadakos and perhaps four or five others.

"She was our prize witness," the agent said gloomily. "The trial started this week and without her it doesn't look too good."

"What about this character Benny Febre?" Short asked. "Is he involved?"

"He's supposed to be one of their big dealers," LePore said, "but we don't have much hard evidence on him."

Short told the strategy session that Patsy Parks had joined six other guests at Febre's table when she arrived at the Hippopotamus; two women, Toni Starr and Marge Jacklone; and Karl Schlossberg, Jay Kaufmann, Aaron Shaw and Barry Lipsky.

"I want to get their checks and find out who was paying for who," Bonora said. "We also better determine where everybody was sitting so we know exactly who Patsy talked to."

The detectives had spent six hours at the Hippopotamus the night of their interrogation, questioning waitresses, bartenders and patrons amid an array of epicurean furnishings reputed to cost more than a quarter of a million dollars. (The decor, designed by Pierre Scapala to imitate the British in India, featured a $20,000 chandelier that once belonged to the Maharajah of Jaipur, simulated Kama-sutra porno-paintings in the ladies' room and a $27,000 high-fidelity speaker system.) From interviews with patrons, the detectives learned that Patsy had been involved in a public quarrel the night of her murder. She had reportedly embarrassed her dancing partner that night by walking off the floor with another man—a South American. Patsy's partner, identified only as a "tall, broad-shouldered guy named Mickey," had cursed her, then turned angrily away to speak with Febre.

This incident was deemed "significant" by a number of participants in the strategy session, who believed Patsy's seventeen knife wounds indicated a crime of passion. Bonora directed Detectives Vincinere and Karwowski to investigate the quarrel, then briefed the squad on the information drawn from Pat Quinn's interview. Afterward he handed out the remainder of the assignments.

It was a relatively subdued meeting, especially after LePore cautioned the detectives against any undue optimism toward solving the murder. Their adversaries were no suburban amateurs, he said, but part of a trained, professional organization that would go to any lengths to protect its membership. The work they did was skilled and efficient. Vincent Pacelli, Sr., now serving eighteen years in Atlanta, Georgia, for drug dealing, had dated a Playboy bunny who was to be a key witness in his trial, just like Patsy in his son's. She disappeared before she could testify and her body had never been found.

The case of Robert Woods had proven just as baffling to the police. Woods was the owner of Salvation, the Greenwich Village disco-theque that Patsy frequented and where Pacelli's ring allegedly did a considerable amount of their dealing. When it was learned he was providing information to his attorney that described how the "mob" was trying to take over the club, Woods was murdered. No one, LePore declared, had even been accused on that score.

"And last year a guy by the name of Rostow—he'd been mixed up with some sort of stock swindle—was found in the trunk of a car at

Kennedy Airport. That car belonged to Papadakos. The New York police haven't solved that one either."

At eleven o'clock John Manzi and his attorney arrived at headquarters for the scheduled polygraph examination. Bonora introduced the two men to LePore and a battle immediately erupted between them. The agent had dealt with Spanakos on numerous other occasions and saw no reason to honor Bonora's prior commitment to limit questioning to the death of Patsy Parks. He was convinced that both the lawyer and Manzi had information that would contribute to his own drug investigations.

As bickering intensified between attorney and agent, Bonora invited them both out to lunch, hoping drinks and a meal would soothe their tempers. Yet at the restaurant LePore became so antagonistic toward Spanakos that Bonora found himself taking the attorney's side. The federal agent was outraged, but the commander was certain Spanakos was about to leave the restaurant with his client. And he needed Manzi on that polygraph. His primary responsibility, after all, was the murder investigation.

Bonora finally did maneuver Manzi into the polygraph room late that afternoon. The test results demonstrated that he had not killed Patsy Parks and did not know her killer. But the exam also confirmed the commander's suspicion that Manzi was withholding information.

While several detectives involved Spanakos in conversation in the Homicide office, Bonora slipped into the examination room to be alone with the witness for the first time.

"The exam says you're holding back information, John," he said, handing over the results so Manzi could study them for himself. "You didn't have any doubts the machine would work, did you?"

"No," Manzi replied. "I knew it was going to work as soon as I saw that card trick. Nobody knows cards like I do."

Before his actual polygraph examination Manzi had been given several practice tests while attached to the machine so that the examiner could adjust the controls. One of these seemed particularly appropriate for a gambler. After Manzi picked a card from a deck, the examiner was asked to guess it from responses Manzi made. He did so without much difficulty, though Manzi did his best to mislead him with a well-practiced poker face.

Bonora said to him now: "John, if you have something else to tell us, it could be very helpful. I promise you it won't go any further than this room."

Manzi pushed his hair back and wet the edge of his lips.

"We're talking about murder, not a simple card game," Bonora added quietly. "You must have had some feeling for Patsy. What kind of animal would do that to her?"

"There is one thing," Manzi said. "When I dropped Patsy off at the Hippo I told her to call me as soon as she made contact. I heard from her about two A.M. She said she had met someone and he had left but he would be coming back."

"When did you hear from her next?" Bonora asked.

"I didn't. I had told her to call me later but I never heard from her again. At first I thought she might have gone back to the apartment, so I drove uptown; but she wasn't there. Then I telephoned my card game and they said she wasn't there either."

"Was that the only call you made from the apartment?"

"That's right."

"What was your conversation?"

"I left a message that if a girl called, to have her phone me at the apartment. I remember because the joker on the other end asked should he relay that message if my wife called. I told him to go fuck himself."

In Bonora's mind that admission moved the investigation measurably forward. If Patsy had been in the Hippopotamus until 2 A.M., only three hours were left to be accounted for—the Medical Examiner having determined her death at 5 A.M. The admission also disclosed that Patsy's contact had left the nightclub at one point in the evening. And Bonora was now confident that Manzi was leveling. His recollection of the message taker's jest was the type of improbability detectives look for in witness testimony–happenings almost too peculiar to fabricate.

Still, in the back of the commander's mind was the thought that Manzi might very well have been planted by the drug ring to keep tabs on Patsy after the Grand Jury testimony. Seeking the gambler's real feelings toward the girl, he brought him into the squadroom and casually handed him several color photographs Identification had shot of the victim's body. As Manzi gazed at what was left of Patsy Parks, a part of her leg chewed away by dogs, her black hair lying in singed wisps about her head, he slumped into a chair and began to weep.

"I'm not afraid of these guys," he cried out. "I don't give a damn who they're connected with."

Bonora put his hand on the witness's shoulder and Manzi looked up at him. "Man, I'll try to help you. Yeah. I'll do anything I can. Those filthy bastards!"

An hour after Manzi left headquarters Patsy Parks was positively identified as the murder victim. The Identification Bureau matched her footprint to the one stamped on her birth certificate. No public announcement was made of this discovery for fear the publicity might improperly influence the jury sitting in the trial of Papadakos and Pacelli. Yet that Friday night there was a frantic quality to the conversation in the Upper East Side bars Patsy had once frequented, places like Eric, Dressner's and P. J. Clarke's. Despite the detectives' precautions, the word of her death had leaked out. Thursday afternoon Anthony Tuttle, the author of a novel about the Upper East Side, *Songs from the Night Before,* had appeared on a television talk show and announced that a "good friend" had been murdered. Last night's surprise raid on the Hippopotamus had only exacerbated the general alarm, the detectives' impatient questions about Patsy Parks breaking down the walls of complacency that normally surround the Upper East Side bar set. Tracy Kendall, a former model, a tall, vivacious girl in her early thirties, later told a reporter, "Patsy was all anyone was talking about Friday. That raid on the Hippo shook everyone up."

What contributed most to the anxiety snaking through Patsy's circle of friends was their inability to understand the crime. Why was Patsy dead?

Mike Furey, bartender at Eric on Second Avenue, remembered her confiding she was in "big trouble." Perhaps it was the drugs, some ventured. It was general knowledge that Patsy had been a heavy cocaine user, but then so were many of the most respectable residents of the Upper East Side. "Cocaine is nothing strange up here," a well-known journalist living in the East Sixties told Bonora privately one afternoon several weeks after Patsy's murder. "All my friends have their connections." If drugs were the key, what then did Patsy's death augur for the rest of those who had become users?

That weekend the Hippopotamus remained empty.

Early Monday morning, February 14, Bonora received a telephone call from William Spanakos. The commander's spirited defense of the attorney before LePore had gained him an ally; Spanakos had been doing some "off the record" research for Bonora over the weekend, given the tacit agreement that such work would benefit his client. Throughout his career Bonora had been able to develop these unlikely relationships with defense attorneys. He had a reputation for square dealing and his promise "to help" a guilty suspect had often been enough to win his lawyer's confidence and the suspect's subsequent confession. (Defense counsel Maurice Edelbaum had been so impressed by Bonora's fair-mindedness during the Pobliner investigation, that at the end of his testimony the lawyer stopped the commander in the foyer outside the courtroom to shake his hand.)

Spanakos had learned that Benny Febre was Pacelli's cousin. "Mickey," he said, appeared to be Mickey Conte, an ex-convict with the reputation of being a "tough guy." The information heightened Bonora's suspicion of both men, and for the second time he sent the detectives into the Hippopotamus to try to speak with them. That night Karwowski and Vincinere found Conte outside the club, a lumbering hulk of a man who in his proper suit and tie looked like a barroom bouncer. Initially Conte denied ever having met a Patsy Parks, but when Karwowski produced her photograph he admitted he had danced with her February 3, though he had not known her name. He said he had left the Hippopotamus alone that night, running into another girl outside who asked for a lift home. Her looks were similar to Patsy's, he conceded, but he was certain it hadn't been she. He had driven the girl across the Fifty-ninth Street Bridge into Queens and dropped her off "somewhere in Forest Hills."

This statement aroused considerable speculation among the detectives during the following morning's strategy session, including the possibility that the girl taken "home" was Patsy Parks, and that Conte was actually her murderer. Yet Bonora was more interested in Benny Febre that day, as he continued to believe Patsy had been killed to prevent her testimony. As a member of the drug ring, Febre had the motive. According to the statements of Karl Schlossberg and Jay Kaufmann, he had the opportunity as well. The two men had admitted that when they departed the Hippopotamus at 2 A.M. Patsy and Febre were still sitting together at the table. In addition, the New York City police had just that morning volunteered a tantalizing fact from their criminal files: Febre was reportedly the last person seen with nightclub owner Robert Woods before his murder.

Sergeant Short had cornered Febre on the second visit to Hippopotamus and obtained a minute-by-minute account of Febre's activity after 2 A.M., the night of February 3. Febre's alibi was Aaron Shaw, a thirty-year-old Dallas businessman with whom he claimed to have stayed until six o'clock that morning. Naturally the next step was to interview Shaw, but Inspector Frank Klecak denied Bonora's request to fly to Texas. The supervisor, citing the expenditure involved in such a trip, suggested Bonora either contact the Dallas Police Department for help or telephone Shaw himself.

Bonora was not surprised at his supervisor's reaction. Klecak, unhappy that he had been passed over for promotion several times, was determined not to be overlooked again. He was anxious not to make waves. Yet understanding the supervisor's psychology did nothing to ease the commander's consternation. Shaw's knowledge could play a crucial role in resolving the case, and telephone interrogations were rarely effective. The witness could hang up at any time. As for the Dallas detectives—how could he properly brief them so their interrogation would be demanding enough, or even be certain there were no leaks in their department?

Bonora decided to postpone any action, but the following day he suddenly changed his mind. Agent LePore phoned from New York and told him that a federal jury had just convicted Pacelli and Papadakos on four out of five counts of narcotics violations. If experience were any teacher, many of the persons on the periphery of the drug ring would be outraged at the now-useless taking of Patsy's life. Perhaps someone like Aaron Shaw might be less reluctant to assist the police.

Bonora picked up the telephone and called the Merchandise Mart, the modern building complex housing Dallas's garment industry. Shaw was the Southwest district manager of Carlett Clothes.

"Aaron," Bonora said authoritatively when Shaw answered. "Aaron, this is Sergeant Bonora. I'm the commanding officer of the Homicide Squad of the Nassau County Police in New York. We have the responsibility for investigating the murder of Patsy Parks."

"Yes, Sergeant. I understand."

"Aaron, we've been doing a lot of digging into this case. We've had twenty-five detectives working twenty-four hours a day and we know almost everything there is to know about this case."

"So what? What does all this have to do with me?"

"We made contact with many of your good friends including Benny and Toni Starr. We know you were with Patsy the night she was killed. You were at her table at the Hippo that Thursday night."

"That's right," Shaw agreed, "but I don't know anything about her death."

"Aaron, as I told you before: we're investigating a murder. This isn't a petty larceny or some nonsense misdemeanor. We're talking about a very serious crime. You realize that Pacelli and Papadakos were convicted today anyway . . ."

Bonora paused, but there was no reaction.

"Now, just so you understand the law, Aaron," the sergeant continued, "and you know we're not playing any games, let me explain to you the legal backing for our actions. The law in the state of New York is this: if you have any knowledge or information regarding the murder of an individual and you fail to convey that knowledge or information—regardless of what it is, no matter how insignificant—we can take action against you.

"Frankly," he added in a confidential tone, "we could have come down there, walked into your office in the middle of the day and hit you with this thing cold. But I know you're a bright businessman, Aaron, and when we're dealing with businessmen we prefer to handle our affairs like businessmen."

Aaron cleared his throat but did not comment. So Bonora mentioned the department's policy of helping "helpful" witnesses, implying the reverse at the same time. Then he announced he was about to start the questioning.

"Many of these questions I already know the answers to," he lied. "How you answer them will determine just how we deal with you."

A strained silence crossed the line until Shaw finally snapped: "All right. What do you want to know?"

Bonora smiled inwardly. "Why don't you start with *your* version of how you spent Thursday night."

The witness began hesitantly. "Benny and Toni Starr came over to the Carriage House around ten o'clock. That's where I was staying . . . on East Thirty-eighth Street. We had some drinks . . . we were watching television until . . . oh, after midnight. We went right to the Hippo. We stayed there . . . until about . . . uh, three o'clock. The three of us left after that . . . went back to Benny's apartment. I didn't leave there until about six . . . got a cab back to the hotel."

"What happened the next day?" Bonora asked.

"Nothing much. I got up around eleven and Benny came over. It wasn't until then that I learned about Patsy's death."

The significance of the last statement did not immediately register on Bonora. He had been making some notes regarding Shaw's whereabouts. Then all of a sudden his thoughts started to race. Patsy's identity had eluded the detectives for five days. Only an "insider" would have known she was dead the day following the murder. Only an "insider" like Febre.

"Aaron, I'm sorry, I didn't quite get you," Bonora said. "There must be something wrong with the connection. You said you learned of Patsy's death on Friday, February fourth?"

"That's right. I remember it vividly. Benny came by and told me she had been murdered during the night."

Bonora tried to maintain his poise as he continued the questioning, wanting another confirmation of the date but worried lest any sudden interest alert Shaw to his statement's significance. Febre had to be the murderer or knew who was. And if this information were confirmed, they had him nailed.

"What time did you say Patsy left the Hippo?" he asked.

"I told you. I didn't see when she left. She was at our table for a while, then she was out on the dance floor. I lost sight of her after that."

"And what about Marge Jacklone, you took her home?" Like a chess player, the commander was working patiently around the needed piece.

"Yeah, Benny had rented a limo and we dropped her off up on Third Avenue."

"What about her date for the evening? Where was he?"

Shaw exhaled nervously. "To tell you the truth, I don't really know. I guess he must have left the table at some point. He wasn't there when we left."

"And it wasn't until the next morning, Friday, that you learned about Patsy's death?"

"Yes, I'm positive that was when."

The third admission—recorded like the other two by the bug on the office telephone—was all that was needed. Bonora told Shaw he wanted him to come to New York—immediately.

"But I can't," Shaw protested. "My wife is ill and there's no one else to watch the business."

"Aaron, we're going to see you one way or another," Bonora

warned. "Now if we have to come to Dallas you're really going to screw things up. I don't think you want that."

"Well . . . would tomorrow be soon enough?"

"No, I want to see you today," Bonora insisted.

"I can't do it. I can't, honestly. I've got to find someone to take care of my wife first."

"Okay," Bonora relented. "You make reservations for a flight tomorrow and let us know the time. We'll pick you up at the airport."

Yet when Shaw called back less than an hour later it was not with the information the detectives had hoped for.

"I've made a terrible mistake," he confessed. "It wasn't Friday February fourth that I learned of Patsy's death. It was the following Friday, February eleventh. I don't know how I could have confused the two days."

Bonora was furious. "Now listen, Aaron. You told me three times, *three times,* you learned of her death on Friday the fourth. Remember, the fourth? What are you trying to pull? Didn't I warn you of the consequences?"

"But I was upset by your phone call. I just confused everything in my head." Shaw's voice was shaking. "I swear. I really didn't learn until the following Friday."

Bonora challenged the story with a rapid succession of questions but despite the machine-gun interrogation, Shaw held his ground, recalling meetings and dates during his ten-day sojourn in New York without further confusion or contradiction. And not long thereafter he declared he was unable to travel to New York the next week.

"Well, then we're going to have to come down there," Bonora said. He sensed Shaw and the case slipping from his grasp. "But let me emphasize something to you, Aaron. We're not coming down there to fool around."

"Oh no, I'll talk to you," Shaw quickly agreed, pouncing on the commander's compromise with obvious relief. "You come to Dallas and I'll tell you what I know."

Bonora returned immediately to Klecak's office and recounted the two phone calls. But once again the supervisor refused to authorize a Dallas trip. He was the antithesis of Bonora in outlook, an inherent pessimist. He suggested that the detectives might travel all the way to Texas only to find they were unable to change Shaw's story or that Shaw might in fact be telling the truth. Even after tapes of the two telephone conversations were played, he continued to cavil. He discounted Shaw's strained voice—a certain indicator of purposeful obfuscation—as nothing more than common nervousness. Growing increasingly desperate, Bonora finally called on Donald Belfi, the Assistant District Attorney assigned to the Parks case. Apprising him of the morning's conversations with Shaw and of Klecak's continued obstinacy, he gained a pledge of assistance. And an hour later, with the weight of the District Attorney's office pushing on one side and Bonora hammering away from the other, Klecak relented. Financial authorization for the Dallas trip was granted.

"I'll be taking the six o'clock plane out of Kennedy," Bonora told the supervisor.

Klecak turned on him with a look of scorn and exasperation. "What the hell are you talking about, Matt, you can't go to Dallas."

"Of course I'm going. Who do you think is interviewing Shaw?"

"Matt, you're the Homicide commander now. You've got detectives to do this work."

"I'm the one who has been dealing with Shaw," Bonora asserted.

"That's not the point," Klecak said. "That's not your job anymore. You are no longer the squeal man."

"Hell, I've opened the line of communication with Shaw. Someone else goes down there and he's liable to clam up."

"What about the squad? Who's going to run the squad in your absence?"

"Short is there," Bonora said. "He's a good man."

Klecak looked at him disdainfully, shaking his head. Then he waved the commander out of his office. Bonora made the six o'clock flight and was in Dallas by nine.

That evening Bonora and Assistant District Attorney Donald Belfi spent six hours with Shaw and his attorney. The witness did not change his story. The following day Shaw took a polygraph examination in the Dallas Police Department with startling results. The test sustained his claim that he had spent the entire night of February 3 with Benny Febre. He had learned of Patsy Parks's death from him eight days later.

CHAPTER

12

THE DALLAS TRIP was not totally without compensation. By putting Shaw on the polygraph the detectives now knew for certain the truth of his statements. They were able to eliminate Benny Febre from suspicion of murder. Still, Bonora was perturbed, feeling the anguish of a gambler on a winning streak who with three bad throws of the dice had suddenly lost his entire stake. He had flown to Texas expecting to solve the case. Returning, the investigation appeared to stretch out endlessly before him.

In his absence the two squeal men, Walker and Book, had been unable to locate Barry Lipsky—the only uninterviewed guest at the Febre table. Nor had they been able to ascertain his place of residence or business. Furthermore, the doors had been closed on further direct consultation with Mickey Conte. In a second interview outside the Hippopotamus, Conte had glibly reminisced about the afternoon he had shot his wife and the jail term he had served for assault and armed robbery of the Central Park Zoo ticket office. But he refused to fill out a written statement or take a polygraph exam in Mineola. The next day his attorney notified the squad that Conte would no longer be answering questions.

Returning from Dallas, Bonora received little sympathy from Hazel, normally so attentive to her husband's needs. While he had been away, Pat Quinn had telephoned the house several times. In each call she asked for "Matt," as if he were some long-time, special friend. And on her last call, when the stewardess requested that Bonora phone her at the friend's apartment where she was staying, Pat smugly refused to leave the number. "Oh, he knows it," she said with a confidence that made Hazel bristle.

Since their initial meeting Bonora had been seeing Pat Quinn on a regular basis. Convinced she had significant information still to impart and believing trust would be established more quickly through an informal relationship, he had interviewed her only in the most casual of circumstances. They had talked over quiet meals in small Italian restaurants in Manhattan, and once at her suggestion at The Palm, a celebrated gathering spot for the literary establishment and the socially prominent. Together they had also toured a number of the Upper East Side bars and singles' hangouts.

Bonora was impressed by the extent of Pat's travels, the famous people she had met, the ease and sophistication with which she moved about the Upper East Side. And by their third meeting he realized his interest in her existed somewhat independently of his professional instincts. He liked her looks and the young, trendy clothes she wore. Her resonant voice with its soft Midwestern twang made vivid the most ordinary conversation.

Pat too seemed affected by their meetings. On two separate occasions she had mentioned how hard she had tried to find her own apartment so they could "spend some time alone together."

Naturally, the commander made no attempt to explain more than the professional side of this relationship to his wife. "She's a young girl and she's scared," he told her. "We need her help and I can't take the chance that she might run away. I'm the only one she trusts."

Hazel remained unsatisfied, sensing there was more to be said. And in her own modest way she continued to make clear her displeasure over the nights Bonora stayed late in New York City.

In the week following the Dallas trip the entire investigation continued to falter. On Monday federal narcotics agents in Dallas notified the squad that their request for a wiretap on Aaron Shaw's telephone was running into difficulty. (The polygraph examination had indicated Shaw knew more about the Parks murder than he cared to admit.) On Tuesday the commander's own request for a bug on Febre's telephone was rejected in court. Wednesday the South American who had taken Patsy from the dance floor was located and he vigorously disparaged the seriousness of her quarrel with Conte. The two had exchanged dirty looks, he said, and that was all. Finally on Friday when it appeared to Bonora that disappointment was the best the squad could expect, Agent LePore called from New York City with propitious news. The FBI had just discovered a Barry Glen Lipsky of Miami Beach on their probation records. He had been convicted in 1970 for stock swindling.

"Jesus! That was Rostow's game," Bonora exclaimed, thinking of the man who had been found in Papadakos's car.

"A strange coincidence if it's the wrong Lipsky," the agent agreed.

Bonora instructed LePore to contact his office in Miami to get a rundown on Lipsky. He wanted the names of Lipsky's associates and the condition of his probation. Then he directed Detectives Walker and Book to canvass the local rent-a-car agencies and American Express to learn what they might have on a Barry Glen Lipsky from Miami Beach.

Lunching with the squad at Lorenzo's that day, Bonora felt a surge of his customary optimism. What did it matter that these men were part of a professional organization, the commander reasoned. Wasn't he? The fact that the previous murders remained unresolved by the New York City cops meant little, for if a narcotics ring of their scope had been permitted to operate as long and as effectively as it had, detectives were obviously being paid off. Indeed, the reports of the Knapp Commission appearing in the newspapers in recent weeks spoke of little else. From Bonora's point of view Patsy Parks's murder was no different from countless others, from hundreds already solved by the Nassau County Police Department. It just needed to be worked a little harder—a push here, a nudge there. Then, maybe a break. Persistence was the name of the game.

Returning from lunch, Bonora found Det.-Sgt. Daniel Lannon seated in his office, waiting for some procedural advice on the Lofton case. Lannon was Bonora's nighttime assistant, presently directing an investigation into the murder of a black drug pusher in Hempstead. The commander hung up his coat and, seating himself, started to consider his assistant's problem. But before he could offer a suggestion Deputy Inspector Archer poked his head into the office and told Lannon: "Danny, I want you to get that tape recorder out of Mrs. Lofton's house. It's been there three weeks and we haven't gotten a thing from it." He left without awaiting a reply or even acknowledging Bonora's presence.

"What the hell is going on here?" Lannon demanded angrily. "Is he my boss or are you, Matt?" It was not the first time the question had been raised.

"I am," the commander said firmly, pounding the desk with his fist. "But that guy wants to run the whole show."

Bonora was fed up. None of his pleas for autonomy had had any effect on the Detective Division's leadership. His troubles with Archer continued unabated, and it appeared that the situation was getting worse.

Late that afternoon the commander appeared in the office of his old friend and hunting partner, Deputy Commissioner James Ketcham. He implored Ketcham to put a stop to Archer's machinations. Archer's persistent interference, he said, was damaging the men's morale and threatening the quality and effectiveness of the Homicide investigations. He cited a recent case in which one of Archer's supporters had taken the unprecedented step of dismissing the Homicide detectives from the scene of a murder while the precinct squad detectives continued to investigate. Not only were the men embarrassed and upset, Bonora said, but the following day when they resumed the investigation a crucial piece of evidence was missing. It was three days later before they learned a precinct squad detective was casually storing the evidence in his filing drawer.

Bonora further accused Archer of trying to undermine his own personal authority. He mentioned that afternoon's incident with Lannon and recounted how several weeks before Archer had approached his deputy, Sgt. Jim Short, with the idea of replacing Bonora as Homicide commander if Short passed the lieutenant's examination. Short, respectful of Bonora's ability and deeply loyal, had spurned the idea.

Deputy Commissioner Ketcham became incensed as the recital of grievances continued. Soft-spoken and unassuming, he had made his own climb through the ranks by dint of hard work and intelligence—not political manipulation. That background moved him immediately to Bonora's defense and he promised to use his influence with the Commissioner to try to right matters. Bonora thanked him gratefully. He left for home that weekend hopeful that his problems with Archer were at last coming to an end.

Yet when the commander returned to headquarters Monday morning, February 28, he recognized at once that they were not. Making the turn into the Homicide squadroom, Bonora saw Archer charging down the hall, yelling hysterically. "You went to the Deputy Commissioner; you went to Ketcham about me. You accused me of heading a conspiracy to replace you." As he reached Bonora he threw back his right shoulder as if he were about to deliver a punch.

The commander shook his head, cautioning him with a glance.

"Then you don't deny it," Archer shouted, his face almost scarlet. "You don't deny it."

"This isn't the time or the place to discuss the matter, George," Bonora said quietly and walked away into his office.

That afternoon Bonora mentioned the encounter to his supervisor, Inspector Klecak, suggesting Archer might need psychological attention. When Archer learned that the commander had characterized his actions as "irrational," he announced his intent to give Bonora a "blue one," that is, file departmental charges against him. He accused the commander of circumventing the chain of command by going to Ketcham, and of falsely reporting the hallway incident to Klecak. The quiet struggle for power had broken out into open warfare.

The following morning Bonora was called to the Chief of Detectives' office. Would he be willing to sit down with Archer in a closed room and talk things out once and for all? Bonora answered that he would. By late in the day Archer, though initially reluctant, had similarly agreed. The meeting was set for Wednesday at 10 A.M., in Room 219.

That Tuesday night Bonora remained at his desk hours past dinnertime, his mind swimming through the confusion of recent developments. As quickly as the controversy with Archer seemed to have moved, the Parks investigation was progressing at an even more substantial clip. Over the past weekend Detectives Walker and Book had learned from American Express that Lipsky maintained an account and had been using his card extensively to fly between Miami and New York. In the fall he had taken a weekend trip to Nice, France–conveniently close to Marseilles, the heroin capital of Europe. Then Monday, Avis reported that Lipsky had rented a car on the morning of February 4 and had returned it a week later at La Guardia Airport. Bonora ordered the car located and this morning the Identification Bureau had photographed it–a dark green 1972 Plymouth with a black vinyl roof. While obviously the rented car could not have transported Patsy Parks to Massapequa, the possibility existed that it might have been used to replace the murder vehicle. Quite often murder vehicles are set ablaze by professional criminals to destroy evidence and the murderer acquires a replica so that his neighbors remain unaware of the car's sudden disappearance.

This morning Bonora had also heard from LePore, who had been speaking with Lipsky's New York City probation officer. Lipsky was to have checked in the previous day but had failed to show. Recalling the difficulties in receiving authorization for the Dallas trip, Bonora had suggested that the probation officer pressure Lipsky to come from Miami Beach to New York as soon as possible. Early in the evening LePore had reported back: Lipsky would come to New York on Thursday–just two days away.

Presently Bonora sat before a yellow pad on his desk, trying to chronicle the history of his conflict with George Archer. His grievances, it seemed, had begun ages ago. Their memories exasperated him yet he worked to recall their minutest details. When tomorrow's meeting concluded, he wanted to be certain that each item of controversy had been brought fully into the open, discussed and dispensed with.

At one point during the evening Detective Frank Cardone wandered into the commander's office. Since the Holder investigation Cardone had left the coffee room whenever Inspector Archer entered. It was evident to Bonora that a problem existed between them, and he mentioned the planned closed-door meeting. He wondered out loud whether there wasn't something the detective wanted to tell him, something that for instance might give further insight into the conflicts Archer had created by his interference. Bonora assured Cardone that anything he said would be held in strictest confidence.

What happened next is still a matter of dispute. According to Bonora, Cardone turned away so that his eyes avoided the commander and he began to speak in a husky, troubled voice. In the next five minutes–perhaps the most momentous in Bonora's career–the detective announced that he had lied before the Grand Jury investigating Joan Holder's murder and claimed he had been pressured into doing so by Archer and Nassau District Attorney William Cahn.

Cardone denies that this admission ever occurred. Called to the witness stand a month later during the pretrial hearing for the Holder-Gershenson conspiracy case, he testified that he had spoken truthfully to the Grand Jury. And in response to a question from the prosecution he denied ever relating any improprieties surrounding this testimony to Bonora.

Bonora would also testify at this pretrial hearing. In his testimony the commander declared that that night in his office Cardone recalled a "big battle" erupting between Cahn and Brooklyn District Attorney Eugene Gold over the arrest of Holder and Gershenson. Archer had been sent to Brooklyn to arrange matters with the District Attorney's office for a local indictment where the conspiracy had allegedly occurred. During this discussion, it seems, a problem arose over the publicity and Gold telephoned Cahn directly. The Nassau District Attorney insisted on handling the trial publicity himself. Gold, however, declared that if he were going to the trouble of holding the trial, his office would damn well get the publicity. Cahn refused to budge on the publicity issue and Gold finally said, "If I can't have the publicity, you can shove the case up your ass."

According to Cardone, Archer met subsequently with District Attorney Cahn. He was told: "You get that case out here any way you can. I don't care how you get it out here, but get it out here."

Archer's solution was to have Cardone tell the Grand Jury that Holder and Gershenson had plotted Joan Holder's murder during one of their rendezvous at the Green Acres Shopping Center in Valley Stream. He was merely to "stretch the truth," Cardone said, spreading his hands apart to demonstrate, as a man sizing a fish.

Bonora was stunned by these revelations, having expected Cardone's problem with Archer to involve some sort of personality conflict. It never occurred to him that corruption might exist in his own department. Yet not for a minute did the commander doubt the veracity of the story. Nor was Bonora particularly surprised to hear of the District Attorney's desire to seek publicity for himself. How many times had Assistant District Attorney Jack Lewis complained of being excluded from talking to the press? When a trial ended, he was ordered to leave by the back door so that the newspaper reporters would get their comments directly from the District Attorney. Indeed, on so many occasions had Cahn taken public credit for the work of some other police agency that the detectives had dubbed him the "Milton Berle of law enforcement."

This propensity for self-glorification had not gone unnoticed outside the police department. *Newsday,* Long Island's Pulitzer Prize-winning newspaper, would later ask in an editorial whether Cahn's penchant for publicity wasn't in fact affecting the just administration of his office. On February 8, 1974, they wrote: "During his third term in office Nassau District Attorney Cahn has twice grappled with large issues that stirred immense public interest—and twice he has come away embarrassed. . . . [One] trial proved little except that television reporters could pronounce Cahn's name and headline writers could spell it. . . . Cahn demonstrated far more proficiency in generating publicity than in obtaining convictions. And in both of these cases innocent men were put to the ordeal of public scrutiny and the expense of legal defense because a District Attorney was overzealous. We hope this dismal record disturbs Cahn as much as it disturbs us."

When Cardone finished his account Bonora recalls that the detective turned to him with a weighty sigh, the tension drained from his face. It was a familiar expression to the commander—the look of a man finally relieved of his burden of guilt, the look of a confessed man. Bonora patted Cardone reassuringly on the shoulder. Then, leading him to the door, he reaffirmed that their conversation had been strictly confidential.

Room 219 on the second floor of police headquarters is used primarily for interrogation. It is small and rectangular in shape. There are two metal desks, a filing cabinet, a storage closet and several chairs. Its walls are purposely bare (a glass-framed photograph could become a dangerous weapon in the hand of an angry suspect). Its single window overlooks the old County Courthouse, a domed tan-stucco structure built in the early 1900's to resemble on a smaller scale the U. S. Capitol building in Washington, D.C. Hidden in the room is a microphone that allows conversations to be monitored and recorded.

Bonora entered Room 219 shortly before 10 A.M. on March 1, along with Archer and Inspector Klecak, who was to mediate the encounter. Klecak locked the door, then took a seat so that he separated the two adversaries. The supervisor explained that this meeting had been ordered by the Deputy Commissioner of Police and that the men were to remain locked in the room until their differences were settled. They were to hold nothing back, to discuss their deepest feelings in full. When the meeting ended, nothing said of a private nature was to be repeated outside these four walls. Their discussion would not be monitored or recorded.

The session began with a clamor of angry accusations but quickly settled into a more reasoned discussion. Through a specific recounting of their clashes Bonora tried to demonstrate the difficulty of directing investigations with someone else constantly interfering. Archer appeared surprisingly sympathetic and even admitted at Klecak's insistent needling that at times he could be overbearing. At the end of a half hour he accepted Bonora's proposal to come to him first if he wanted something accomplished during a Homicide investigation. In turn, the commander agreed to do his utmost to see that the request was expedited.

With this agreement there was a lull in the conversation. Klecak turned to both men and asked if anything had been left unsaid, that if not, he would adjourn the meeting. Bonora mentioned there was one further matter needing review, and at this point reiterated the ground rules for the session: that their conversation was for the purpose of clarifying all issues between Archer and the commander and everything said was to be held strictly in confidence. Receiving the concurrence of the other two men, Bonora related Cardone's account of the perjury. He added that he believed the allegations and that they diminished his respect for Archer, who had placed one of his men in such a vulnerable position. If found out, Cardone could be sent to jail, separated for years from his wife and children.

Here again there is strong disagreement as to what followed. Archer (also in testimony at the Holder-Gershenson pretrial hearing) stated that he denied Cardone's accusation, explaining that he had gone to Brooklyn only to make the Brooklyn District Attorney "aware of the evidence that we had and our plan to make the arrest."

He swore that Nassau District Attorney Cahn never ordered him to get the case out here "any way you can," nor did he himself ever direct Detective Cardone to testify falsely before the Grand Jury.

Bonora, on the other hand, claims Archer did not try to refute the accusations during the meeting. And in response to his questioning admitted there had been a bitter fight over the publicity in the Holder case. The Deputy Inspector repeated Cardone's account of the meeting in the Brooklyn District Attorney's office almost verbatim, including Gold's alleged salty remark to Cahn. After that he fell silent, seeming to withdraw into a shell.

When the meeting in Room 219 ended, Klecak shook Bonora's hand, remarking that at last he had a full picture of the conflict between Archer and the commander, that he understood what had been troubling him. Bonora replied that he was pleased for the opportunity to have expressed his grievances in this kind of private forum; that he thought Archer and he might hereafter be able to work together. Then the Homicide commander extended his hand toward Archer, stating that he harbored no ill feelings and that he wanted to let all of their past differences drop. He assumed the Nassau indictment, if falsely brought, could be dismissed on some pretense and Holder and Gershenson properly charged in Brooklyn.

Archer put out his hand as if to shake, then suddenly withdrew it; he mumbled that he wanted to think further. Bonora, disturbed by the rejection, urged Archer to shake now as a sign their controversy had been resolved. Klecak advised him to exchange handshakes as well. But even though Archer agreed the meeting had been helpful, he was adamant about not shaking hands with the commander. He said he needed some more time to think and would probably shake in the morning. Not wanting to stand on ceremony, Bonora finally gave an acquiescent shrug. Klecak unlocked the door.

Nine hours later Bonora stood before another door—this one painted a glossy black on the sixteenth floor of a New York City apartment building. He had spoken with Pat Quinn earlier in the day and the stewardess had mentioned that her roommates would be gone the entire evening. Yet it was not this information that was responsible for the commander's present exuberance. Rather it was the phone call he had received prior to leaving headquarters late that afternoon. A detective friend had just seen Archer requesting his retirement forms from the police department's Office of Personnel and Accounting. The Deputy Inspector had apparently decided to resign!

The news made Bonora ecstatic. No more would he have to worry about incursions into his authority, about the continued existence of his job, about the future of the Homicide Squad. With Archer out of the way, he could concentrate his energies purely on the task he had been assigned: investigating homicides.

Bonora rang the doorbell again, this time more impatiently. The loud buzz brought a woman's high heels clicking sharply across the apartment's parquet floor.

"C'mon in," Pat Quinn said gaily as she opened the door. Her hair was freshly washed and she was wearing a low-cut maroon satin dress, tight around the waist and hips. Her expression suggested to Bonora that she wanted to sleep with him, an opportunity that ordinarily would have flattered the commander's ego, relaxed him in the knowledge that he was in control of the encounter. Tonight, however, the situation produced an uncharacteristic anxiety.

"Let's have a drink in the restaurant," he said abruptly.

Pat smiled and with forced cheeriness responded, "That's a good idea. How about P. J.'s?"

The reference was to P. J. Clarke's, one of Manhattan's most fashionable saloons. Housed in a former row house on the corner of Fifty-fifth Street and Third Avenue, Clarke's has changed little over the past twenty-five years. In the midst of Third Avenue's flashy commercialism it has managed to preserve a bit of old New York, from its surly, aproned waiters, its blackboard menus, its stained-glass windows to the two-story landmark structure itself—an anomaly amid the surrounding skyscrapers. The clientele is a garrulous mixture of advertising executives, athletes, politicians, actors, models and writers.

Bonora and Pat were given a table in the rear of the main wood-paneled room in front of the large polished wall clock. The light there was richly shadowed and other-worldly, a reconverted Victorian gas lamp attached to the wall above them leaving half their table in the dark. They began with drinks, then steaks and a bottle of wine. Then a second bottle of wine. They both loved conversation and they talked incessantly with the familiarity of old friends; about Patsy and the investigation, about Bonora's work and Pat's travels. The jukebox played. Restaurant hoppers came and went. The time passed quickly. Before Bonora realized, it was midnight and the young girl was pressed against his side, her head resting on his shoulder. He felt a warm glow within him, a combination of the wine and the good food and the smell of perfume. He leaned over and kissed Pat affectionately on the forehead. She looked up and smiled tenderly. A moment later she was whispering in his ear. "Matt, Matt, I have to tell you something . . . something important."

Bonora watched her now as she searched for the words, his eyes unmoving. Their table seemed suddenly cocooned in a blanket of silence and he was certain she could hear his heart.

"When Patsy left the apartment she told me what she had to do." Pat's voice was thick, strained. "She said, 'I'm going to see Vinnie.' . . . Vinnie Pacelli!"

"You're sure? You could testify to that?" Bonora asked.

Pat nodded.

"What else did she say?"

"That was all. Just that she had to see Vinnie."

"Why didn't you tell me any of this before?" Bonora's tone reflected disappointment, not anger.

"I was scared," Pat answered. "I guess I didn't trust you. I didn't want to get involved."

Bonora squeezed her hand gently, shaking his head. Pat moved closer and kissed him.

For the next hour the two remained at the table, saying little, drinking a third bottle of wine. When they left the restaurant Bonora put his arm around Pat and began to stride up Third Avenue. Reaching Sixty-sixth Street, where Pat was now staying, he began to envision the imminent pleasure of the next several hours. He entered the lobby of her modern apartment house only distantly aware of his surroundings. At the bank of elevators they stopped and Pat snuggled contentedly against him, whispering something incoherent in his ear that ended with "I love you." But those three words were enough. They exploded all the commander's fantasies.

At once Bonora felt a dull throb in his stomach, and the girl became a weight on his arm. By the time they reached the sixteenth floor the anxiety had turned sharp and painful. Now that Pat had told him what he needed, was there any reason for his being here? As she unlocked the apartment door Bonora stared at the carpeted hallway with its gold-filigree wallpaper, thinking of Hazel, his wife of twenty-three years, home now in bed, unknowing, asleep.

Pat walked into the apartment and turned on the lights. She turned around to find Bonora standing at the door's edge.

"I've got to do some thinking," he said in a slow, surprised voice.

She gazed at him curiously, then slowly her upper lip curled into a bemused smile. "It's okay," she said.

Bonora wanted to say something then, something to explain what was going through his mind. But before he could finish groping for the words she was gone. He was gazing once again at the shiny black apartment door.

Thursday morning was bright and clear, a string of white clouds hanging over the distant horizon. Bonora came to work relieved of his concerns, ready to throw himself fully into the Parks case. When Klecak entered his office he thanked the supervisor once again for his role in the previous day's meeting. He expressed his pleasure at the prospect of settling down to "do some police work."

Klecak's expression reflected none of the commander's euphoria. And with good reason. Archer had arrived at headquarters early that morning and called for a full-scale investigation of the charges raised at Wednesday's meeting.

Bonora was flabbergasted by the news. "You've got to be joking," he exclaimed. The supervisor assured him he was not. Deputy Inspector Archer wanted to clear his name of all possible wrongdoing and was presently composing a written report of the meeting. Klecak directed the commander to do the same.

Bonora adamantly refused. The meeting had been conducted on an agreement of confidentiality, he said. He could not break that covenant.

At Klecak's request Bonora accompanied him to Room 219, where he was left with Capt. Andrew Mulrain, a boyish-looking detective who made a halfhearted attempt to persuade Bonora to reconsider his refusal, obviously displeased by the task assigned him. Though Bonora was thankful for that loyalty, the door to the room nevertheless remained closed. For the first time in his life the commander sensed the anxiety and helplessness of a suspect in a police interrogation. He was being pressured to talk.

Bonora had never before considered himself a maverick. He appreciated the importance of discipline in police work, the necessity of subordinates to carry out the commands of their superiors. Yet his acceptance of this rule had never blinded him to the consequences of his actions. Often in his career he had refused to execute what he considered incompetent orders. As a young patrolman he would not be pressured into giving out parking tickets to bolster his sergeant's reputation. And when Hazel left the house to give birth to their second child he disobeyed the command of his supervisor to maintain his post and raced to the hospital to be by his wife's side. The refusal to break the agreement of confidentiality was an equally principled decision on Bonora's part. It did not waver even after Klecak returned with an order from the Chief of Detectives to write the report.

Eventually Bonora was allowed to return to Homicide. Reaching the squadroom, the commander immediately called Cardone into his office and, behind a locked door, recounted the morning's events. He needn't have done so. Klecak had already informed the detective of Bonora's accusations.

"Mattie, what are you doing to me?" Cardone said. "Do you realize what you did to me? You went across the hall and accused me of a crime."

Bonora advised Cardone to hire an attorney. He further urged him not to change the testimony he had given before the Grand Jury unless he received immunity. It would mean a certain indictment for perjury, and a jail sentence.

"Frank, whatever you do, don't let your emotions overcome your responsibility to yourself and your wife and children," Bonora said. "I'm sure I'm going to take a fall on this. I'm probably going to lose my job. But they can't send me to jail. Remember that."

The two men shook hands and Bonora wished the detective good luck. Then, feeling his emotions suddenly welling up inside, he asked Cardone to leave the room.

Bonora kept to himself most of the remainder of the day. When he finished lunch and returned to headquarters, he closed his office door and spent the next two hours preparing a strategy for the surveillance and pickup of Barry Glen Lipsky, arriving that night at La Guardia Airport. At 5 P.M. he brought his plans to Inspector Klecak, who approved them with one stipulation: someone other than Bonora was to direct the operation.

"You've been working long hours," Klecak said. "You've had a lot of things on your mind. I want you to take the evening off."

"What the hell are you talking about?" Bonora exclaimed. "Lipsky could be crucial to this case. He could hold the key." Aaron Shaw had indicated that Barry Lipsky "disappeared" for more than an hour from the Hippopotamus during the early morning of February 4. According to John Manzi, so had Patsy Parks's contact. "He's got to be broken," Bonora said determinedly. "And surprise is our only advantage. Tomorrow may be too late."

"You've got good men under you," Klecak responded. "They can handle it. I know you're tired. I know what you've been through."

Bonora immediately understood the problem. Cardone had denied Bonora's account to the supervisor and Klecak no longer trusted him.

"None of my men working tonight are experienced interrogators," the commander protested weakly.

"They'll do fine," Klecak responded. "Believe me. You have to have confidence in your men."

Bonora thought of Sgt. Dan Lannon, the assistant in charge that night. An old-timer, he had been brought into Homicide by the Chief of Detectives.

"All right, blow the fucking case," the commander said, standing up. "It obviously doesn't mean much around here anyway."

He marched angrily out of the office and returned to the Homicide squadroom. Lannon had already arrived and was seated in the commander's office, awaiting his assignment. In a cold, brusque manner Bonora outlined the evening's strategy:

Instead of approaching Lipsky on the airplane when it arrived, Lannon was to allow Lipsky to walk to the baggage claim by himself. This would enable the detectives to observe anyone who came to meet him. If Lipsky were met by another man, LePore was to step forward and identify himself as a federal agent. He could then arrest Lipsky for parole violation without disclosing to anyone else the real nature of the detectives' interest. If, however, Lipsky arrived at the baggage claim alone, the Nassau detectives were to approach him. In either instance he was to be brought to Mineola for interrogation.

"Okay?" Bonora said. "Any problems, you give me a call. I'll be home."

At 6 P.M. Barry Lipsky left Miami, Florida, for New York, aboard National Airlines Flight 90. He was dressed in jeans, boots and a leather vest. With his long curly hair and dark sunglasses he might have been an advance man for a touring rock group. In fact, he was the "chemist" in the Pacelli organization, the person who tested the quality of the heroin they purchased, who cut it with quinine and packaged it for sale on the street. It was a relatively new occupation for the thirty-two-year-old Lipsky, a graduate of the University of Miami. For ten years he had worked as a stockbroker until 1970, when he was arrested for conspiracy to transfer stolen securities. A year later he joined up with Pacelli.

Lipsky had left Miami with great apprehension. In the past week he had received two unsettling phone calls from the Pacelli organization, each caller wanting to be certain he would not miss the check-in date with his parole officer in New York. This sudden concern gravely troubled Lipsky and during the three-hour flight he ate little and spoke to no one. There had been rumors that a "contract" was out on his life. He believed he was in danger by coming to New York. Still, out of a sense of loyalty to the organization he refused to disclose those fears to his surprise visitors at La Guardia Airport. For more than an hour he sat completely stone-faced in the squadroom of the Nassau County Homicide Squad while the detectives bombarded him with questions. At ten o'clock their efforts ceased; Lannon called Bonora.

"We decided to go on the airplane and take Lipsky off ourselves," Lannon said. "We've got him in here now, but he won't give us anything but name, rank and serial number. The bastard is telling us nothing, Matt."

Bonora had been sitting home anxious and concerned. The news that his hard-worked plan had been arbitrarily abandoned piqued him.

"What are you going to do?" he asked coolly.

"What else can we do? We'll have to release him. We sure as hell don't have anything to hold him on."

"All right, Danny. I'm giving you a direct order," Bonora said. "Don't release Lipsky until I get there. I'll be right in."

The commander ran upstairs, put on a clean shirt and tie, grabbed his briefcase and raced toward the car. He was worried. The extra time was giving Lipsky a chance to acclimate himself, to prepare an alibi. Then while driving toward headquarters Bonora recalled from the federal records that of the six men indicted in the stock swindle, only Lipsky had gone free. Probably the man had cooperated before.

Reaching Mineola, the commander began to think of how to approach the witness. The records showed Lipsky to possess near-genius intelligence, so he discounted any attempt to deceive him by pretending sympathy to the crime–implying, for instance, that there might be mitigating circumstances or that Patsy herself had provoked the incident. Nor did an offer of blanket immunity seem particularly suitable. What if Lipsky were directly involved in the crime? His best chance, Bonora concluded, was to play a bluffing game, working on the witness's fears.

He arrived in the squadroom at 10:30 P.M. and found Lipsky sitting next to his desk. He was built on the heavy side, with a soft face, round dark eyes and a slanting jaw. About him, grouped in a semicircle, were six detectives. Bonora nodded to the men and introduced himself to the witness. He asked Lipsky whether he'd been advised of his constitutional rights. The witness said he had, but the commander read him his rights anyway.

Seating himself directly opposite Lipsky, Bonora began to talk in almost a whisper, his words building sentences slowly, with calm and certainty.

He said, "Barry, we didn't pick you up out of the blue. We've been investigating you for some time now. We know who your friends are and who *you think* your friends are. We know just about everything you've ever done since you were born. We know this Parks story from beginning to end.

"Barry, you're here to make a decision. You can decide to work with us and I swear to you we'll do all we can to help. Or you can go your own way."

Lipsky glanced around the room. He seemed unconcerned.

"The door you came through is wide open," Bonora said, pointing his finger dramatically at the outer office. "Let me say right now you're free to leave here any time you want. You're not under arrest. But there is one thing I ought to tell you if you're thinking about leaving, Barry. You know we can't guarantee your safety if you remain in the street."

Lipsky looked sharply at the commander, then turned away.

"In fact, we can't even tell you whether you'll see the sun come up tomorrow morning." Bonora smiled grimly. "As I said, we'd like to help you. But it's all up to you, Barry. You know what you're involved in. We both know the trouble you're in. At this moment in your life you have to choose sides. Think about that, Barry. Think about that hard. There's the door. Choose a side."

Lipsky's complexion had suddenly grown pale. He gazed questioningly about him, at the stark green walls of the room, at the stolid faces of the seven detectives measuring his every move. He turned to Bonora with a plaintive look.

"Are you the boss here?" His voice was barely audible.

Bonora nodded affirmatively.

Lipsky looked at the other detectives, then back to the commander. "I'll talk to you."

Bonora motioned to the other detectives to leave and pulled his chair in closer.

"I think they're going to kill me," Lipsky said when the last detective had departed and the door had closed. "They've been calling Miami to make sure I didn't miss my probation check-in. I've been too scared to come up."

Bonora made a vague, sympathetic gesture. "Let me hear the whole story, Barry."

"Where should I begin?" The witness's voice was timid, but Bonora sensed a quiet challenge.

"Oh, start from the moment you picked up Marge."

Lipsky stiffened, eyeing Bonora uncertainly. Then he let out a deep sigh and began to shake his head. It was clear these men knew everything. . . .

At 3 A.M., four and one half hours later, Bonora left his office with Barry Lipsky's twenty-eight-page confession. As the commander had suspected, Lipsky had been Patsy's contact. He had left the Hippopotamus when she insisted on speaking with Vincent Pacelli, Jr., about her subpoena and had taken a cab to the Pacelli apartment in New Rochelle.

In his statement Lipsky recalled that Pacelli became instantly upset when informed of Patsy's dilemma. "Said she had ratted him out, had been to the Grand Jury and knew about a box. He hit one fist into his palm and said, 'It's about that goddam box.' He said, 'All right. I know what I have to do.'"

The two men had left immediately for New York in Pacelli's car. It was a 1972 Plymouth, dark green with a black vinyl roof. (As Bonora had theorized, it was later set on fire.)

"Vinnie was driving and wearing gloves as he usually does. He stopped at a gas station on FDR Drive and East Seventy-third Street. He said, 'We are going to have to burn her up with gas.' So he told me to go into the station and buy a bunch of gasoline. I bought one can from a kid working there and paid about two dollars for it. Vinnie was parked just a little south of the station on the service road, out of sight.

"When he saw I only had one can, he told me to go back and get more. I returned to the station and bought three more cans."

They drove within a few blocks of the Hippopotamus and Lipsky went inside the club to get Patsy. In order not to be seen leaving together, he remained at his table for about ten minutes. When he joined the others in the car Patsy was seated in the front with Pacelli. He climbed into the back seat behind her.

Pacelli drove over the Fifty-ninth Street Bridge and westward on through Queens, all the while revealing his "plans" to Patsy for flying her out of the country so she wouldn't have to testify. Soon they were in Long Island and Pacelli began driving in and out of dead-end streets. He explained that he was looking for his friend's place so he could switch the car. At 5 A.M. he stopped before an outdoor phone, got out and pretended to make a call.

This was the prearranged signal. When he returned Lipsky was already in the driver's seat. Pacelli climbed into the back seat directly behind Patsy.

"I didn't want to watch what was going to happen because I knew that he was going to kill her," Lipsky said. He drove off and the struggle started between Patsy and Pacelli. "Her feet came up by the wheel and Vinnie was stabbing her. She fought but he hit her several times in the chest with the knife. I could hear the thud with each thrust. . . .

"When Vinnie started to stab her, she screamed, 'Please don't hurt me. My baby, I am a mother.'

"He said very calmly, 'What, are you kidding?' and continued to strike her with the knife.

"She slumped over in the seat on the right-hand side. She had a fur coat on. He said that she was dead and I continued to drive. He told me to find the road that we had been on before.

"He located the area where he felt was a good spot to get rid of the body. There was woods on both sides and the main road was nearby. I stopped the car and he jumped out and opened the door and pulled her out in one motion. He said to me to open the trunk and get the gasoline. He pulled her in a few feet off the road and took the gasoline, which I gave him, and he poured the gasoline over her body—all four cans, and he said he had gas all over his gloves so would I light the match.

"It was a match from a pack that I had picked up at the Hippo for this purpose. I lit the match and threw it on her body. I watched her body go up in flames. . . ."

CHAPTER

_____

13

THE CONFESSION of Barry Glen Lipsky carried enough authority in court to convict Vincent Pacelli, Jr., of murder on a federal civil rights charge. (Pacelli had deprived Patsy Parks of her civil rights by causing her death.) Subsequent information Lipsky gave Bonora also provided the foundation for a federal narcotics investigation that would culminate a year later in one of the largest roundups of drug dealers in the history of the United States. During a two-day period in April, 1973, federal agents and local policemen arrested eighty-six alleged operators in what Daniel P. Casey, New York director of the U. S. Bureau of Narcotics and Dangerous Drugs, termed "one of the most significant domestic conspiracy cases in some time."

For neither of these successes did Bonora receive recognition. The day following Lipsky's confession, while the commander was forty miles away interviewing Pacelli in Manhattan's Federal House of Detention, District Attorney William Cahn called a press conference. Standing before a covey of television cameras, radio and newspaper reporters, the fifty-year-old District Attorney, smiling and confident in a well-cut suit and his expensive toupee, dramatically explained how his office with the help of the police department had solved the Parks murder. Bonora's name was never mentioned.

Accustomed to such self-serving exhibitions on the part of the District Attorney, Bonora nevertheless felt the neglect of his role and that of the Homicide Squad more acutely this time. With the department questioning his credibility, his career seemingly on the line, the commander could have used a morale booster. His immediate reaction on reading the specious account of the murder's solution was to strike back, to confront Cahn directly, perhaps by going to the media himself. Certainly he had good friends among the reporters, having dealt with them over the years in a candid, straightforward manner. However, at the urgings of Deputy Commissioner Ketcham, Bonora contained his anger. "Let him have this one," Ketcham suggested over the weekend. "Maybe this will finally settle the situation in the department."

Yet it did not. When Bonora returned to work Monday morning he found Inspector Klecak unimpressed by the success of the Parks case. Klecak even reproved him for disobeying his orders and reappearing at headquarters Thursday night. Then in the next several days the controversy took a turn that eliminated forever the possibility of easy resolution and filled Bonora with an impending sense of doom. He was ordered by the Police Commissioner to the office of the District Attorney to give a sworn statement. Cahn, apprised of the controversy, had arrogated its investigation. Hereafter the District Attorney would be investigating charges of his own misconduct.

Friday afternoon Bonora appeared in the prosecutor's offices on the second floor of the Nassau County Courthouse. He had been assured by the Commissioner, as had Archer and Cardone, that Cahn would take no punitive action as long as the detectives cooperated with the investigation. Bonora was not fully convinced. Given a friendly wave by the receptionist, he passed warily through the double doors leading into the long corridor of offices belonging to the ninety-two Assistant District Attorneys, ninety-one of whom were registered Republicans like their boss. And for once the commander could find little humor in the series of candid photographs of the District Attorney that approached his office along one hundred feet of hallway, referred to by staff members as the "thirteen stations of the Cahn."

Bonora passed the Vice Bureau; inside, men wearing earphones were listening to wiretap recordings. Next came the Homicide Bureau—familiar surroundings to the commander. Then, finally, the office of Robert Roberto, Cahn's third-in-command. Roberto was a recent appointment to the District Attorney's staff, but already he had made a name for himself. During an investigation of local massage parlors, he had allowed a young woman to complete fellatio upon him before revealing his identity—a questionable interpretation of his duties about which he freely testified in open court to the embarrassment of both defense attorneys and his own colleagues. Bonora had little faith in Roberto's independence of mind and he was pleased when Don White, a court stenographer, opened the door to his office. The commander had worked with White on several occasions, most recently the Dallas trip. He had found him competent and trustworthy.

Roberto's office was small and gloomy, its appearance an accurate reflection of the occupant, whose gray suits were invariably stained and wrinkled. He was a slender man with slumped shoulders, a pockmarked face, thick black eyebrows and black hair that was greased straight back. He sat behind a desk piled high with pornographic magazines that had been seized during a raid but were creased and dog-eared as if they had been often perused.

Bonora seated himself in front of the desk and, raising his right hand, gave Don White his oath to tell the truth. As soon as he was finished, Roberto leaned forward, hunching over the magazines as if he were trying to get as close to the commander as possible. He examined him carefully in a moment of silence, his dark eyes coolly confident in their task. Then he began to speak in a friendly, solicitous voice:

"Matt, this is a very serious situation we're involved in. But you don't have to worry; I'm on your side. I'm here to help you. If you want my help, though, you're gonna have to tell the truth. If you do that, if you tell the truth, then I'll do every—"

Bonora cut him off. The commander had used that routine from the moment he became a detective.

"Of course I'm going to tell the truth," he said crossly. "I always tell the truth. I've got nothing to hide."

Roberto, slightly taken aback, nodded self-consciously and began his questioning. In the next half hour, while Don White recorded his words, Bonora set down for the first time the substance of his private meeting with Archer and Klecak. He spoke in a firm, bold voice, yet he was troubled and uneasy throughout his testimony. The illegality of the Nassau indictment of Holder and Gershenson was of minor concern to the commander. That in his mind was a jurisdictional mistake easily remedied; it posed no severe threat to the cause of justice. What truly disturbed him was the decision to break the pledge of confidentiality he had given Cardone. His testimony jeopardized the detective's future and Bonora felt a special loyalty to Cardone, not only as he was one of his staff members, but because he had recently worked to bring the detective and his wife together again after a lengthy estrangement. On the other hand, Bonora had promised the Police Commissioner to cooperate in the investigation. And he could not perjure himself. Otherwise he too could be indicted. Disturbed and upset when the questioning ended, he rose abruptly, shook hands with Don White and walked silently from the room.

Over the weekend Deputy Commissioner Ketcham came to Bonora's house in Wantagh and helped him compose a written report outlining the full history of his troubles with Deputy Inspector Archer. Bonora had continued to oppose such a project, but Ketcham, a perceptive student of departmental politics as well as an attorney, managed to convince him he had protected Cardone as well and as long as he could. Now was the moment to guard his own interest, Ketcham warned gravely. The reference was to the commander's job—his continuing livelihood as a cop.

Monday morning Bonora submitted the five-page document to

Inspector Klecak along with another proposal he had kept under wraps since Archer first called for the investigation. The commander asked that he be given a polygraph examination to confirm his account of what had occurred between Cardone and himself. Klecak agreed to forward the request to Chief of Detectives Curran.

Bonora returned to the squadroom and spent the day awaiting a response, growing more and more impatient. The Police Commissioner had proscribed his participation in new Homicide cases until completion of the District Attorney's investigation and the commander had little else to occupy his attentions. Finally at five o'clock, having heard nothing, he returned to the supervisors' office and confronted Klecak about his request for the polygraph. The Inspector claimed he had been unable to reach Chief Curran.

By the following morning Bonora had still received no response. At eleven o'clock he approached Klecak again and demanded to see the Chief at once.

"Gee, I don't know," Klecak said, rubbing the chin of his pink Rotarian face. "He's probably busy."

"Well, you pick up that phone and find out," Bonora ordered angrily. "You tell him it's urgent."

Klecak's call found Curran free and Bonora paid him a hasty visit. He explained his proposition, this time broadening its scope. He wanted Archer and Cardone to take a polygraph examination as well, "and also Mr. Cahn."

Curran, a tall, handsome Irishman with long straight features and a thick shock of wavy gray hair, had not retained his post through the administrations of three successive Police Commissioners by making rash judgments. He promised to take Bonora's proposal under advisement.

During the next several days Bonora inquired each morning of Inspector Klecak about the status of his polygraph examination and that of Archer and Cardone. Klecak put him off. The commander learned secretly, however, from Assistant Chief of Detectives John Cummings that Archer and Cardone had been asked and both had refused to take the exam. Cummings, uninvolved from the start of the controversy, had become an open supporter of Bonora once informed of his proposal. Any doubts he may have held concerning the validity of the commander's charges had been erased by Bonora's willingness to have his statements judged by the polygraph machine. From twenty-five years' experience as a detective Cummings recognized that a guilty man aware of the polygraph's near infallibility never *volunteered* to take the test.

Unfortunately, Chief Curran, Cummings's boss, had not been similarly influenced. According to Ketcham, Curran had so far ignored two directives from the Police Commissioner to inform Bonora that both Archer and Cardone had refused polygraphs. This revelation had profoundly shaken Bonora's faith in the department. Earlier he had been able to write off Klecak's defection as the result of personal animosity and petty jealousy. (He remembered how often he had brushed aside Klecak's urgings to use his influence with the Deputy Commissioner so as to insure the Inspector's future promotion.) Yet Curran's apparent partisanship could not be dismissed so easily. He was not just some supervisor, but the leader of the entire division of 429 detectives, a man Bonora had long admired. For years he had respected his ability both as an investigator and an administrator. Above all, Curran appeared in the commander's mind as a consummate representative of the department's ethos: its honesty, impartiality and dedication.

Bonora had become aware that it was Curran who had gone to the District Attorney with news of the commander's accusations. But he had hesitated drawing the conclusion that this might be a purely political move. The sudden realization that Curran cared only about bolstering his own position brought a new critical perspective to Bonora's thoughts. As he looked around the Homicide squadroom, at the detectives engaged in their varied tasks, it struck him that not one man had come to offer his support since the District Attorney had jumped into the investigation. Naturally the commander did not expect a demonstration. This was a police department. A nod would have been sufficient, a pat on the shoulder. Yet there had been nothing, and the indifference made him feel like a marked man, his friends having deserted him on all sides.

Wednesday morning Bonora received a phone call from Deputy Commissioner Ketcham. Commissioner Louis Frank had just *ordered* Chief Curran to tell the commander about Cardone's and Archer's refusal to take polygraph examinations. Five minutes later Bonora was summoned to Chief Curran's office and there, before Klecak and Assistant Chief Cummings, he was finally given the information.

"Well, I guess we know who's telling the truth now," Bonora said pointedly. He suggested that he be given the polygraph right away. "In fact, I insist on it. I don't want any doubts left in anyone's mind."

Once again Curran put him off. Nevertheless, leaving for home that evening Bonora felt his vindication all but complete. Even Curran could not deny the significance of a man willing to be polygraphed.

The office of the Police Commissioner is located on the second floor of Nassau County headquarters, overlooking a landscaped lawn on the south side of the building. It is a spacious, carpeted room with wood-paneled walls that are hung with photographs of the County Executive and other local and state dignitaries. Adjacent to the Commissioner's desk is a highly polished conference table with wine-red leather chairs. Scattered about are plaques and trophies awarded to the department for accomplishments in both police work and league athletics.

Bonora arrived there early Thursday morning, March 23. Unexpectedly summoned by the Commissioner, he sensed that the controversy had come to a head, that something momentous was about to occur. Yesterday's meeting with Curran had given him a certain degree of confidence. And he trusted Deputy Commissioner Ketcham to protect his position. Yet over the past several weeks so much of an unanticipated nature had taken place—Archer had once been counted out only to bounce back with renewed zeal—that the commander didn't quite know what to expect. Was he slated to be commended? Would Archer be dismissed? Or was the reverse about to happen?

He entered the Commissioner's office with Archer and Chief Curran by his side. Seated behind his grand mahogany desk, Commissioner Frank appeared almost magisterial in his gray pinstripe suit, his white hair neatly combed and parted. Behind him were the American flag and the blue and orange Nassau County flag; to his side was Deputy Commissioner Ketcham.

Frank had been appointed Commissioner in 1971 after serving more than twenty-five years as a uniformed officer concerned with traffic control. The victim of a severe stomach ulcer, he continued to look somewhat fragile, like a man who had lost thirty pounds too quickly. Mild-mannered and affable, his promotion had been highly applauded by much of the department, who resented the innovations of his predecessor, the domineering Commissioner Francis Looney. In this respect, Bonora was in the minority. He believed that only Looney's tenacity had allowed the department to remain impartial and independent from the politicized District Attorney's office. (When District Attorney Cahn insisted on naming the head of the police vice squad, which operated out of Cahn's office, Looney simply withdrew the squad to headquarters.) Bonora wasn't certain Frank could be counted on for that kind of staunchness.

In a solemn voice the Commissioner opened the meeting by commending both Bonora and Archer for the fine work they had performed on behalf of the department, for the excellent quality of their personal records. He regretted that either of them had become involved in a controversy and that it had grown to such traumatic proportions. Their conflicts had been mishandled from the beginning, Frank declared. But now that the District Attorney had completed his investigation he was left no alternative other than the step he was about to take. Archer, the Commissioner said, was being sent back to uniform, transferred to the Marine Division. Bonora would become a special investigator assigned to the Commissioner's office.

Bonora was stunned. "Wait a minute," he said. "Have I done anything wrong?"

The Commissioner acknowledged that he had not.

"Why then am I being transferred?" From Bonora's point of view Archer's transfer to the Marine Division was fitting punishment. It was a dead end in the department and meant the certain denial of all his ambitions. But the loss of his own command struck the sergeant as grossly unfair. He had worked more than twenty years to achieve that goal; it gave his life its meaning. As for becoming the Commissioner's investigator, a "shoofly" prying for corruption among other cops—there was no worse job the commander could consider.

Commissioner Frank explained to Bonora that effective administrative practices dictate "that if two good men are butting heads and you can't resolve the problem, transfer both of them."

"I appreciate that," Bonora said. "But you're telling me I'm going to lose my command. Yet you haven't told me that I've done anything wrong."

It was then Frank confessed he had received a communication from the District Attorney's office two days before. It said in part:

> After a complete and thorough investigation of the allegations made by Sgt. Matthew Bonora, it is the consensus of this office that Sgt. Bonora is lying and that the charges he made against the police officers involved in the Howard Holder case are without foundation.
>
> It is the suggestion of the District Attorney that the matter be handled departmentally, but it is urged, however, that Sgt. Bonora be immediately transferred from the Homicide Bureau and that he be given no position of authority wherein he at any time might be used in court as a witness.

"The District Attorney is the chief law enforcement officer in the county," the Commissioner said. "So you see, Matt, I don't have any choice."

"Well, I do," Bonora replied heatedly. "I don't have to accept the transfer. I don't have to identify with the politicizing of the police department."

He left the room bitter and heartbroken, though it was several hours later before he sensed the true weight of the decision. As he was leaving headquarters for home Inspector Klecak stopped him and demanded the keys to the squad car permanently assigned to the Homicide commander.

The trip to Wantagh in the car of Homicide detective Daniel Stark was long, silent and oppressive. Entering the house through the back door, Bonora could no longer control his emotions. He collapsed into a kitchen chair and began to sob. Hazel ran to comfort him, throwing her arms around his shoulders, murmuring over and over, "Oh my God, my God, my God..."

For a few minutes Bonora could not collect himself. The pain of betrayal was too profound. He felt alone and rejected, abandoned by the department that had been both a refuge and a creed for twenty-two years. Then his children entered the room and, sensing their loyalty, feeling their love, he gained the strength to compose himself. He knew instinctively that he had to set a proper example, that he had to show them how to stand up when you're knocked down.

He dried his eyes and calmly explained to the entire family that he had lost his command. Then he fixed himself a cup of hot tea and asked Hazel to put dinner on the table. They could discuss their options afterward.

Two hours later the supper dishes had been rinsed and placed in the washer, the pots and pans cleaned. Bonora, Hazel, John, Nancy, Jeanne and Betty sat down around the kitchen table to decide what was to be done. It was a grim moment in all their lives, each of them feeling the betrayal in his own way. They found it difficult to talk, recognizing the choice was fairly straightforward. Either Bonora drove to Albany and handed in his retirement papers or he remained a cop, working for the Commissioner.

Bonora was of the mind to retire immediately. His faith in the Nassau County Police Department had been brutally crushed. He didn't want to be part of an organization that had lost its independence, that would now handle law enforcement subject to the political considerations of the District Attorney. By retiring he would be stating his outrage and disgust.

There were monetary advantages to be gained as well from such a move. Retiring this year, Bonora's pension would be based on last year's salary, which as a Homicide commander working overtime had amounted to $22,400. Reassignment to the Commissioner's office would lower his salary to the sergeant's base of $16,900 and thus cut drastically into his pension if he retired a year later. Freed of his faith in the department, Bonora could for the first time consider his future pragmatically.

Yet throughout these deliberations the question kept arising in his mind: What would he do if he left the department? How would he support his family, send the rest of the children through college? He had been a policeman twenty-two years, trained to do little else. Though no one seated at the table that night suggested another specific career, each of the family members expressed the conviction that Bonora would succeed at anything he put his mind to. The commander was not so certain.

The next day was typical of March on Long Island. The sun was meshed in strands of gray, the air cold and damp. Bonora arose early and left the house in his gold Ford station wagon, passing under the leafless maple trees near his home. As usual his eyes searched for anything out of the ordinary—for prowlers, perhaps, hidden among the bushes surrounding the neat brick and wood houses lining his street, for stolen cars that had been abandoned. Finding nothing amiss, he glanced warmly at his son seated beside him, thankful he would not be making this trip alone. Then with a sigh that beckoned anxiously to the unknowable future ahead, he pulled out onto the highway, blending quickly into the stream of commuter cars as he headed north toward Albany.

EPILOGUE

FOURTEEN DAYS after Bonora quit the Nassau County Police Department George Archer was promoted to Inspector in the Detective Division. On that same day Frank Klecak became Deputy Chief Inspector. Frank Cardone retained his position as a member of the Homicide Squad.

Bonora remained in retirement into the summer, physically and emotionally exhausted from the battles and disappointments of the spring. He needed time to relax, to clear his mind so that he could properly consider the future. By the end of that five-month period he had come to only one firm conclusion: he needed to work, but not in a job that was merely nine to five.

Since that time there has been little Bonora has not tried. He has written newspaper articles and become a private investigator, organized a public-interest organization and run for political office (he lost to the Republican incumbent in a hectic race for Hempstead Town Supervisor). He was looking for a niche wherein his ambitions and energies would be fully satisfied, as they once were in his work for the police department. The pursuit has not been dull nor his accomplishments unnoteworthy.

Initially uncertain what to do, Bonora took a crack at investigative journalism, offering his services on a part-time basis to a local radio station. Within a month he had produced an award-winning five-part series that revealed how the glaringly high automobile fatality rate in Suffolk County was the result of a backward and provincial rescue system. (This system relied on voluntary ambulance squads that often took up to an hour to transport injured passengers to the hospital.)

Unfortunately New York State's Elliot Stuart Award for Excellence in Radio Journalism carried no cash award. With little money forthcoming from the radio station, Bonora decided to return to home ground. He became a private investigator and was hired by a man trying to retrieve $80,000 he had handed over to a con artist; by a mother searching for her lost child; by several married men with questions about their wives. Then came his first major case: the defense of twenty-four Nassau County Jail guards who had been arrested on assorted charges of corruption and misconduct.

Nassau County District Attorney Cahn had announced the guards' indictments with a great display of public outrage that political observers noted followed conveniently close on the heels of the scourge of bad publicity arising from Bonora's retirement and his denunciations of the District Attorney in court and to the press. Cahn indicated the indictments were based on evidence uncovered by a professional research group hired from California to infiltrate the Nassau County Jail. In fact, it was later disclosed that the $200,000 study had found no evidence of misconduct. The actual basis for the indictments was the testimony of a felon from an upstate prison who had been transferred to the Nassau County Jail after the professionals departed.

Bonora was assigned to research the background of this man, the prosecution's star witness. Through his many contacts in the prison system, he managed to unearth a confidential psychiatric report describing the felon as a "pathological liar." It served as the basis for the dismissal of nearly all the indictments.

The success of this investigation gained the commander considerable personal publicity and before long he was approached by Norman Blankman, a wealthy North Shore businessman. Blankman had decided to run as an independent for Nassau County Executive and needed a strong campaign issue. Would Bonora be willing to investigate political corruption in the county? The former detective answered a hesitant yes. The following month he located some county employees willing to testify they were forced to pay Republican party dues in order to keep their jobs. County and party officials denied the charges; Blankman was swamped in the 1973 election.

This was Bonora's first taste of politics and like a kid in his first snowfall, he couldn't get enough. Following the election he learned of a public watchdog organization in Chicago that developed political corruption investigations, then fed the information to newspapers and the local U. S. attorney's office. He took the idea to Blankman, who liked it, and who subsequently founded AWARE (Action Where Action Requires the Electorate). Bonora was appointed the executive director, a part-time post that paid $34,000 a year.

It was during this period that Bonora was first contacted by William Timothy, a former inmate at Green Haven State Prison, who had shared a cell with Jay Pobliner. Timothy told Bonora that Pobliner and his father had arranged to kill three witnesses who had testified at Jay's 1970 trial. The witnesses—Joe Hall, Eddie Gaines and Illis Jurisson—were to be slain to prevent them from testifying again after being forced to write statements clearing Jay.

Bonora did a bit of independent checking and found some corroboration for Timothy's accusations. He then recorded the former inmate's testimony and sent the tapes to the FBI, who turned the evidence over to the Nassau County District Attorney's office. Naturally, District Attorney Cahn made no mention of Bonora's role when he announced the indictments of Jay, Herman Pobliner and their attorney, Herbert Handman. (Herman Pobliner eventually pleaded guilty in a deal that insured he would receive only a probationary sentence and the remaining charges would be dropped against the other defendants.) Nor was this indictment the only reminder Bonora had in the years following his retirement of his final detective investigations. Periodically he received a copy of a new petition submitted by George McKie, who was attempting to gain another trial or an early release from jail. And soon he would read of the marriage of Howard Holder and Lynnor Gershenson during a prison furlough the two had been given over the Christmas holidays.

Yet the commander was too busy in his new work to take more

than hasty glances into the past. He had developed further evidence on the Republican "dues" matter and had managed to have the investigation brought before a federal Grand Jury. The results of his other research had also prompted federal probes into the operations of Nassau Community College, the Nassau County Medical Center, the Long Island State Park Commission and municipal construction contracts in the towns of Oyster Bay and Hempstead.

Clearly all these investigations put Bonora at odds with District Attorney Cahn, who by implication had failed to do his job or was covering up corruption. Rumors were bruited about that Bonora was out to "get" Cahn; and likewise that Cahn was out to "get" Bonora. Neither man made much effort to conceal his animosity, but swords were not formally drawn until the fall of 1974 when Bonora announced he had joined the campaign team of Denis Dillon.

A former head of the federal Strike Force in New York City, Dillon had captured the Democratic nomination for Nassau County District Attorney. It was a position that had lately gone for the asking in the predominantly Republican county as Cahn was the largest vote getter on Long Island and had already won three four-year terms by large pluralities.

Bonora put his full investigative skills to work for Dillon, feeding him a constant stream of information that the Democratic challenger used to hammer away at Cahn's purported failure to prosecute political corruption in the county. Two weeks before the election Dillon called his major press conference of the campaign. He publicly charged Cahn with tax evasion and outright thievery. On the basis of Bonora's research Dillon presented documents that he contended showed that Cahn, as president of the National District Attorneys' Association, had traveled around the country on the Association's account, yet had billed Nassau County for more than $100,000 of the same expenses.

Cahn angrily denied the charges, but in the aftermath of Watergate his statements apparently were not enough to counteract the force of the documents. On November 5, 1974, Denis Dillon engineered the greatest upset in the history of Nassau County elections. He defeated Cahn by more than fifty thousand votes.

The victory proved even sweeter than Bonora had imagined. Eighteen months later the former District Attorney was convicted in a federal court on forty-five counts of mail fraud stemming from the alleged double billing. On July 2, 1976, Judge Orrin Judd sentenced Cahn to a year and a day in prison.

Today Bonora remains a private citizen. He has his own investigating firm, and on any given day he can be found tracking a murderer or looking into political corruption for his newest client, *The New York Times*. The demands are different from police work, but so are the challenges and rewards. He has returned to sixty- and seventy-hour work weeks, and once more his voice pulses during accounts of his newest endeavors. He's no longer a policeman, but for a man of Bonora's needs, for his dedication and ambition, for his idealism too, it's a job to thrive on.